Aviation Law and Drones

The aviation industry is being transformed by the use of unmanned aerial vehicles, or drones – commercially, militarily, scientifically and recreationally. National regulations have generally failed to keep pace with the expansion of the fast-growing drone industry.

Aviation Law and Drones: Unmanned Aircraft and the Future of Aviation traces the development of aviation laws and regulations, explains how aviation is regulated at an international and national level, considers the interrelationship between rapidly advancing technology and legislative attempts to keep pace, and reviews existing domestic and international drone laws and issues (including safety, security, privacy and airspace issues). Against this background, the book uniquely proposes a rationale for, and key provisions of, guiding principles for the regulation of drones internationally – provisions of which could also be implemented domestically. Finally, the book examines the changing shape of our increasingly busy skies – technology beyond drones and the regulation of that technology. The world is on the edge of major disruption in aviation – drones are just the beginning.

Given the almost universal interest in drones, this book will be of interest to readers worldwide, from the academic sector and beyond.

David Hodgkinson is a partner at HodgkinsonJohnston and an associate professor at the University of Western Australia. He is the author of books and numerous journal articles on aviation and climate change, and was Director of Legal at IATA, the organisation of the world's airlines.

Rebecca Johnston is a partner at aviation and aerospace law firm, HodgkinsonJohnston, and teaches at the University of Western Australia. She is admitted to practise law in Australia and New York. Together with David Hodgkinson, she is the author of *International Air Carrier Liability, Safety and Security* (Routledge).

Aviation Law and Drones

Unmanned Aircraft and the Future of Aviation

**David Hodgkinson and
Rebecca Johnston**

Routledge
Taylor & Francis Group

LONDON AND NEW YORK

First published 2018 by Routledge

2 Park Square, Milton Park, Abingdon, Oxfordshire OX14 4RN

52 Vanderbilt Avenue, New York, NY 10017

Routledge is an imprint of the Taylor & Francis Group, an informa business

First issued in paperback 2020

Copyright © 2018 David Hodgkinson and Rebecca Johnston

The right of David Hodgkinson and Rebecca Johnston to be identified as authors of this work has been asserted by them in accordance with sections 77 and 78 of the Copyright, Designs and Patents Act 1988.

All rights reserved. No part of this book may be reprinted or reproduced or utilised in any form or by any electronic, mechanical, or other means, now known or hereafter invented, including photocopying and recording, or in any information storage or retrieval system, without permission in writing from the publishers.

Notice:
Product or corporate names may be trademarks or registered trademarks, and are used only for identification and explanation without intent to infringe.

British Library Cataloguing in Publication Data
A catalogue record for this book is available from the British Library

Library of Congress Cataloging in Publication Data
Names: Hodgkinson, David (David Ivor), author. | Johnston, Rebecca (Lawyer), author.
Title: Aviation law and drones : unmanned aircraft and the future of aviation / David Hodgkinson and Rebecca Johnston.
Description: New York, NY : Routledge, 2018. | Includes bibliographical references and index.
Identifiers: LCCN 2017059478 | ISBN 9781138572447 (hardback) | ISBN 9781351332323 (ebook)
Subjects: LCSH: Drone aircraft--Law and legislation. | Aeronautics--Law and legislation. | Aeronautics, Commercial--Law and legislation.
Classification: LCC K4105 .H63 2018 | DDC 343.09/75--dc23
LC record available at https://lccn.loc.gov/2017059478

ISBN: 978-1-138-57244-7 (hbk)
ISBN: 978-0-367-66984-3 (pbk)

Typeset in Bembo
by Taylor & Francis Books

Contents

Preface

> Man must rise above the Earth – to the top of the atmosphere and beyond – for only thus will he fully understand the world in which he lives.
>
> – Socrates

It is estimated that the number of unmanned aircraft operations will surpass manned aircraft operations in the next 20 years. The world is now on the edge of a technological revolution in aviation. Drones are the ultimate disruptive technology, and while the consumer market has been quick to adopt this technology, legal and regulatory systems around the world are responding much more slowly to it.

Drones represent the most significant disruption to the aviation industry since World War II.

To keep pace with these developments, aviation regulatory authorities across the globe have devised different methods to regulate drones in their airspace. Inevitably, though, technology will continue to outstrip regulation for the foreseeable future.

It is the framework for drone regulations which forms the subject of this book.

We extend our sincere appreciation and thanks to a number of people and organisations for assistance in the production of this book. In particular, we would like to thank our commissioning editor, Guy Loft from Routledge.

We are indebted to our contributors, Dr Jonathan Aleck, General Manager of the Legal Affairs, Regulatory Policy and International Strategy Branch of Australia's Civil Aviation Safety Authority (CASA); Auguste Hocking, Assistant General Counsel at the International Air Transport Association (IATA); James Coyne, Technical Director at Unmanned Aircraft Systems International; and those who have contributed anonymously.

We acknowledge the support of our aviation and aerospace law firm, HodgkinsonJohnston. We thank our tireless research associates: Alexandra Ioppolo, Dylan Hindle, Marché Bantum, Monica Hamid, Nicole Courtney, Ricardo Napper and, in particular, Aheli Guha.

Finally, David would like to thank his wife, Lucy Young. Rebecca would like to thank her husband, Hudson Wheeler, her parents, James and Sandra Johnston and her sister, Laura Johnston.

Foreword

It is common ground that modern technological developments occur at such a pace nowadays as to leave those responsible for devising fair and workable rules to govern the use of the products, as well as the by-products, of those innovative enterprises ever further behind. Nowhere, perhaps, is this more apparent than it is in relation to the proliferation of unmanned aerial vehicles, remotely piloted aircraft or, as they have conveniently come to be known, *drones*.

Born of the same kind of disruptive technological inventiveness, it may be that the distinctively legal challenges posed by the still relatively new, if now virtually ubiquitous, phenomenon of social media, will prove to be more enduringly daunting than those thrown up by the widespread commercial and recreational use of unmanned aircraft. In a remarkably similar way, however, the increasingly ready accessibility of drones that can be used in ways that are capable of bringing about a seemingly limitless range of social and economic advantages and, at the same time, can seriously threaten our safety, security and legitimate expectations of personal privacy, raises the same kind of political, ethical and perforce legal questions about where, when and how limitations can and should be imposed, without unduly discouraging creativity, entrepreneurial success and real public benefits.

The dilemma itself is not new. Questions of the same kind have attended scientific advances and innovation throughout the course of modern history. Indeed, neither the technological foundations of electronic mass communication nor those of remotely piloted aircraft are entirely new or fundamentally radical. Rather, it is their sudden, pervasive and largely unchecked availability that make the problems of law they throw up remarkable and unprecedented.

In the case of drones, as in that of social media, because of the contested political and legal terrain they traverse, the discussions and debates engendered by these matters often tend to shed more polemical heat than pragmatic light on the questions they raise. What is necessary to surmount this kind of tendentious freneticism is a balanced and comprehensive framing of the field, and the development of rational proposals and propositions informed by a thoughtful and dispassionate understanding of the issues. And this is precisely what David Hodgkinson and Rebecca Johnston so effectively and refreshingly offer in *Aviation Law and Drones: Unmanned Aircraft and the Future of Aviation*.

The first three chapters of the volume succinctly set out the historical, conceptual and functional parameters of the field within which existing regulatory considerations must necessarily be considered in the first instance. The utility of this approach is demonstrable, giving the reader both a clear sense of contemporary national and international regulatory arrangements, and a firm basis on which a deeper analysis can (and does) proceed. This utility is enhanced by the inclusion of pertinent industry and environmental perspectives that compellingly elucidate the critical areas in law, policy and practice where shortcomings and deficiencies in existing arrangements need to be addressed.

Chapter 4 is especially valuable for its depiction and discussion of the overarching features of the relevant international law, along with the crucially important differences in the ways in which that law is recognised and applied in different national jurisdictions. Here readers also find an exceptionally useful consideration of the distinctive implications of federal and unitary political structures for the application of relevant international legal principles. In this context, Australia, as much as the United States, provides a usefully instructive example for all readers interested in the application of general principles of international law in the context of a federal state. From a constitutional perspective, these issues are coming to take on particular significance in federal jurisdictions like Australia and the United States, where the extent to which federal laws governing the use of drones should or should not be regarded as effectively precluding state and local regulation is the subject of an important emerging jurisprudence.

In Chapter 5 the authors draw on, but lead readers well beyond, the searching narrative and analysis provided in the preceding chapters. Here they introduce a cogent set of Guiding Principles reflecting a prudent and realistic recognition of the need for the domestic implementation of internationally accepted norms and standards, free from the problematic encumbrances that arguably inhere in the kind of multilateral agreements some might otherwise too easily fasten on as the optimal vehicle for the effective regulation of unmanned aircraft. In the concluding chapter, the disutility of existing international aviation agreements in relation to a number of drone-related developments that were only recently just-over-the-horizon, and the implications of these innovations for existing and contemplated regulatory options, are thoughtfully explored.

In the rapidly expanding body of contemporary literature touching on various aspects of the law related to unmanned aircraft and aerial systems, *Aviation Law and Drones: Unmanned Aircraft and the Future*, stands out as a welcome beacon for lawyers, legislators, regulators, current and prospective drone users and anyone interested in these important issues, offering readers an informed and highly informative study that is measured, comprehensive and thought-provokingly forward looking.

Dr Jonathan Aleck
Executive Manager
Legal and Regulatory Affairs
Civil Aviation Safety Authority
Australia

Introduction

The aviation industry is being transformed by the use of unmanned aerial vehicles, or drones – commercially, militarily, scientifically and recreationally. National regulations have generally failed to keep pace with the expansion of the fast-growing drone industry.

Aviation Law and Drones: Unmanned Aircraft and the Future of Aviation traces the development of aviation laws and regulations, explains how aviation is regulated at an international and national level, considers the interrelationship between rapidly advancing technology and legislative attempts to keep pace, and reviews existing domestic and international drone laws and issues (including safety, security, privacy and airspace issues).

Against this background, the book uniquely proposes a rationale for, and key provisions of, guiding principles for the regulation of drones internationally – provisions of which could also be implemented domestically.

The world is on the edge of major disruption in aviation; drones are just the beginning.

Given almost universal interest in drones, we hope that this book has worldwide application and finds a global audience (both general and academic).

Chapter 1 explores the interrelationship between rapidly advancing technology and legislative attempts to keep pace with that technology. It provides a brief history of drones in an aviation context and explores the various challenges and limitations for law makers in regulating drones.

Chapter 2 examines existing domestic and international drone regulations and major issues which attend them. The legal and policy complexities of drone laws are increasing as their use becomes more widespread and diverse. Those complexities are also examined. It also includes valuable insights into the drone industry by way of commentary from industry thought leaders.

Chapter 3 sets out the history of the development of aviation laws and regulations from the origins of flight. It traces the course of international air carrier liability, safety and security conventions.

Chapter 4 explains how aviation is regulated at an international level – that is, through treaties and other international instruments as agreed by states. It then considers the relationship between international and national law, and instruments through which states at the national level implement international treaties.

Chapters 1 to 4 set the foundation for Chapter 5 – the rationale for guiding principles for the regulation of drones internationally by states, provisions which would also be implemented domestically. It addresses the difficulties associated with any multilateral agreement to regulate drones.

The final chapter examines the changing landscape of our increasingly busy skies – technology beyond drones and the regulation of that technology.

The law stated in this book is as it appeared to us on 19 March 2018. Any errors or inaccuracies are entirely the responsibility of the authors.

Acronyms

AMC	Acceptable means of compliance
ANO	Air Navigation Order
AOC	Air Operator's Certificate
APPs	Australian Privacy Principles
ARN	Aviation Reference Number
ATM	air traffic management
C2	command and control
CAA	United Kingdom Civil Aviation Authority
CASA	Australian Civil Aviation Safety Authority
CASR	Australia's Civil Aviation Safety Regulation
CIA	United States Central Intelligence Agency
CIDPA	Conférence Internationale de Droit Privé Aérien
CITEJA	Comité International Technique d' Experts Juridiques Aériens
CS	certification specifications
DAA	detect and avoid
EASA	European Aviation Safety Agency
EPIC	United States Electronic Privacy Information Center
EU	European Union
FAA	United States Federal Aviation Administration
GPS	global positioning system
IATA	International Air Transport Association
ICAO	International Civil Aviation Organisation
JARUS	Joint Authorities for Rulemaking on Unmanned Systems
MRTD	machine readable travel document
PANS	Procedures for Air Navigation Services
ROC	Remote Pilot Operators' Certificate
RPA	remotely piloted aircraft
RPAS	remotely piloted aircraft system
RPV	remotely piloted vehicle
SARPs	ICAO's Standards and Recommended Practices
SDR	special drawing right
UA	unmanned aircraft
UAS	unmanned aircraft system

UTM	Unmanned Aircraft Systems Traffic Management
UAV	unmanned aerial vehicle
VLOS	visual line of sight
VTOL	vertical take-off and landing

1 Drones, innovation and the challenge for law makers

1.1 The drone revolution

1.1.1 Definition

'Drone' is one of the many names for an unmanned aircraft. Various origins of the word have been suggested. It could have emerged as a term descriptive of the 'dull and dry' reconnaissance work performed early in its history.[1] It has also been traced to the target drone 'Fairey Queen', the success of which led to the creation of the 'Queen Bee' drones. This could then have led to the use of 'drone' as the male counterpart of the queen bee.[2] What is known is that the word drone was used in a 1936 report by Lieutenant Commander Delmer Fahrney of the US Navy who was in charge of a radio-controlled unmanned aircraft project.[3] As is evident from the origin of the term itself, drones have been associated with the military in the popular imagination,[4] and carry a negative connotation because they have been used to kill remotely.[5] However, these associations are slowly changing as drones are increasingly used in a civilian setting.[6]

While 'drone' is in popular usage, drones were previously called 'pilotless aircraft'.[7] This is the term used in Article 8 of the *Chicago Convention of*

---

1 Muhammad Nadeem Mirza et al, 'Unmanned Aerial Vehicles: A Revolution in the Making' (2016) 31 *Research Journal of South Asian Studies* 625, 627.
2 Laurence R. Newcombe, *Unmanned Aviation: A Brief History of Unmanned Aerial Vehicles* (American Institute of Aeronautics and Astronautics, 2004) 4.
3 Ibid.
4 Bart Custers, 'Drones Here, There and Everywhere: Introduction and Overview' in Bart Custers (ed), *The Future of Drone Use: Opportunities and Threats from Ethical and Legal Perspectives* (Springer, 2016) 3, 11.
5 Benjamyn I. Scott, 'Terminology, Definitions and Classifications' in Benjamyn I. Scott (ed), *The Law of Unmanned Aircraft Systems: An Introduction to the Current and Future Regulation under National, Regional and International Law* (Wolters Kluwer, 2016) 9, 9.
6 Bart Custers, 'Drones Here, There and Everywhere: Introduction and Overview' in Bart Custers (ed), *The Future of Drone Use: Opportunities and Threats from Ethical and Legal Perspectives* (Springer, 2016) 3.
7 Muhammad Nadeem Mirza et al, 'Unmanned Aerial Vehicles: A Revolution in the Making (2016) 31 *Research Journal of South Asian Studies* 625, 627.

International Civil Aviation 1944.[8] In the 1960s, the term 'Remotely Piloted Vehicle' (RPV) was used,[9] replaced by 'Unmanned Aerial Vehicles' (UAV) in the 1980s.[10] Other terms that have been used are 'Unmanned Aircraft Systems' (UAS), 'Unmanned Aircraft' (UA), 'Remotely Piloted Aviation Systems' (RPAS), 'Unmanned Drones', and 'Autonomous Drones'.[11]

There are subtle distinctions in these definitions. A UAV can be defined as an unmanned reusable vehicle, and as such would exclude missiles and aerial targets.[12] Theilmann's definition of a UAV contains further description in that the vehicle is also 'capable of being operated remotely or with onboard software, capable of carrying a payload that is not essential to its flight'.[13] UAVs have also been defined so as to exclude 'gliders, balloons, [and] tethered objects'.[14] Jha, however, provides a much broader definition of a UAV when he writes that a UAV is 'essentially … an aircraft without a human pilot'.[15] The term UAV is not well known amongst the general public.[16] It is more often used in media reports and legal commentaries.[17] However, it has not been adopted by the European Union, the International Civil Aviation Organisation (ICAO) and most states.[18]

UAS is widely used by international organisations such as ICAO and the European Aviation Safety Agency (EASA).[19] It is a 'whole of system' term that

---

8   Benjamyn I. Scott, 'Terminology, Definitions and Classifications' in Benjamyn I. Scott (ed), *The Law of Unmanned Aircraft Systems: An Introduction to the Current and Future Regulation under National, Regional and International Law* (Wolters Kluwer, 2016) 9, 10.

9   Muhammad Nadeem Mirza et al, 'Unmanned Aerial Vehicles: A Revolution in the Making' (2016) 31 *Research Journal of South Asian Studies* 625, 627.

10   Ibid.

11   Benjamyn I. Scott, 'Terminology, Definitions and Classifications' in Benjamyn I. Scott (ed), *The Law of Unmanned Aircraft Systems: An Introduction to the Current and Future Regulation under National, Regional and International Law* (Wolters Kluwer, 2016) 9, 10–12.

12   Gregory K. James, *Unmanned Aerial Vehicles and Special Operations: Future Directions* (Postgraduate Thesis, Moterey California Naval Postgraduate School, 2000) 3.

13   Connor A. Theilmann, *Integrating Autonomous Drones into the National Aerospace System* (Senior Capstone Thesis, University of Pennsylvania, 2015) 8.

14   Laurence R. Newcombe, *Unmanned Aviation: A Brief History of Unmanned Aerial Vehicles* (American Institute of Aeronautics and Astronautics, 2004) 1.

15   A. R. Jha, *Theory, Design, and Applications of Unmanned Aerial Vehicles* (CRC Press, 2017).

16   Bart Custers, 'Drones Here, There and Everywhere: Introduction and Overview' in Bart Custers (ed), *The Future of Drone Use: Opportunities and Threats from Ethical and Legal Perspectives* (Springer, 2016) 3, 11.

17   Benjamyn I. Scott, 'Terminology, Definitions and Classifications' in Benjamyn I. Scott (ed), *The Law of Unmanned Aircraft Systems: An Introduction to the Current and Future Regulation under National, Regional and International Law* (Wolters Kluwer, 2016) 9, 10.

18   Ibid.

19   Ibid 11.

includes components such as the control station from where the aircraft is flown. It is defined by ICAO as:

> [a]n aircraft and its associated elements which are operated with no pilot on board.[20]

'UA' refers to the aircraft within the UAS system and is defined by ICAO as:

> [a]ny aircraft intended to be flown without a pilot on board … [it] can be remotely and fully controlled from another place (ground, another aircraft, space) **or pre-programmed to conduct its flight without intervention.**[21] (emphasis added)

For ICAO, RPAS is a subcategory of UAS – this subcategory relating only to unmanned aircraft which are piloted from a remote pilot station.[22] ICAO defines RPAS as:

> [a] remotely piloted aircraft, its associated remote pilot station(s), the required command and control links and any other components as specified in the type design.[23]

Notwithstanding ICAO's standard definitions, it notes that:

> UA are commonly referred to as drones. However, many large RPA are also called drones making the term all encompassing for unmanned aircraft in common vernacular.[24]

'Drone' is used throughout this book as it is recognised more widely and by the general public.

1.1.2 History

The history of drones is ancient.[25] In China, kites carrying explosives were used by a warlord to assault the walled city of his enemies.[26] In 425 BC, Archytas, an

---

20 International Civil Aviation Organization, *Frequently Used Terms* <https://www4.icao.int/uastoolkit/Home/FAQ>.
21 International Civil Aviation Organization, *Frequently Used Terms* < https://www4.icao.int/uastoolkit/Home/FAQ>.
22 Ibid.
23 Ibid.
24 International Civil Aviation Organization, *Background* <https://www4.icao.int/uastoolkit/Home/Narrative>.
25 Benjamyn I. Scott, 'Overview' in Benjamyn I. Scott (ed), *The Law of Unmanned Aircraft Systems: An Introduction to the Current and Future Regulation under National, Regional and International Law* (Wolters Kluwer, 2016) 3, 3.
26 Gregory K. James, *Unmanned Aerial Vehicles and Special Operations: Future Directions* (Postgraduate Thesis, Monterey California Naval Postgraduate School, 2000) 5.

ancient Greek philosopher reputedly built and designed a steam propelled 'pigeon' which apparently flew 200 metres before running out of steam.[27] In 400 BC, a vertical flight device, the 'Chinese top', was invented in China, which consisted of feathers at the end of a stick.[28] The stick was spun between the hands to generate enough lift before it could be released into free flight'.[29] The Egyptian Saqqara bird, a bird-shaped artefact, with its 150 millimetre length and 180 millimetre wingspan is dated to 200 BC.[30] It may have been able to glide; its wings were angled at that of modern aircraft, and this indicates that the ancient Egyptians may have understood some of the processes of aerodynamics.[31]

In 1818, 'a French solider designed an aerial balloon that would use a time delay to float over enemies and launch rockets down on top of them'.[32] In 1849, Austrians launched 200 pilotless balloons to bomb Venice during their siege of the city.[33] Although the balloon raid was not entirely successful (some balloons were blown back by the wind over Austria),[34] Venice surrendered after five weeks.[35] Balloons were also used in the siege of Paris in the 1870s.[36]

In 1863, two years after the start of the American Civil War, a New York-based inventor, Charles Perley, invented the 'Perley Aerial Bomber', a hot-air balloon that carried explosives and was connected to a timing device.[37] However, this device proved to be very inaccurate and dangerous.[38] Nevertheless, Confederacy and Union forces were already using unmanned balloons for bombing and reconnaissance.[39]

27 Kimon P. Valvanis and M.P. Kontitsis, 'A Historical Perspective on Unmanned Aerial Vehicles' in Kimon P. Valvanis (ed) *Advances in Unmanned Aerial Vehicles* (Springer, 2007) 16.
28 Ibid.
29 Ibid.
30 Doug Aamoth, *Cryptids: The Saqqara Bird* (9 June 2010) Time <http://techland. time.com/2010/06/09/cryptids-the-saqqara-bird/>.
31 Ibid.
32 Gregory K. James, *Unmanned Aerial Vehicles and Special Operations: Future Directions* (Postgraduate Thesis, Moterey California Naval Postgraduate School, 2000) 5.
33 Connor A. Theilmann, *Integrating Autonomous Drones into the National Aerospace System* (Senior Capstone Thesis, University of Pennsylvania, 2015) 5.
34 Benjamyn I. Scott, 'Overview' in Benjamyn I. Scott (ed), *The Law of Unmanned Aircraft Systems: An Introduction to the Current and Future Regulation under National, Regional and International Law* (Wolters Kluwer, 2016) 3, 3.
35 Brett Holman, *The First Air Bomb: Venice, 15 July 1849* (22 August 2009) Airminded: Airpower and British Society 1901–1941 <https://airminded.org/2009/08/22/the-first-air-bomb-venice-15-july-1849/>.
36 Muhammad Nadeem Mirza et al, 'Unmanned Aerial Vehicles: A Revolution in the Making' (2016) 31 *Research Journal of South Asian Studies* 625, 629.
37 *Pre-Aviation UAV's: Perley's Aerial Bomber (USA)* NOVA <www.pbs.org/wgbh/nova/spiesfly/uavs_01.html>.
38 Ibid.
39 Benjamyn I. Scott, 'Overview' in Benjamyn I. Scott (ed), *The Law of Unmanned Aircraft Systems: An Introduction to the Current and Future Regulation under National, Regional and International Law* (Wolters Kluwer, 2016) 3, 3.

In 1887, British meteorologist Douglas Archibald attached a camera to a kite to take aerial pictures.[40] And in 1898, kites with cameras were used by the United States for reconnaissance in the Spanish-American War.[41] Beyond military use, unpowered gliders or rubber band-powered flying devices preceded manned flight.[42] Examples include, the Cayley Model Helicopter (1796), and the Cayley Model Glider (1804) both built by Sir George Cayley,[43] and the Penaud Planophore (1871), designed by Alphonse Penaud.[44]

In 1893, Lawrence Hargrave, an Australian, invented the Hargrave box kite.[45] In 1894, he was able to fly the kite 4.9 metres above the ground by linking some of his box kites together.[46] Other examples of early precursors to drones include Samuel Franklin Cody's unmanned powered kite in 1907, and John Stringfellow's success in flying a steam powered glider designed by William Samuel Henson in 1848.[47]

Drones in the military

Although this book is primarily concerned with the use of drones in a civilian context, the military has most significantly engaged in drone development.[48] As a result, we include a short analysis of drone use by the military.

The origin of the modern drone can be traced to the First World War in which drones were created as target practice for the British army.[49] The prototype of these target drones was named the 'Ruston Proctor Aerial Target' and is credited to Sir Archibald Low who worked for the Royal Flying Corps.[50] The other early precursor to modern drones was the Hewitt Sperry

40 Douglas Archibald, *The Story of the Earth's Atmosphere* (George Newnes, 1897).
41 Benjamyn I. Scott, 'Overview' in Benjamyn I. Scott (ed), *The Law of Unmanned Aircraft Systems: An Introduction to the Current and Future Regulation under National, Regional and International Law* (Wolters Kluwer, 2016) 3, 3.
42 Ron Bartsch, James Coyne and Katherine Gray, *Drones in Society: Exploring the Strange New World of Unmanned Aircraft* (Routledge, 2017) 29.
43 Charles H. Gibbs-Smith, 'Sir George Cayley: 'Father of Aerial Navigation' (1773–1857)' 17 *Notes and Records of the Royal Society of London* 36.
44 John David Anderson, *The Airplane: A History of its Technology* (American Institute of Aeronautics and Astronautics, 2002) 40.
45 Janeen Webb and Jack Dann, 'Lawrence Hargrave: Unheralded Aeroplane Engineer' 17 *Omni* 24.
46 Ibid.
47 Laurence R. Newcombe, *Unmanned Aviation: A Brief History of Unmanned Aerial Vehicles* (American Institute of Aeronautics and Astronautics, 2004) 43.
48 Thomas D. Lovett, 'Ruling the Skies or Drowning in Rules? A Look at the FAA's Sluggish Progress in Developing Rules and Forces that Might Be Shaping the Future of Drone Use in the United States' (2016) 21 *Barry Law Review* 251, 253.
49 Muhammad Nadeem Mirza et al, 'Unmanned Aerial Vehicles: A Revolution in the Making' (2016) 31 *Research Journal of South Asian Studies* 625, 629.
50 Ron Bartsch, James Coyne and Katherine Gray, *Drones in Society: Exploring the Strange New World of Unmanned Aircraft* (Routledge, 2017) 24.

Automatic Airplane, an aerial torpedo from 1917,[51] made by Elmer Sperry and Peter Hewitt.[52] The Hewitt Sperry Automatic Airplane could fly at speeds up to 80 kilometres per hour and carry a bomb weighing at 135 kilograms.[53] The plane was particularly remarkable because it represented a technological progression; it incorporated a gyrostabiliser – a breakthrough in flight as it prevented aircraft from rolling.[54] In 1918, Charles Franklin Kettering at Delco (such company later renamed General Motors), successfully flew a 'more sophisticated unmanned aircraft', an aerial torpedo, called the Kettering Bug which could strike at 120 kilometres distances, travel at 80 kmph and carry 136 kilograms of bombs over short distances.[55] Modern cruise missiles are a variant of the Kettering Bug.[56]

During the interwar years, aircraft were converted to drones.[57] Examples of such converted aircraft were the Larynx from 1927, a cruise missile,[58] and the 'Queen Bee', which successfully tested as target practice in 1933.[59] The Queen Bee could reach up to 17,000 feet, travel at over 160 kmph, and travel more than 400 kilometres.[60]

The Second World War necessitated commercial level production of low-cost radio-controlled planes as target practice.[61] The Radioplane company built close to 15,000 target practice drones named OQ-2 for the US army.[62] These drones were launched with a catapult and recovered with a parachute.[63] Some interesting trivia surrounds the OQ-2 drones. The company was owned by

---

51 Bart Custers, 'Drones Here, There and Everywhere: Introduction and Overview' in Bart Custers (ed), *The Future of Drone Use: Opportunities and Threats from Ethical and Legal Perspectives* (Springer, 2016) 3, 9.

52 Connor A. Theilmann, *Integrating Autonomous Drones into the National Aerospace System* (Senior Capstone Thesis, University of Pennsylvania, 2015) 5.

53 Benjamyn I. Scott, 'Overview' in Benjamyn I. Scott (ed), *The Law of Unmanned Aircraft Systems: An Introduction to the Current and Future Regulation under National, Regional and International Law* (Wolters Kluwer, 2016) 3, 4.

54 Laurence R. Newcombe, *Unmanned Aviation: A Brief History of Unmanned Aerial Vehicles* (American Institute of Aeronautics and Astronautics, 2004) 16.

55 Muhammad Nadeem Mirza et al, 'Unmanned Aerial Vehicles: A Revolution in the Making' (2016) 31 *Research Journal of South Asian Studies* 625, 629.

56 Ibid.

57 Bart Custers, 'Drones Here, There and Everywhere: Introduction and Overview' in Bart Custers (ed), *The Future of Drone Use: Opportunities and Threats from Ethical and Legal Perspectives* (Springer, 2016) 3, 9.

58 Ibid.

59 Laurence R. Newcombe, *Unmanned Aviation: A Brief History of Unmanned Aerial Vehicles* (American Institute of Aeronautics and Astronautics, 2004) 47.

60 Ron Bartsch, James Coyne and Katherine Gray, *Drones in Society: Exploring the Strange New World of Unmanned Aircraft* (Routledge, 2017) 25.

61 Connor A. Theilmann, *Integrating Autonomous Drones into the National Aerospace System* (Senior Capstone Thesis, University of Pennsylvania, 2015) 6.

62 Bart Custers, 'Drones Here, There and Everywhere: Introduction and Overview' in Bart Custers (ed), *The Future of Drone Use: Opportunities and Threats from Ethical and Legal Perspectives* (Springer, 2016) 3, 9.

63 Ibid.

Reginald Denny, a well-known Hollywood actor, and a part-time aviation enthusiast.[64] A Mrs Norma Jane Dougherty was working in the OQ-2 factory as a technician, and Captain Ronald Reagan, an army publicist, instructed photographer David Conover to take photographs of Mrs Dougherty.[65] Mr Conover persuaded Mrs Dougherty to become a model. Mrs Dougherty went on to become Marilyn Monroe, and Captain Ronald Reagan went on to become the fortieth president of the United States.[66]

Together with the use of drones for target practice, a further development in unmanned aircraft was the construction by Germany of the Vergeltungswaffe-1 (V-1).[67] The V-1 was a flying bomb that used Archibald Montgomery Low's radio guidance system.[68] Its targets were Britain and Belgium.[69] It could travel 240 kilometres and reach nearly 800 kmph.[70] It could be directed towards a target and programmed to crash after a set time, dropping 900 kilograms of explosives.[71]

During the Cold War the use of drones was primarily focused on surveillance and reconnaissance.[72] The first aerial reconnaissance drone developed was the MQM-57 Falconer; its first flight was in 1955.[73] The Falconer could carry cameras and illumination flares; 73,000 of these drones were made, and used in 18 countries.[74] In 1959, Ryan Aeronautical began its development of the Firebee series of long-range reconnaissance drones.[75] The development of the Firebee was hastened by US concern over 'pilot losses and aircraft losses over hostile territory'.[76] Such concerns were reinforced by the shooting down of the U-2 spy plane piloted by Gary Powers over the Soviet Union in 1960.[77] The

---

64 Robert Guttman, 'Drones: The Hollywood Connection: Actor Reginald Denny was Instrumental in Launching the Target Drone, and His Factory Launched a New Star' 27 *Aviation History* 48.
65 Ron Bartsch, James Coyne and Katherine Gray, *Drones in Society: Exploring the Strange New World of Unmanned Aircraft* (Routledge, 2017) 26.
66 Ibid.
67 Muhammad Nadeem Mirza et al, 'Unmanned Aerial Vehicles: A Revolution in the Making' (2016) 31 *Research Journal of South Asian Studies* 625, 629.
68 Ron Bartsch, James Coyne and Katherine Gray, *Drones in Society: Exploring the Strange New World of Unmanned Aircraft* (Routledge, 2017) 26.
69 Ibid 27.
70 Ibid.
71 Benjamyn I. Scott, 'Overview' in Benjamyn I. Scott (ed), *The Law of Unmanned Aircraft Systems: An Introduction to the Current and Future Regulation under National, Regional and International Law* (Wolters Kluwer, 2016) 3, 4.
72 Christopher J. Coyne and Abigail R. Hall-Blanco, 'The Drone Paradox: Fighting Terrorism with Mechanized Terror' (2016) 16 *GMU Working Paper in Economics* 1, 6.
73 Bart Custers, 'Drones Here, There and Everywhere: Introduction and Overview' in Bart Custers (ed), *The Future of Drone Use: Opportunities and Threats from Ethical and Legal Perspectives* (Springer, 2016) 3, 9.
74 Ibid.
75 A. R. Jha, *Theory, Design, and Applications of Unmanned Aerial Vehicles* (CRC Press, 2017).
76 Ibid.
77 Ibid.

Lightning Bug, a drone in the Firebee series, could be remotely controlled or could fly over pre-programmed routes.[78] These drones were used for spying on Cuba, China, and North Korea.[79] And drones for reconnaissance were used on a large scale during the Vietnam War.[80]

During the post-Cold War era, drones have been used in the global war on terror for targeted attacks on humans.[81] Although Zaloga traces the beginning of robotic warfare to 2002 (when an automobile carrying an Al Qaeda leader was blown up by a CIA Predator drone),[82] the US Air Force and the Central Intelligence Agency (CIA) have, from as early as 1995, used Predator drones for both reconnaissance and combat in Afghanistan, Pakistan, Bosnia, Serbia, Iraq, Yemen, Libya, Syria, and Somalia.[83] In some of these countries, targeted attacks were conducted in non-conflict situations.[84]

Before a discussion of drones in a civilian context, it is necessary to briefly mention the contributions of the radio pioneers without whom modern drones would not have been possible; the defining feature of modern drones is the ability to be remotely controlled. The earliest contributor was James Clerk Maxwell. He first proposed an electromagnetic theory of light in 1865.[85] Heinrich Hertz then proved Maxwell's theory through his experiments.[86] In 1894, Sir Oliver Joseph Lodge investigated the properties of Hertzian waves, and realised the possibility of using them for transmission of messages.[87] In 1895, Jagdish Chandra Bose first transmitted radio signals.[88] The following year, in 1896, Guglielmo Marconi transmitted radio signals over 2.4 kilometres,

78 Benjamyn I. Scott, 'Terminology, Definitions and Classifications' in Benjamyn I. Scott (ed), *The Law of Unmanned Aircraft Systems: An Introduction to the Current and Future Regulation under National, Regional and International Law* (Wolters Kluwer, 2016) 9, 4.

79 Ibid.

80 Steven J. Zaloga, *Unmanned Aerial Vehicles: Robotic Air Warfare 1917–2007* (Bloomsbury Publishing, 2011).

81 Christopher J. Coyne and Abigail R. Hall-Blanco, 'The Drone Paradox: Fighting Terrorism with Mechanized Terror' (2016) 16 *GMU Working Paper in Economics* 1, 6.

82 Steven J. Zaloga, *Unmanned Aerial Vehicles: Robotic Air Warfare 1917–2007* (Bloomsbury Publishing, 2011).

83 Bart Custers, 'Drones Here, There and Everywhere: Introduction and Overview' in Bart Custers (ed), *The Future of Drone Use: Opportunities and Threats from Ethical and Legal Perspectives* (Springer, 2016) 3, 10.

84 Benjamyn I. Scott, 'Terminology, Definitions and Classifications' in Benjamyn I. Scott (ed), *The Law of Unmanned Aircraft Systems: An Introduction to the Current and Future Regulation under National, Regional and International Law* (Wolters Kluwer, 2016) 9, 4.

85 Philip L. Marston, 'James Clerk Maxwell: Life and Science' (2016) 178 *Journal of Quantitative Spectroscopy and Radiative Transfer* 50, 50.

86 John H. Bryant, 'The First Century of Microwaves – 1886 to 1986' (1988) 36 *IEEE Transactions on Microwave Theory and Techniques* 830, 831.

87 Richard Shelton Kirby, *Engineering in History* (Courier Corporation, 1990) 345.

88 Theodore S. Rappaport, Wonil Roh and Kyungwhoon Cheun, 'Mobile's Millimeter-Wave Makeover' (2014) 51 *IEEE Spectrum* 34, 36–37.

marking the beginning of long distance radio.[89] In 1898, Tesla patented the first radio-controlled device, a boat called the 'teleautomaton'.[90] Archibald Montgomery Low invented the first wireless rocket guided systems in 1918.[91] Edward M. Sorensen developed radio-controlled planes that could be flown beyond visual line of sight; 'altitude, attitude and flight dynamics' could be determined from the ground.[92] His remote control system was patented in 1946 and forms the basis for radio-controlled systems now.[93]

Another contribution came from the Hollywood actress Hedy Lamarr who, with the help of her pianist friend George Anthiel, 'invented frequency hopping and spread spectrum, a concept for having wireless radio signals switch quickly among many different frequency channels so that the signal cannot be jammed'.[94] This technology was patented in 1942 and it is used extensively in military and civil aviation.[95] Modern drones such as the General Atomics MQ-1 Predator drone are able to be controlled remotely through satellite relay rather than nearby ground station line-of-sight links.[96]

Civilian drones

Civilian drones have been termed radio-controlled model aircraft or unmanned aircraft.[97] The only difference between the terms is perhaps that a model aircraft is associated with leisure and recreation; unmanned aircraft are associated with commercial use.[98] The earliest example of radio-controlled model aircraft appears to be hydrogen filled model airships.[99] Another early example is when a converted Nortrhop P-61 Black Widow warplane was flown into thunderstorms to collect metereological data for the US Weather Bureau in April 1946.[100]

89 James C. Lin and Paolo Bernadi, 'Editorial: Exposure Hazards and Health Protection in Personal Communication Services' (1997) 3 *Wireless Networks* 435, 435.
90 Ron Bartsch, James Coyne and Katherine Gray, *Drones in Society: Exploring the Strange New World of Unmanned Aircraft* (Routledge, 2017) 23.
91 Ibid.
92 Ibid 26.
93 Connor A. Theilmann, *Integrating Autonomous Drones into the National Aerospace System* (Senior Capstone Thesis, University of Pennsylvania, 2015) 6.
94 Ron Bartsch, James Coyne and Katherine Gray, *Drones in Society: Exploring the Strange New World of Unmanned Aircraft* (Routledge, 2017) 25.
95 Ibid.
96 Connor A. Theilmann, *Integrating Autonomous Drones into the National Aerospace System* (Senior Capstone Thesis, University of Pennsylvania, 2015) 6.
97 Ron Bartsch, James Coyne and Katherine Gray, *Drones in Society: Exploring the Strange New World of Unmanned Aircraft* (Routledge, 2017) 30.
98 Ibid.
99 Ibid.
100 Benjamyn I. Scott, 'Terminology, Definitions and Classifications' in Benjamyn I. Scott (ed), *The Law of Unmanned Aircraft Systems: An Introduction to the Current and Future Regulation under National, Regional and International Law* (Wolters Kluwer, 2016) 9, 5.

The non-military use of drones increased significantly in the 1990s when, according to DeGarmo, '[s]cientific endeavors, such as persistent environmental monitoring, were seen as [an] ideal function for UAVs'.[101] So, for example, the solar-powered Helios and Pathfinder aircraft from the late 1990s, developed by NASA and the Aerovironment Corporation, represented research innovation.[102] In 1998, AAI, an Australian company, produced the Aerosonde Laima, 'which crossed the Atlantic Ocean autonomously on only 1.5 gallons of automotive gasoline'.[103] Also in the 1990s, Japan reached full-scale production and use of drones for spraying crops with fertiliser and pesticides. Non-military uses of drones have, needless to say, continued beyond the 1990s.[104] In 2007, an Aerosonde drone flew into the eye of hurricane Noel at the low altitude of 300 feet, with winds of 80 mph, a feat too dangerous for manned aircraft.[105]

According to Perritt, in addition to the military, model aircraft and hobbyists have played an important role in the civilian use of drones.[106] Perritt distinguishes between macro and micro drones, where micro drones are less than 55 pounds and are powered by '4–8 electrically driven rotors' and macro drones are heavier than 55 pounds and are 'powered by internal combustion engines driving conventional propellers or fan jets'.[107] He argues that micro drones 'evolved from miniaturization of imaging, flight, and electrical propulsion systems that, for the first time, enabled air vehicles to fly in close quarters, down low, and in circumstances where manned aircraft would simply be too big'.[108] Such micro drones have spread from the model aircraft hobbyist community to the commercial world.[109] Macro drones, however, now used in the civilian world, were originally designed for combat and, therefore, find their origin in the military.[110]

The recent jump in popularity of drones amongst consumers has coincided with the technology that has enabled it.

The development of smartphone technology has allowed drones to know their orientation movement direction.[111] Smartphones themselves served as easily available remote controls for the drones.[112] Consumer demand, however,

---

101 Matthew T. DeGarmo, 'Issues Concerning Integration of Unmanned Aerial Vehicles in Civil Airspace' (2004) *MITRE* 4, 4.
102 Ibid.
103 Ibid.
104 Mark E. Peterson, 'Regulatory Construct for Integration into the National Airspace System' (2006) 71 *Journal of Air Law and Commerce* 521, 546.
105 Rebecca Powell, *NASA and NOAA Fly Unmanned Aircraft into Hurricane Noel* (3 April 2008) National Aeronautics and Space Adminstration <https://www.nasa.gov/centers/wallops/news/story105.html>.
106 Henry H. Perritt and Eliot O. Sprague, *Domesticating Drones: The Technology, Law and Economics of Unmanned Aircraft* (Routledge, 2017).
107 Ibid.
108 Ibid.
109 Ibid.
110 Ibid.
111 Civilian Drones (2017) The Economist <www.economist.com/technology-quarterly/2017-06-08/civilian-drones>.
112 Ibid.

has also played a part. A 2014 news article attributes the increasing popularity of modern drones to the fact that 'they allow the selfie generation to take spectacular pictures of themselves or their homes from the air'.[113] Quadcopters have become the most popular drones because of their cheaper cost and reduced complexity.[114] Theilmann traces the current boom in consumer use of drones to the 2010 Las Vegas Consumer Electronics show which showcased the French-based Parrot AR 1.0; it could be controlled by an iPhone app and 'allowed users to take low quality photos and videos'.[115]

However, it was in 2013 that the China-based DJI 'introduced what many consider to be the precursor to modern consumer drone technology'; it included a high quality GoPro camera and live stream camera feed through a smartphone app.[116] While commercial drones, in contrast to consumer drones, are yet to achieve large-scale use (primarily due to government regulations), companies clearly anticipate the use of drones for business purposes. In 2013, Amazon unveiled its 'PrimeAir' project involving delivery by drones.[117] In 2014, Google revealed its home delivery drone.[118] The BBC in 2013 used a hexacopter to conduct its first drone assisted reporting.[119]

In 2016, according to *The Economist*, 2 million consumer drones and 110,000 commercial drones were sold.[120] As with the smartphone 'the fastest innovation is taking place in the consumer market and then being adopted by companies'.[121]

1.1.3 Turning points

The first major turning point in aviation history was the invention of the aircraft. It was used in First World War for military purposes and then commercially, eventually on a global scale. It is now a crucial mode of global transport. The

113 Harry Wallop, Drones – How they Became the Gadget of 2014 (9 December 2014) *The Telegraph* <www.telegraph.co.uk/technology/news/11280750/Drones-how-they-became-the-gadget-of-2014.html>.

114 Richard Williams, Boris Konev and Frans Coenen, 'Multi-Agent Environment Exploration with AR. Drones' in Michael Mistry et al, *Advances in Autonomous Robotics Systems* (Springer, 2014) 60, 60.

115 Connor A. Theilmann, *Integrating Autonomous Drones into the National Aerospace System* (Senior Capstone Thesis, University of Pennsylvania, 2015) 7.

116 Ibid.

117 *Amazon Unveils Futuristic Plan: Delivery by Drone* (1 December 2013) CBS News <https://www.cbsnews.com/news/amazon-unveils-futuristic-plan-delivery-by-drone/>.

118 Dominic Rushe, *Google Reveals Home Delivery Drone Program Project Wing* (30 August 2014) The Guardian <https://www.theguardian.com/technology/2014/aug/29/google-joins-amazon-in-testing-home-delivery-drones>.

119 Trevor Mogg, *BBC News Launches Hexacopter 'Flying Camera' to Give Viewers the Bigger Picture* (29 October 2013) Digital Trends <https://www.digitaltrends.com/cool-tech/bbc-news-hexacopter/>.

120 Civilian Drones (2017) *The Economist* <www.economist.com/technology-quarterly/2017-06-08/civilian-drones>.

121 Ibid.

second, more modest turning point was the *Convention on International Civil Aviation 1944* (the 'Chicago Convention'). The Chicago Convention established a set of basic guidelines and ICAO as a permanent aviation regulatory body.[122]

Drones represent a third turning point. The evolution of drones can be compared to that of the car, early on known as 'locomobiles' or 'horseless carriages'.[123] Cars represented a revolutionary technology. They raised new legal issues, and they moulded the geography of the world around them; roads were built around the globe to accommodate cars.[124] New industries grew up around cars.[125] The drone is an equivalent twenty-first century development.

Drones are being used for a variety of purposes. Drones carrying flame-throwers are used in China to clean powerlines, a highly dangerous occupation for human workers.[126] Portable delivery drones are now a reality; a team from Switzerland has created an origami-inspired delivery drone which can carry loads of up to 500 grams over 2 kilometres and can be folded into a flat pack.[127] Drones have also been of assistance in search and rescue missions, damage assessment, infrastructure safety assessment, and insurance investigations in the aftermath of hurricanes such as Harvey in the United States.[128]

On a lighter note, in May 2014, an Italian restaurant, Francesco's Pizzeria, in Mumbai, India delivered a pizza by drone to the rooftop of a 21-storey apartment building in 10 minutes, avoiding the minimum 30-minute wait for pizza by the traditional method of motorcycle delivery through the city's infamous traffic jam.[129]

These select examples demonstrate the diversity of functions that drones perform and the vast scope of drone use.

Despite the multitude of innovative uses for drones, further evolution of drone technology faces challenges in overcoming significant legal and ethical issues and regulatory systems that are slow to respond to such issues. Some of

---

122 *Convention on International Civil Aviation (Chicago Convention)*, opened for signature 7 December 1944, 15 UNTS 295 (entered into force 4 April 1947).

123 Peter W. Singer, *The Predator Comes Home: A Primer on Domestic Drones, their Huge Business Opportunities, and their Deep Political, Moral and Legal Challenges* (8 March 2013) <https://www.brookings.edu/research/the-predator-comes-home-a-primer-on-domestic-drones-their-huge-business-opportunities-and-their-deep-political-moral-and-legal-challenges/>.

124 Ibid.

125 Ibid.

126 Peter Farquhar, *China is Using a Flamethrower Drone to Clean Rubbish off Powerlines* (20 February 2017) Business Insider <www.businessinsider.com/china-is-using-a-flamethrowing-drone-to-clean-rubbish-off-power-lines-2017-2?IR=T>.

127 *EPFL Develops New Origami-Inspired Delivery Drone* (14 September 2017) Aerospace Technology <www.aerospace-technology.com/news/newsepfl-develops-new-origami-inspired-delivery-drone-5926689>.

128 Kelly McSweeney, *Drones Help with Hurricane Recovery Efforts* (26 September 2017) ZD Net <www.zdnet.com/article/drones-help-with-hurricane-recovery-efforts/>.

129 *India Delivers First Pizza by Drone, Kind Of…* (29 May 2014) NBC News <https://www.nbcnews.com/news/world/india-delivers-first-pizza-drone-kind-n117611>.

the main problems in integrating drones into civil airspace are privacy, security, and safety.

The capacity of drones as surveillance vehicles carries significant implications for privacy and civil liberties. Drones can, for example, be fitted with thermal imaging capability which can be highly intrusive in private spaces such as homes.[130] Such privacy intrusions are made more problematic because drone surveillance is not neutral in its use.[131] Finn and Wright argue that drones in policing and border security roles are already used to a disproportionate extent in relation to marginalised groups, thus raising the problem of discrimination.[132] A survey of US, UK, and EU laws show that the current regulatory regimes are not adequate to meet these challenges.[133] In addition to issues of privacy and discrimination, drones can pose a serious threat to security. In the twenty-first century, terrorists use technology to carry out their activities.[134] Drones, while logistically difficult to operate, may be a possible terrorist tool.[135]

Drones are also a challenge to safety. According to the Australian House of Representatives Standing Committee on Social Policy and Legal Affairs Inquiry, *Eyes in the Sky*, the current quality and technological limitations of drones make drones a safety issue in addition to cluttered airspace.[136]

1.2 Keeping pace with technology

1.2.1 Current use of drones and the pace of technological growth

Drones are being used for a variety of purposes. They are being used by police for 'forensic examination of crime scenes' and for special emergency responses in 'high-risk and significant operations'.[137] They are also being used for the filming of sporting events and making documentaries. The video and photography capabilities of drones are being used by event photographers, real estate agents and tourism guides.[138] They are being used for border patrol, traffic surveillance, pipeline patrol, port security, flood mapping, forest fire rescue, high-altitude imaging, humanitarian aid, environmental monitoring and

---

130 Rachel L. Finn and David Wright, 'Unmanned Aircraft Systems: Surveillance, Ethics and Privacy in Civil Applications' 28 *Computer Law and Security Review* 184, 188.
131 Ibid 190.
132 Ibid 188–189.
133 Ibid 193.
134 Ajay Lele and Archana Mischra, 'Aerial Terrorism and the Threat from Unmanned Aerial Vehicles' (2009) 3 *Journal of Defence Studies* 54, 63.
135 Ibid 64.
136 *Eyes in the Sky: Inquiry into Drones and the Regulation of Air Safety and Privacy* (July 2014) House of Representatives Standing Committee on Social Policy and Legal Affairs, Parliament of Australia <https://www.aph.gov.au/Parliamentary_Business/Committees/House/Social_Policy_and_Legal_Affairs/Drones/Report>, 13.
137 Ibid 7.
138 Ibid 9.

mapping, atmospheric monitoring, soil moisture imaging, crop monitoring, agricultural application and much more.[139]

The scope of drone use grows every year. In 2016, the world's first passenger drone, developed by the Chinese firm Ehang, was cleared for testing in Nevada in the United States.[140] In September 2017, Aire, purportedly the world's first self-flying drone, was launched for development on Kickstarter (a crowd funding site).[141] This drone is a quiet, hovering robot that can be used for surveillance inside domestic homes while the inhabitants are away and is controlled through a mobile app.[142] Facebook is developing a drone to provide Internet services to remote regions of the world.[143] It completed its first successful flight in May 2017.[144]

According to Business Insider, as at 2016, sales of drones were worth $8.5 billion. Such sales are expected to surpass $12 billion by 2021.[145] A 2016 report by Goldman Sachs, *Drones: Reporting for Work*, forecasts a $100 billion market opportunity for drones.[146] The report predicts the commercial drone market to be the fastest growing, particularly in the construction sector.[147]

1.2.2 Drones – some challenges

Privacy

There are several rationales as to why privacy is instinctively important to humanity. Reiman argues that privacy is fundamentally linked to the 'person-hood' of an individual as it is an acknowledgement by society that a person has 'moral title to his existence' and an 'exclusive moral right to shape his

---

139 Matthew T. DeGarmo, 'Issues Concerning Integration of Unmanned Aerial Vehicles in Civil Airspace' (2004) *MITRE* 4.
140 Samuel Gibbs, World's First Passenger Drone Cleared for Testing in Nevada (8 June 2016) The Guardian https://www.theguardian.com/technology/2016/jun/08/worlds-first-passenger-drone-testing-ehang-nevada>.
141 Luke Dormehl, 'The Home-Inspecting Aire Drone Looks Like a Flying Amazon Echo' (19 September 2017) Digital Trends <https://www.digitaltrends.com/cool-tech/aire-flying-security-guard/>
142 Ibid.
143 *Facebook Drone That Could Bring Global Internet Access Completes Test Flight* (3 July 2017) *The Guardian* <https://www.theguardian.com/technology/2017/jul/02/facebook-drone-aquila-internet-test-flight-arizona>
144 Ibid.
145 Divya Joshi, '*Commercial Unmanned Aerial Vehicle (UAV) Market Analysis – Industry Trends, Companies and What You Should Know*' (8 August 2017) Business Insider <www.businessinsider.com/commercial-uav-market-analysis-2017-8/?r=AU&IR=T>.
146 *Drones: Reporting for Work* (9 October 2016) Goldman Sachs <www.goldmansachs.com/our-thinking/technology-driving-innovation/drones/>.
147 Ibid.

destiny'.[148] Moor, on the other hand, argues that privacy is a manifestation of the need for security.[149] It allows us to ensure that no one can use our private information to do us harm.[150] This is especially true in a large, highly inter-active and computerised world.[151] Rachels argues that privacy is important because it allows us to maintain a variety of relationships with other people; we can choose to shape the relationship we have with them by having control over our private information.[152] These rationales all hold that privacy is important to individuals.

Drones pose a particular challenge to privacy because of their technological capacity. Many drones are small; they can conduct surveillance on individuals without being observed. This is especially true of new and innovative drones the size of insects. Unlike conventional aircraft, drones can look into private spaces at very close quarters. Drones can be fitted with ordinary and infrared cameras and heat sensing mechanisms that give them unique capabilities to access private spaces.[153] Further, unlike conventional aircraft, drones are more widely available to the general public; with greater access comes greater risk of misuse.

Security

Whether it be the threat of terrorism by non-state actors or conventional criminal activity, drones are a significant security concern. Drones can be hacked from over a mile away.[154] Given most drone software is in C+ or C++ language, they are easy to hack.[155] Drones can be hacked so as to stop them from responding properly to their operator.[156] Hacking can also result in con-trol of the drone being shifted to someone other than the operator. In April 2014, in Australia, a triathlete suffered injuries when a drone that was being used to take footage of the race fell.[157] The drone appeared to have been

148 Jeffrey H. Reiman, 'Privacy, Intimacy, and Personhood' (1976) 6 *Philosophy and Public Affairs* 26, 39.
149 James H. Moor, 'Towards a Theory of Privacy in the Information Age' (1997) 27 *Computers and Society* 27, 29.
150 Ibid 28.
151 Ibid 29.
152 James Rachels, 'Why Privacy is Important' (1975) 4 *Philosophy and Public Affairs* 323, 326.
153 Rachel L. Finn and David Wright, 'Unmanned Aircraft Systems: Surveillance, Ethics and Privacy in Civil Applications' 28 *Computer Law and Security Review* 184, 184.
154 Manimaran Mohan, *Cybersecurity in Drones* (Senior Capstone Thesis, Utica College, 2016) 26.
155 Ibid 25.
156 Ibid 26.
157 *Eyes in the Sky: Inquiry into Drones and the Regulation of Air Safety and Privacy* (July 2014) House of Representatives Standing Committee on Social Policy and Legal Affairs, Parliament of Australia <https://www.aph.gov.au/Parliamentary_Business/Committees/House/Social_Policy_and_Legal_Affairs/Drones/Report> 17.

hijacked.[158] That drones can be operated for illegal purposes is evident from an incident in Oklahoma prison where an out-of-control drone crashed on the prison grounds.[159] It was being used to smuggle items such as hacksaw blades and drugs into the prison.[160] There is also a possibility that drones will be used by cyber criminals for hacking mobile devices and accessing sensitive data.[161] Drones can also be used for unauthorised surveillance of areas sensitive to national security. Further, as drones are difficult to detect and can carry lethal loads, they are an ideal terrorist tool.[162]

Safety

Even ignoring the threat of harm by terrorists or criminals, drones pose a threat to safety. This is due to multiple reasons. First, there are significant safety concerns regarding drones interacting with traditional air traffic.[163] Due to their small size, drones are difficult for pilots to see and avoid.[164] This makes them a danger in the air. If a small drone is swallowed by the engine of a passenger aircraft, for example, it can lead to a major accident endangering many lives.

Second, drones today may not be built to a very high standard. For example, the *Eyes in the Sky* Inquiry by the Australian Parliament cites a submission which states that many drones, even ones from premium brands, are made of components that are of a hobbyist standard.[165]

Further, as noted previously, there are significant issues regarding the reliability of the technology that controls the behaviour of a drone. For example, in October 2013, a recreational drone landed on a train line on the Sydney Harbour Bridge after the owner lost control of it.[166] The Inquiry noted that drones 'have not yet achieved the reliability expected of mature technologies'.[167] The lack of reliability of drones at this stage of their development poses a safety risk to people and property on the ground. The safety issues raise questions of liability for harm to third parties, such as who should be responsible for the harm caused.[168]

158 Ibid.
159 Manimaran Mohan, *Cybersecurity in Drones* (Senior Capstone Thesis, Utica College, 2016) 13–14.
160 Ibid.
161 Ibid 15.
162 Ajay Lele and Archana Mischra, 'Aerial Terrorism and the Threat from Unmanned Aerial Vehicles' (2009) 3 *Journal of Defence Studies* 54, 63.
163 Kristian Bernauw, 'Drones: The Emerging Era of Unmanned Civil Aviation' (2016) 66 *Collected Papers of Zagreb Law Faculty* 223, 228.
164 Ibid 240.
165 *Eyes in the Sky: Inquiry into Drones and the Regulation of Air Safety and Privacy* (July 2014) House of Representatives Standing Committee on Social Policy and Legal Affairs, Parliament of Australia <https://www.aph.gov.au/Parliamentary_Business/Committees/House/Social_Policy_and_Legal_Affairs/Drones/Report> 14.
166 Ibid 15.
167 Ibid 13.
168 Anna Masutti, 'Proposals for the Regulation of Unmanned Air Vehicle Use in Common Airspace' (2009) 34 *Air and Space Law* 1, 9.

1.2.3 Current regulation of drones

As shown above, as a new and rapidly developing technology, drones pose significant regulatory challenges. The various regulatory regimes for drones, both international and domestic, are still evolving. The current state of development of these regulatory regimes is set out below.

International regulations

CHICAGO CONVENTION AND ICAO

Article 8 of the Chicago Convention, regulates 'pilotless aircraft'.[169] As set out in Article 8, in order for a pilotless aircraft to fly over a contracting state to the Chicago Convention, special authorisation will be required from that state.[170] Further, when flying over areas open to civil aircraft, contracting states must prevent pilotless aircraft from endangering civil aircraft.[171] That UAVs (or drones) fall within the definition of 'pilotless aircraft' was affirmed at the Eleventh Air Navigation Conference held in Montreal in late 2003.[172]

As drones are a species of 'aircraft', many Articles of the Chicago Convention may apply to them; these articles regulate 'aircrafts'. For example, Article 36, in allowing contracting states to 'prohibit or regulate the use of photographic apparatus in aircraft over its territory',[173] may apply to drones.[174] As a type of aircraft, drones must also follow the 'rules of the air' (Article 12).[175] Other articles that may apply to drones are 3, 15, 31, 29, 32, and 33.[176] Drones are also capable of being regulated by ICAO which is mandated to regulate matters concerned with 'safety, regularity, and efficiency of air navigation' (Article 37).[177]

Annexes to the Chicago Convention are not binding, but they provide a framework regulatory regime. Annex 2 – Rules of the Air 'constitutes Standards relating to the flight and manoeuvre of aircraft' and these standards must

169 *Convention on International Civil Aviation (Chicago Convention)*, opened for signature 7 December 1944, 15 UNTS 295 (entered into force 4 April 1947) art 8.
170 Ibid.
171 Ibid.
172 Ron Bartsch, James Coyne and Katherine Gray, *Drones in Society: Exploring the Strange New World of Unmanned Aircraft* (Routledge, 2017) 53.
173 *Convention on International Civil Aviation (Chicago Convention)*, opened for signature 7 December 1944, 15 UNTS 295 (entered into force 4 April 1947) art 36.
174 Kristian Bernauw, 'Drones: The Emerging Era of Unmanned Civil Aviation' (2016) 66 *Collected Papers of Zagreb Law Faculty* 223, 242.
175 International Civil Aviation Organisation 'Circular 328 AN/190: Unmanned Aircraft Systems (UAS)' (Paper presented at the Seminar on Unmanned Aircraft Systems (UAS), Lima, Peru, 18 April 2012 to 20 April 2012) 12.
176 Ibid 11–14.
177 *Convention on International Civil Aviation (Chicago Convention)*, opened for signature 7 December 1944, 15 UNTS 295 (entered into force 4 April 1947) art 7.

be adhered to in relation to drones.[178] Annex 2 was specifically amended to include new Appendix 4 – *Remotely Piloted Aircraft Systems* in 2012 (Amendment 43). Annex 7 – Aircraft Nationality and Registration Marks also applies to drones.[179]

ICAO released *Circular 328-AN/190* in 2011, outlining its view of integrating drones into the international regulatory regime.[180] The organisation also released the 'Manual on Remotely Piloted Aircraft Systems' in 2015 to provide guidance on the technical and operational issues for commercial drones.[181] ICAO is also developing Standards and Recommended Practices (SARPs) specifically for drones; existing SARPs apply to a significant degree.[182]

INTERNATIONAL CONVENTIONS APPLICABLE TO DRONES?

Treaties are fundamental to the regulation of aviation at an international level. Such treaties typically do not refer to drones. However, a broad interpretation of 'aircraft' as adopted by ICAO (from an interpretation of the Chicago Convention) brings drones within the scope of relevant international treaties.

Significant instruments relating to civil aviation which may well be applicable to drones include the *Convention for the Unification of Certain Rules Relating to International Carriage by Air* 1929 (Warsaw Convention), *Convention on Damage Caused by Foreign Aircraft to Third Parties on the Surface* 1952 (Rome Convention), *Convention for the Suppression of Unlawful Seizure of Aircraft* 1970 (Hague Convention), *Convention on Offences and Certain Other Acts Committed on Board Aircraft* 1964 (Tokyo Convention), and the *Convention for the Suppression of Unlawful Acts against the Safety of Civil Aviation* 1971 (Montreal Convention).[183]

However, some instruments, such as the Tokyo Convention, may be of limited use in terms of the regulation of drones because they are aimed at criminal behaviour of people on board an aircraft and, currently, the vast majority of drones are unmanned.[184]

These conventions are discussed more substantially in Chapter 3.

---

178 International Civil Aviation Organisation 'Circular 328 AN/190: Unmanned Aircraft Systems (UAS)' (Paper presented at the Seminar on Unmanned Aircraft Systems (UAS), Lima, Peru, 18 April 2012 to 20 April 2012) 15.
179 Ibid 29.
180 Ibid.
181 International Civil Aviation Authority, *Manual on Remotely Piloted Aircraft Systems (RPAS): ICAO Doc 10019* (1st ed, 2015).
182 See ICAO circular
183 Benjamyn I. Scott, 'Key Provisions in Current Aviation Law' in Bart Custers (ed), *The Future of Drone Use: Opportunities and Threats from Ethical and Legal Perspectives* (Springer, 2016) 241, 249–256.
184 Ibid 255.

EUROPEAN UNION

EU regulation *EC 216/2008* provides a mandate to the EASA to regulate drones that are 150 kilograms and above.[185] *EC 216/2008* regulates significant areas of aviation such as airworthiness, operations, licensing and certification.[186] EASA is in the process of developing a new prototype regulation that will allow it to further regulate drones that are below 150 kilograms.[187] The prototype regulation makes drones subject to privacy regulations.[188] Further, the EU has adopted a geo-fencing system that prevents drones from entering into certain areas.[189] Drones can also be regulated under *Directive 2009/48/EC* which regulates the safety of toys including flying toys.[190]

Domestic regulations

SAFETY AND SECURITY

In the absence of clear guidelines from international bodies, many domestic jurisdictions have chosen to draft their own regulations. Many countries have chosen to exempt small drones below a certain weight level from compliance with standard rules applicable to aircraft. States have also chosen to differentiate between drones used for commercial and recreational purposes in applying regulations. Drones for recreational purposes generally tend to be less regulated. In order to improve safety, various jurisdictions have adopted a maximum flying height above which drones would require permission to operate. Many states prohibit drones from operating over areas that are highly populated, areas sensitive to national security, and the area within a wide circumference surrounding airports.

Some jurisdictions aim to regulate drones to a standard of safety required for manned aircraft.

With regard to the registration of drones, some jurisdictions require mandatory registration of drones above a certain weight (or even all drones). Other jurisdictions only require registration above a certain weight. Pilot licensing requirements apply to drones unless they fall within the small drone exception. Certification

---

185 *Regulation (EC) No 216/2008 of the European Aviation Safety Agency of 20 February 2008 on Common Rules in the Field of Civil Aviation and Establishing a European Aviation Safety Agency, and Repealing Council Directive 91/670/EEC Regulation (EC) No 1592/2002 and Directive 2004/36/E* [2008] OJ L 79/1.
186 Ibid.
187 *Unmanned Aircraft* (14 November 2017) European Commission <http://ec.europa.eu/growth/sectors/aeronautics/rpas_en>.
188 Ibid.
189 *Aviation: Commission is Taking the European Drone Sector to New Heights* (16 June 2017) European Commission <http://europa.eu/rapid/press-release_IP-17-1605_en.htm>.
190 *Directive 2009/48/EC of the European Parliament and of the Council of 18 June 2009 on the Safety of Toys* [2009] OJ L 170/1.

for drones is mostly required for larger drones. In relation to insurance requirements, some jurisdictions require mandatory insurance for drones.

Domestic regulation of drones in a select number of jurisdictions is addressed below by way of example and comparison.

AUSTRALIA

Australia was the first jurisdiction to introduce regulation relating to drones.[191] The *Civil Aviation Safety Regulation (CASR)* Part 101 (CASR Part 101) was introduced in 2002. Australian regulation of drones categorises drones by reference to the purpose of their use (recreational or commercial), and by their weight. For recreational drones, approval is not required as long as certain safety rules are followed.[192] To operate drones weighing above 2 kilograms commercially, the operator must acquire authorisation from the Australian Civil Aviation Safety Authority (CASA) in the form of a Remote Pilot's License and a RPA Operator's Certificate.[193] The amendments to CASR Part 101, effective from 29 September 2016, allow drones weighing between 100 grams to 2 kilograms to be operated without requiring a Remote Pilot's License or an RPA Operator's Certificate.[194] However, the operator must first acquire an Aviation Reference Number (ARN) and then notify CASA five business days prior to flying via an online form.[195] The notification is valid for two years.[196]

UK

Small drones, defined as those weighing less than 20 kilograms, for recreational use, are regulated by Articles 241, 94 and 95 of the *Air Navigation Order 2016* (ANO), the primary document for aviation regulation in the UK.[197] Small drones, if fitted with a camera, must acquire permission from the Civil Aviation Authority (CAA) in order to fly below the minimum distance requirements from people and objects.[198] Model aircraft are also regulated in a similar

---

191 *Regulation of Drones: Australia* (26 July 2016) Library of Congress <https://www.loc.gov/law/help/regulation-of-drones/australia.php>.

192 *Flying Drones or Model Aircraft Recreationally* (23 October 2017) Civil Aviation Safety Authority <https://www.casa.gov.au/modelaircraft>.

193 *Gaining Your Remote Pilot Licence (RePL) and RPA Operator's Certificate (ReOC)* (31 October 2017) Civil Aviation Safety Authority <https://www.casa.gov.au/aircraft/standard-page/commercial-unmanned-flight-gaining-your-remotely-piloted-aircraft-pilot>.

194 *Commercially Unmanned Flight – Remotely Piloted Aircraft Under 2kg* (2 November 2017) Civil Aviation Safety Authority <https://www.casa.gov.au/standard-page/commercial-unmanned-flight-remotely-piloted-aircraft-under-2kg>.

195 Ibid.

196 Ibid.

197 *Recreational Drone Flights* (2015) UK Civil Aviation Authority <www.caa.co.uk/Consumers/Unmanned-aircraft/Recreational-drones/Recreational-drone-flights/>.

198 Ibid.

way.[199] For small commercial drones, the articles relating to small unmanned aircraft also apply.[200] Additionally, operators must obtain permission from the CAA in order to operate the drone commercially.[201] Large drones weighing 20 kilograms or more are subject to the entirety of the ANO.[202] Additionally, operators must apply for specific approval (Exemptions) to fly large drones.[203] Exemptions may also allow large drones to be exempt from certain requirements under the ANO.[204] Similar rules apply to large model aircraft.[205] Guidance documents such as the *Model Aircraft: A Guide To Safe Flying* (CAP 658) and the UK Civil Aviation Authority's *Guidelines on the use of Unmanned Aircraft in UK Controlled Airspace* (CAP 722) relate to large model aircraft and drones respectively.

UNITED STATES

Regulations governing drones in the United States are found in *Title 14 of the Code of Federal Regulation* (14 CFR) Part 107 and section 336 of *Public Law 112–95 (Special Rule for Model Aircraft).*[206] Under these regulations, there are no pilot requirements for recreational drones; commercial drones, however, require the operator to hold a Remote Pilot Airman Certificate, be 16 years of age, and pass TSA vetting.[207] Unless operated exclusively in compliance with section 336, drones weighing above 0.55 pounds must be registered.[208] Commercial drones must be less than less than 55 pounds and 'must undergo pre-flight check to ensure UAS is in condition for safe operation'.[209]

Privacy

While the rules discussed above deal primarily with issues of safety and security, usually, privacy is not dealt with under drone-specific regulations. The UK

---

199 *Model Aircraft* (2015) UK Civil Aviation Authority <www.caa.co.uk/Consumers/Unmanned-aircraft/Model-aircraft/>.
200 *Regulations Relating to the Commercial Use of Small Drones* (2015) <www.caa.co.uk/Commercial-industry/Aircraft/Unmanned-aircraft/Small-drones/Regulations-relating-to-the-commercial-use-of-small-drones/>.
201 Ibid.
202 *Large Unmanned Aircraft* (2015) UK Civil Aviation <www.caa.co.uk/Commercial-industry/Aircraft/Unmanned-aircraft/Large-unmanned-aircraft/>.
203 Ibid.
204 Ibid.
205 *Model Aircraft* (2015) UK Civil Aviation <www.caa.co.uk/Consumers/Unmanned-aircraft/Model-aircraft/>.
206 *Getting Started* (31 July 2017) Federal Aviation Administration <https://www.faa.gov/uas/getting_started/>.
207 Ibid.
208 Ibid.
209 Ibid.

restriction on small drones carrying cameras is perhaps the exception. However, there are general privacy principles that may apply to drones.

The common law doctrine of *cuius est solum, eius est usque ad coelum et ad inferos* (meaning whoever owns the soil, it is theirs all the way to Heaven and all the way to hell) implies that ownership of land conveys ownership of airspace above and ground below the land. This doctrine, although limited by the right of conventional aircraft to fly over private land, can be interpreted to prevent the use of drones; by operating at close quarters to the land, they may constitute direct and immediate interference with the land.[210] This may, to some extent, provide protection for breaches of privacy.

In the United States, there are a variety of statutory and common laws that can regulate drones such as those relating to trespass, privacy and stalking in addition to State-specific laws regulating wiretapping, paparazzi and anti-voyeurism.[211] In Australia, there are privacy laws at the State and national level as well as the *Surveillance Devices Act 2004* (Cth).[212] Further, there are common law torts of trespass, nuisance and breach of confidence which may protect privacy.[213]

1.2.4 Limitations of current regulation of drones

Limitations of international regulations

Articles in the Chicago Convention that may apply to drones were clearly aimed at manned aircraft. Hence, applying those articles to drones could result in compliance being impractical or inappropriate. For example, Article 29 requires that every aircraft carry on board certain paper originals of documents such as a certificate of registration and certificate of airworthiness.[214] This may be practically impossible for many kinds of drones.[215] Article 31 requires that every aircraft has a certificate of airworthiness from its state of registration.[216] However, the criteria for what constitutes airworthiness may differ for

---

210 Kristian Bernauw, 'Drones: The Emerging Era of Unmanned Civil Aviation' (2016) 66 *Collected Papers of Zagreb Law Faculty* 223, 242.
211 Ethan N. Brown, 'Please, Don't Let Me Drone On: The Need for Federally-Led and State-Collaborated Action to Promote Succinct and Efficient Drone Regulations' 16 *Kansas Journal of Law and Public Policy* 48, 63.
212 *Eyes in the Sky: Inquiry into Drones and the Regulation of Air Safety and Privacy* (July 2014) House of Representatives Standing Committee on Social Policy and Legal Affairs, Parliament of Australia <https://www.aph.gov.au/Parliamentary_Business/Committees/House/Social_Policy_and_Legal_Affairs/Drones/Report> 34–37.
213 Ibid 37.
214 International Civil Aviation Organisation 'Circular 328 AN/190: Unmanned Aircraft Systems (UAS)' (Paper presented at the Seminar on Unmanned Aircraft Systems (UAS), Lima, Peru, 18 April 2012 to 20 April 2012) 13.
215 Ibid.
216 Ibid.

drones.[217] Article 32 requires the licensing of personnel.[218] However, international standards have not yet been developed for licensing of remote pilots.[219]

ICAO is developing standards which are drone-applicable; it is understood that such standards are not far away. In the absence of such regulations, domestic jurisdictions create their own regulations which leads to issues of harmonisation.[220] These issues also arise in relation to EU regulations as, currently, all drones below 150 kilograms are regulated by the various EU states.[221]

The international conventions that apply to drones are limited in their ability to effectively regulate drones. For example, although the Warsaw Convention, by virtue of applying to aircraft, most likely applies to drones, Article 17 of the convention is unlikely to be applicable to drones at this stage of the technology's development because it relates to death or injury of passengers on board or in the process of embarking or disembarking.[222] Similarly, The Hague Convention targets acts related to hijacking by people on board the aircraft.[223] Therefore, it cannot regulate drones because at present the vast majority of drones do not carry any people on board.[224] The Montreal Convention, although applicable to drones because it is aimed at actions against the aircraft, is most likely to be ineffective to regulate civilian drones at present because it is only confined to the international arena.[225] The Tokyo Convention is unlikely to apply because the Convention is aimed at criminalising behaviour of people on board.[226]

In relation to the Rome Convention, there are four major limitations. First, the Rome Convention is not widely ratified.[227] As such it is not able to effectively regulate an internationally recognised framework for liability. Second, the Rome Convention caters for 'poor compensation as the limits are set at a 1958 value'.[228] This is a problem for harm caused by both manned and unmanned aircraft as it leaves victims undercompensated. Third, in the Rome Convention, liability is determined according to the weight of aircraft (manned or unmanned).[229] This can cause significant imbalance between the damage caused and the extent of liability that attaches to that damage as even small

217 Ibid.
218 Ibid.
219 Ibid 14.
220 Kristian Bernauw, 'Drones: The Emerging Era of Unmanned Civil Aviation' (2016) 66 *Collected Papers of Zagreb Law Faculty* 223, 234.
221 Ibid 237.
222 Benjamyn I. Scott, 'Key Provisions in Current Aviation Law' in Bart Custers (ed), *The Future of Drone Use: Opportunities and Threats from Ethical and Legal Perspectives* (Springer, 2016) 241, 249–250.
223 Ibid 255.
224 Ibid.
225 Ibid 255–256.
226 Ibid 255.
227 Sofia Michaelides-Mateou and Chrystel Erotokritou, 'Flying into the Future with UAVs: The Jetstream 31 Flight' (2014) 39 *Air and Space Law* 111, 123.
228 Ibid.
229 Ibid.

drones can cause significant harm. The fourth limitation is that the strict liability regime may not be appropriate for remotely piloted aircraft.[230] For example, if a drone is operating using defective software, the question arises as to whether the manufacturer or the remote operator is liable.[231] This problem is compounded by the fact that modern drones are still in their technological infancy and there are limited airworthiness requirements for drones. Although in *Convention for the Suppression of Unlawful Acts against the Safety of Civil Aviation* 2009 (General Risks Convention) and *Convention for the Suppression of Unlawful Acts against the Safety of Civil Aviation* 2009 (Unlawful Interference Compensation Convention), modernised the Rome Convention, their applicability to drone regulation is limited because issues relating to strict liability and weight-based liability continue to be a part of these conventions.[232] Furthermore, these conventions are not yet in force.

Limitations of domestic regulations

DRONE-SPECIFIC REGULATIONS

Federal jurisdictions face similar harmonisation issues to those of the EU as regulations are spread over the federal and State jurisdictions. Further, while some States may implement regulations regarding drones, other States might not. This creates inconsistency.

The other issue in domestic regulation of drones is that, in many jurisdictions, small drones are largely omitted from the regulatory framework. This is especially true if the drones are for recreational use. As small drones become increasingly accessible to the general public, the current state of regulations become inadequate. Further, an increase in small drones increases collision risks significantly. Additionally, in relation to security threats, detection may be an issue as drones can be used by terrorists to avoid detection by radar networks.[233] The regulation of small drones is particularly problematic because the definition of small drones can include vehicles that are quite heavy. For example, small drones can weigh up to 55 pounds (in the US) and 20 kilograms (in the UK).[234] Drones of that weight pose significantly greater threats to air traffic than more typical hazards such as birds.[235]

---

230 Pam Stewart, 'Drone Danger: Remedies for Damage by Civilian Remotely Piloted Aircraft to Persons or Property on the Ground in Australia' (2016) 23 *Torts Law Journal* 290.
231 Ron Bartsch, James Coyne and Katherine Gray, *Drones in Society: Exploring the Strange New World of Unmanned Aircraft* (Routledge, 2017) 91.
232 Hodgkinson and Johnston, *International Air Carrier Liability* (Routledge, 2017) 216–217.
233 Ajay Lele and Archana Mischra, 'Aerial Terrorism and the Threat from Unmanned Aerial Vehicles' (2009) 3 *Journal of Defence Studies* 54, 55.
234 Brian F. Havel and John Q. Mulligan, 'Unmanned Aircraft Systems: A Challenge to Global Regulators' (2015) *65 DePaul Law Review* 107, 118.
235 Ibid.

Subjecting large drones to similar rules as manned aircraft may be appropriate – for the most part – as they pose similar threats to safety and security. However, liability imposed on operators may need to be reassessed, especially in the context of autonomous drones as they require little human input to operate.[236]

It may also be argued that in some ways drones are being over-regulated, specifically those for commercial purposes.[237] For example, in many jurisdictions, commercial drones require certification from the relevant national aviation agency. Differential treatment may not achieve safety and security objectives as similarly sized recreational drones may not be regulated to the same extent.[238] This might just have a cooling effect on the commercial drone market.

Research and study continues on striking the appropriate balance between commercial, safety and security considerations which is no easy feat. One suggestion has been to introduce classifications for drones that correspond to the harm they can cause rather than the purpose for which they are used.[239]

PRIVACY

The main privacy issue for both national and international aviation agencies is that privacy is beyond the scope of regulation.[240] That is, privacy is beyond their power to regulate; it is outside their mandate. Thus, privacy does not feature largely in the regulations of drones. Non-industry-specific laws are often referred to as a mechanism to protect privacy. Often, these laws do not provide adequate protection.

Many statutory privacy laws are inadequate because those laws are only applicable to government or private commercial entities, and do not apply to private individuals.[241] As such, for example, they are unlikely to cover situations such as a person spying on his or her neighbour through a drone fitted with video cameras. Anti-voyeurism laws may provide significant privacy protection. However, these laws are not universal; for example, they vary from

236 Kristian Bernauw, 'Drones: The Emerging Era of Unmanned Civil Aviation' (2016) 66 *Collected Papers of Zagreb Law Faculty* 223, 244–245.
237 Ethan N. Brown, 'Please, Don't Let Me Drone On: The Need for Federally-Led and State-Collaborated Action to Promote Succinct and Efficient Drone Regulations' 16 *Kansas Journal of Law and Public Policy* 48, 59–60.
238 Konstantin Kakaes et al, *Drones and Aerial Observation: New Technologies for Property Rights, Human Rights, and Global Development* (New America, 2015) 31.
239 Brian F. Havel and John Q. Mulligan, 'Unmanned Aircraft Systems: A Challenge to Global Regulators' (2015) *65 DePaul Law Review* 107, 119.
240 Ibid 112–113.
241 *Eyes in the Sky: Inquiry into Drones and the Regulation of Air Safety and Privacy* (July 2014) House of Representatives Standing Committee on Social Policy and Legal Affairs, Parliament of Australia <https://www.aph.gov.au/Parliamentary_Business/Committees/House/Social_Policy_and_Legal_Affairs/Drones/Report>.

state to state in the US.[242] The same is true for Australia, where harassment and stalking laws may protect privacy but are inconsistent across jurisdictions.[243] Further, the privacy legislation in Australia is concerned with data protection only, not unrecorded surveillance.[244]

In Australia, there is currently no tort of privacy.[245] This limits Australian courts from protecting people from privacy breaches by drones. However, in other common law jurisdictions, torts and other rules of common law may evolve to protect people's privacy from drones. In the US, there are four torts relating to privacy, 'publicity which places the plaintiff in a false light', 'appropriation of the plaintiff's likeness', 'intrusion upon the plaintiff's seclusion or solitude', and 'public disclosure of private facts about the plaintiff'.[246]

The tort of public disclosure of private facts about the plaintiff has also been adopted by the courts in New Zealand.[247] Although the UK does not have an explicit tort of privacy, it has expanded the tort of breach of confidence to protect privacy to a large extent.[248] In Canada, there is a statutory tort of privacy.[249] These torts may be able to provide some privacy protections in the drone context. However, case law relating to existing torts was developed in substantially different circumstances to that of drones breaching privacy.[250] Perhaps the flexibility of the common law will allow the courts to apply privacy protections in the context of drones. However, the ability of the common law to protect privacy from drones must be viewed as uncertain.

1.3 Challenges for law makers

As shown in the previous section, while there are laws and regulations relevant to drones, they are significantly limited in their ability to adequately regulate drones. This section briefly explores the challenges faced by law makers in overcoming these limitations.

---

242 Ethan N. Brown, 'Please, Don't Let Me Drone On: The Need for Federally-Led and State-Collaborated Action to Promote Succinct and Efficient Drone Regulations' 16 *Kansas Journal of Law and Public Policy* 48, 63.
243 *Eyes in the Sky: Inquiry into Drones and the Regulation of Air Safety and Privacy* (July 2014) House of Representatives Standing Committee on Social Policy and Legal Affairs, Parliament of Australia <https://www.aph.gov.au/Parliamentary_Business/Committees/House/Social_Policy_and_Legal_Affairs/Drones/Report> 37.
244 Ibid 35.
245 Jillian Caldwell, 'Protecting Privacy Post *Lenah*: Should the Courts Establish a New Tort or Develop Breach of Confidence?' (2003) 26 *UNSW Law Journal* 90, 91.
246 Ibid 96.
247 Ibid.
248 Ibid 109–112.
249 Douglas Camp Chaffey, 'The Right to Privacy in Canada' (1993) 108 *Political Science Quarterly* 117, 120–121.
250 Ron Bartsch, James Coyne and Katherine Gray, *Drones in Society: Exploring the Strange New World of Unmanned Aircraft* (Routledge, 2017) 87.

1.3.1 Balancing risks and benefits

Perhaps one of the most significant challenges to lawmakers is to regulate drones in such a way as to allow society to reap the benefits of drones while at the same time preserve the privacy, safety, and security of individuals. CASA, the Australian aviation safety regulator, has made progress towards creating a regime that balances safety and usability by introducing a new category of drones below 2 kilograms for commercial use that does not require the operator to have a licence.[251] Privacy, however – which is outside the scope of CASA's mandate – has not been addressed sufficiently (if at all) by lawmakers.

1.3.2 Law, technology and retrofitting

One of the main challenges faced by lawmakers in regulating drones is the rapid pace of development in drone technology and the diversity of drone use. Domestic legislation and international treaties take significant lengths of time to negotiate, draft and enter into force. This is particularly true for multilateral treaties, presenting significant challenges for consensus-building, that may be required to create uniform laws for drones. Lawmakers and regulators have often dealt with these issues by retrofitting old laws to new technology.

One of the areas in which retrofitting of the law is most evident is the area of privacy. It is clear from earlier analysis that common law privacy protections and legislative instruments are the only sources of privacy protection. However, *existing* privacy protections may not be adequate in effectively protecting individuals from breaches of their privacy from drones.

As set out previously in this chapter, transposing regulations from manned aviation to drones can lead to unwanted results. It can also lead to regulatory stifling of the development of unmanned aircraft.

Applying the laws of manned aircraft to drones also raises concerns with respect to apportionment of liability. Given that the drone and its operator are at some remove, there are potential issues associated with the application of a strict liability regime (such as the one currently applicable to some manned aircraft) to drones.

Jurisdictional issues

DOMESTIC

Jurisdictional issues pose yet another challenge to lawmakers. Concerns such as privacy are usually beyond the jurisdiction and competence of aviation

---

251 *Commercially Unmanned Flight – Remotely Piloted Aircraft Under 2kg* (2 November 2017) Civil Aviation Safety Authority <https://www.casa.gov.au/standard-page/commercial-unmanned-flight-remotely-piloted-aircraft-under-2kg>.

authorities, both national and international.[252] Privacy protections are usually afforded through legislation and, to some extent, by the common law. As set out in the previous section, these protections are not tailored to address the special challenge to privacy posed by drones.

At a domestic level, this issue could be circumvented by the development of privacy regulations as a combined effort between authorities responsible for aviation and the legislature. Otherwise, aviation authorities may require their scope of operation to be expanded to include privacy. This is not such a novel idea as aviation authorities such as the United States Federal Aviation Administration (FAA) has expanded its jurisdiction post-9/11 to include security as a core issue for regulation.

INTERNATIONAL

ICAO suffers a similar limitation in terms of its jurisdiction regarding privacy issues. However, the limitation to its jurisdiction is not easily overcome. First, ICAO derives its mandate from the Chicago Convention; that mandate does not include regulation of privacy.[253] Second, even if ICAO did have such a mandate, as an international organisation involved with multiple nations with differing ideologies and cultures, it is difficult (and, perhaps, undesirable) for ICAO to create regulations regarding socio-political issues such as privacy.[254]

FEDERAL STATES

Problems also arise in the context of federal states where there are jurisdictional divisions between the federal and state level. In the US, federal drone policy does not deal with privacy concerns.[255] However, 26 States in the US have instituted drone regulation, mainly dealing with privacy issues.[256] This creates significant inconsistencies in large federal systems. It is difficult for lawmakers to comprehensively address issues arising from drone use in a system where regulation applies in a fragmented manner.

252 Brian F. Havel and John Q. Mulligan, 'Unmanned Aircraft Systems: A Challenge to Global Regulators' (2015) *65 DePaul Law Review* 107, 112.

253 *Convention on International Civil Aviation (Chicago Convention)*, opened for signature 7 December 1944, 15 UNTS 295 (entered into force 4 April 1947) art 37.

254 Brian F. Havel and John Q. Mulligan, 'Unmanned Aircraft Systems: A Challenge to Global Regulators' (2015) *65 DePaul Law Review* 107, 113.

255 Allyn K. Milojevich, 'Proliferation of Unmanned Aerial Systems (Drones) and Policy Challenges on the Horizon: A Policy Memorandum to John P. Holdren' 8 *Journal of Science* 1, 2.

256 Ibid.

1.3.3 Problems of enforcement

Practical problems for law enforcement authorities

Lawmakers also face the issue of implementing the regulations they make. Many jurisdictions have guidelines relating to drones such as those prohibiting the flying of drones in restricted zones such as highly populated areas.[257] However, the enforcement of regulations is difficult. First, there are very few technologies that can detect drones in restricted airspace.[258] Second, there are few technologies that can safely land drones.[259] Finally, it is difficult to determine ownership of a drone once it is captured and thus, difficult to proceed with prosecution.[260] Such hurdles must be overcome for enforcement of regulations to be effective. The first two problems of enforcement depend on advances in drone technology. The third, however, can be overcome through regulations such as restrictions on the purchase of drones and more comprehensive licensing systems.

International enforcement mechanisms

As with most international treaties or agreements, enforcement is left to sovereign States. Enforcement is generally achieved through political pressure or sanctions; there is no international law enforcement body.

257 Konstantin Kakaes et al, *Drones and Aerial Observation: New Technologies for Property Rights, Human Rights, and Global Development* (New America, 2015) 30.
258 Allyn K. Milojevich, 'Proliferation of Unmanned Aerial Systems (Drones) and Policy Challenges on the Horizon: A Policy Memorandum to John P. Holdren' 8 *Journal of Science* 1, 2.
259 Ibid.
260 Ibid.

2 Existing drone regulation and its issues

2.1 Introduction

While drone technology and its advancement present opportunities and possibilities for a broad range of industries and communities, such technology also presents regulatory challenges for governments – either federal or unitary, developed or developing – around the world. An increasing number of countries have implemented domestic drone regulations to prevent a potential influx of drones in their skies without appropriate protections.

This chapter examines the various regulatory structures that States have adopted to regulate drone use. It also identifies common features and unique differences across jurisdictions both federal and unitary.

2.2 Drones – challenges

2.2.1 Privacy issues

Privacy has always been a fundamental public concern and the rise of drones has only exacerbated such concern. There is clear difficulty in maintaining an acceptable level of privacy given the relative ease with which a suitably equipped drone can breach that privacy. Privacy laws are necessary to close this gap. Currently, the pace at which privacy laws are being developed is well behind that of advancements in drone surveillance technology. In addressing the privacy issues, States have, thus far, tended to 'retrofit' existing privacy laws.

In a number of jurisdictions including Australia, New Zealand, Canada and the United States, the approach has been to apply existing legislation to drones. As existing legislation often does not contemplate drones, the scope of these privacy laws, and powers to enforce them, can be less than ideal.

Scope of existing privacy laws

For many jurisdictions, no law specifically prohibits surveillance conducted by individuals operating drones. In Australia, for example, privacy law comprises *Australian Privacy Principles* (APPs) which provide an overall framework by which official authorities must abide. These principles only apply to an 'APP entity' which is defined in Australian law as an organisation or agency. While an APP entity may apply to an individual in limited circumstances, individuals who act in a non-business capacity are specifically exempt.

In Canada, unlike Australia, government departments are subject to separate legislation than private commercial entities. Government officials are bound by the *Privacy Act* (1985) and private commercial entities are governed by the *Personal Information Protection and Electronic Documents Act* (2000). However, like Australia, private individuals are not restricted in their use of drones to conduct surveillance on another individual provided that it is for non-commercial reasons.

New Zealand does offer some *limited* protection against breach of privacy by drones. The main difference between New Zealand and other States is that its privacy law applies to individuals. Specifically, it contains an 'interference with privacy' provision which may be breached where a drone collects private information involving an unreasonable interference with the personal affairs of an individual.[1] Again, this only refers to data collection, not unrecorded surveillance.

The European Union has directly implemented privacy requirements in its proposed regulation for drones. Article 4 of the Prototype Regulation stipulates that

> [t]he operator of a [drone] shall be responsible for its safe operation. The operator shall comply with the requirements laid down in this Regulation and other applicable regulations, in particular those related to security, privacy, data protection, liability, insurance and environmental protection.[2]

Privacy is addressed in Regulation (EU) 2016/679 which is concerned with data protection. While no regulation exists relating to surveillance, the EU has proposed the adoption of a geofencing system as part of mandatory requirements for drone operations.

Federal and unitary States

A common issue for federal systems is possible inconsistency of privacy laws at the state and local levels. In the United States, in 2017, at least 38 states considered legislation directly related to drones.[3] Among those states there are a

---

1   Andrew Shelley, 'Application of New Zealand Privacy Law to Drones' (2016) 12 Policy Quarterly 73; *Privacy Act 1993* (NZ) s 66.
2   *Prototype Commission Regulation on Unmanned Aircraft Operations* (22 August 2016) European Aviation Safety Agency <https://www.easa.europa.eu/system/files/dfu/UAS%20Prototype%20Regulation%20final.pdf>.
3   *Current Unmanned Aircraft State Law Landscape* (25 July 2017) National Conference of State Legislatures <www.ncsl.org/research/transportation/current-unmanned-aircraft-State-law-landscape.aspx#1>.

limited number who have privacy laws that directly relate to drones. In South Dakota, surveillance law was amended to include unlawful drone surveillance on private property.[4] In Oregon, a person is prohibited from operating a drone in a way that intentionally, knowingly or recklessly harasses or annoys the owner or occupant of privately owned premises.[5] At the same time, US states – Kentucky, Louisiana and Nevada, for example – do not have rules that directly relate to privacy within their drone legislation.[6]

Australia has a range of state laws that relate to privacy and trespass which vary among states. In contrast, in Germany, the federal and state governments have published a common set of guidelines on drone operations. These stipulate that any proposed drone operation must have a signed data collection statement, authorised on a case-by-case basis.

These issues, of course, are not faced by unitary systems where one set of laws apply. For example, in France, all aerial photography and videos captured by drones are subject to data privacy law.

Who is the enforcer?

Civil aviation authorities are not responsible for protecting privacy. In the United States, the Electronic Privacy Information Center (EPIC) sued the US FAA because it claimed that the FAA failed to implement the necessary safeguards for privacy when developing a 'comprehensive plan' to 'safely' integrate drones into national airspace. The FAA denied the assertion on the basis that privacy did not constitute a safety concern (its only concern). Similarly, Australia's CASA has stated that privacy is not within its remit; it is solely concerned with aviation safety.[7] Transport Canada has stated that it would involve local police if privacy laws have been broken,[8] and the Civil Aviation Authority of New Zealand has referred the issue to the Office of the Privacy Commissioner.[9] None of these authorities directly enforce any privacy law, nor have they implemented any drone regulations that protect privacy, relying on other governmental authorities and existing laws. The difficulty is that members of the general public may not be able to easily identify the relevant authority or laws.

4 National Conference of State Legislature, *Current Unmanned Aircraft State Law Landscape* <www.ncsl.org/research/transportation/current-unmanned-aircraft-state-law-landscape.aspx>.
5 Ibid.
6 Ibid.
7 *Flying Drones/Remotely Piloted Aircraft in Australia* (26 February 2018) Civil Aviation Safety Authority <https://www.casa.gov.au/aircraft/landing-page/flying-drones-australia>.
8 *Flying Your Drone Safely and Legally* (9 March 2018) Government of Canada <https://www.tc.gc.ca/eng/civilaviation/opssvs/flying-drone-safely-legally.html>.
9 *RPAS, UAV, UAS, Drones and Model Aircraft* (March 2016) Civil Aviation Authority of New Zealand <https://www.caa.govt.nz/rpas/>.

Other laws?

Other laws may assist in protecting privacy against intrusion from drones. Property law is one such example. The common law maxim – *cujus est solum ejus est usque ad coelum, et ad inferos* – whoever has the soil, also owns to the heavens above and to the centre beneath – while not applicable to the 'modern world'[10] still forms the basis of protection for common law jurisdictions.

As the maxim suggests, land owners own a certain amount of airspace. In *United States v Causby*, the Supreme Court stated that a landowner owned 'at least as much as the space above the ground as he can occupy or use in connection with the land'.[11] In Australia, it has been held that an aircraft which flies 500 feet above an owner's property and takes a photograph is not trespassing upon that property.[12] In *Bernstein*, Griffiths J stated that:

> The problem is to balance the rights of an owner to enjoy the use of his land against the rights of the general public to take advantage of all that science now offers in the use of air space. This balance is in my judgment best struck in our present society by restricting the rights of an owner in the air space above his land to such height as is necessary for the ordinary use and enjoyment of his land … and declaring that above that height he has no greater rights in the air space than any other member of the public.[13]

Criminal law may also provide an indirect form of privacy protection. Some jurisdictions may have offences the elements of which can be met through drone operations. For example, the offence of voyeurism is already being used to convict drone operators. In the Australian states of Queensland[14] and New South Wales,[15] voyeurism is an offence under their criminal codes. In the United States, certain states have specifically enacted drone laws with a voyeurism offence, including Florida and Indiana. Utah has amended the voyeurism offence to include any type of technology.[16] In the United Kingdom, the voyeurism offence in the *Sexual Offences Act* 2003 can apply to drones as well. Any voyeurism offence which is broad in its application also may apply to drones.

---

10 See *United States v Causby* 328 US 256 (1946), 260–261.
11 Ibid, FN 9.
12 *Bernstein of Leigh v Skyviews and General Ltd* [1978] 1 QB 479.
13 Ibid.
14 *Criminal Code 1899* (Qld) s 227A.
15 *Crimes Act 1900* (NSW) s 91J
16 Madalyn MCrae, Drone Legislation Tackles Privacy Concerns (July 28 2017) *The Daily Universe* <http://universe.byu.edu/2017/07/28/drone-legislation-tackles-privacy-concerns1/>.

By way of example, the Canadian criminal code sets out as follows:

> 162. (1) Every one commits an offence who, surreptitiously, observes – **including by mechanical or electronic means** – or makes a visual recording of a person who is in circumstances that give rise to a reasonable expectation of privacy, if
>
> (a)   the person is in a place in which a person can reasonably be expected to be nude, to expose his or her genital organs or anal region or her breasts, or to be engaged in explicit sexual activity;
>
> (b)   the person is nude, is exposing his or her genital organs or anal region or her breasts, or is engaged in explicit sexual activity, and the observation or recording is done for the purpose of observing or recording a person in such a State or engaged in such an activity; or
>
> (c)   the observation or recording is done for a sexual purpose. [emphasis added]

2.2.2 Safety and security issues

As with manned aviation, safety of drone operations is of paramount importance. A balance must be struck in the regulation of drones between freedom of operations and safety for both third parties and other airspace users.

Drones pose a significant safety risk for people on the ground. In 2015, a drone almost hit champion skier Marcel Hirscher during a skiing competition.[17] With the increasing use of drones, without adequate regulation for safety of drone operations – and drones themselves – the authors anticipate this kind of incident to become a much more common occurrence. Regulatory safeguards must be put in place to minimise safety risks that drones pose to third parties on the ground.

Drones also pose a safety risk to other airspace users. A drone may, for instance, lose contact or fly out of range of its remote pilot and, thus, ceases to act in a predictable or planned manner – a clear threat to safety. The risk of mid-air collision with other airspace users is high. This is further compounded by the ability (or inability) for drones to cope with inclement weather and the limitations of the technology to facilitate drone operations.

National security is also, needless to say, fundamentally important. And by their very nature, drones have the ability to compromise national security. The potential for drones to intrude on airspace has authorities considering a range of regulatory restrictions.

---

17 See, *Drone Almost Hits Marcel Hirscher* (22 December 2015) Youtube <https://www.youtube.com/watch?v=p9T6-KPFRq8>.

2.3 Current domestic regulations

2.3.1 Operational rules

Operational rules form the basis for drone operations in any jurisdiction. From the jurisdictions previously examined, each has adopted rules for drones in some form. While countries define drone operations in different ways, there appear to be two main approaches to such definition.

The first approach is to define drone operations by the weight of the drone. As a general principle, the larger the drone, the more stringent the operating rules. The weight-based approach in each jurisdiction varies. For instance, Australia's smallest weight category for drones (termed 'micro') is 100 grams or less, while China's smallest weight category (also termed 'micro') is 7 kilograms or less.

A common trend is the attempt to cut the 'red tape' for smaller drones to allow easier use of drones. Australia, the United States, the United Kingdom, New Zealand and Canada contain exemptions for smaller drones to operate without complying with otherwise applicable rules. Variations across each jurisdiction go to the weight threshold qualifying for an exemption. That threshold ranges from less than 1 kilogram up to 25 kilograms.[18]

The second approach is to define operations by purpose. Drones are generally flown either for recreational, commercial or scientific purposes. Drones flown for a commercial purpose (usually termed Remotely Piloted Aircraft or Unmanned Aircraft Systems) are usually subject to more strict operating rules depending on the jurisdiction. While drones are flown for a variety of purposes and may effectively be carrying out the same operations, the regulatory treatment of drone operations can differ greatly according to a flight's purpose.

2.3.2 Safety regulations

Drones present a range of benefits and challenges for society. And it is fundamentally important to govern the use of drones from an aviation safety perspective. Drone safety rules are designed to protect people both in the air and on the ground.

Approaches to the regulation of smaller drones are generally consistent across jurisdictions. In most jurisdictions, drones can be flown to a maximum altitude of 400 feet above ground level.[19] To fly any higher, approval must be sought from the relevant regulatory body, and any associated conditions must be adhered to. Drones must be flown within visual line of sight and can only be flown in visual meteorological conditions. Drones must not be flown over populated areas (such as parks, beaches, stadiums and cities) or in close proximity to

---

18 Interestingly, Austria adopted a rule where a drone operating at 79 joules or less and up to 30 metres from the ground are exempt from all regulations.
19 *Civil Aviation Safety Regulations 1998* (Cth) reg 101.085; *Federal Aviation Regulations*, Small Unmanned Aircraft Regulations CFR §107.51 (2016).

other people. In most jurisdictions, there is also a right of way rule requiring drones to give way to manned aircraft. Licensing or certification from an appropriate authority is generally required for larger drones or drones flown for a commercial purpose.

2.3.3 Security regulations

Airspace is a particularly important issue for State regulation in terms of drones. National airspace, a finite resource, now has to accommodate drones, and in often significant numbers. States have generally retro-fitted drones into their existing airspace structure.

Most drones will tend to occupy uncontrolled airspace with some requiring controlled airspace. Drones occupying controlled airspace are generally not distinguished from manned aircraft, without posing many additional regulatory concerns.

Concerns do lie with uncontrolled airspace where drone operators can fly drones more freely (though generally subject to several conditions).

One particular concern is that certain drone activities may conflict with national interests, particular security interests. Drones, as is well known, are capable of conducting surveillance; this will necessitate the creation of rules that prohibit drones from entering airspace over sensitive areas.

Prohibited airspace generally includes airports, military bases, prisons and power stations. Such prohibition is generally accepted across nearly all jurisdictions for national security purposes. In Australia, the Victorian Government has amended laws to establish no-fly zones near or above prisons to try to stop contraband (including drugs and mobile phones) being delivered via drone.[20]

2.3.4 Insurance

The increasing prevalence of drone use brings with it new liability exposures; such that, one can anticipate numerous types of liability claims associated with their use. The insurance industry has provided coverage to address liability concerns. A significant number of States now require mandatory insurance, including Canada, China, Austria, Belgium, Cyprus, Germany and Italy. Jurisdictions which do not require mandatory insurance include the United States, Australia, Indonesia and Brazil.

Within those jurisdictions requiring mandatory insurance, the type of insurance varies. Each jurisdiction with mandatory insurance will either require insurance that covers all aspects of an operation, or only third-party insurance. The Canadian Aviation Regulations require that:

20 Department of Justice and Regulation, Drone Ban Near Victorian Correctional and Youth Justice Facilities (1 February 2018) *Victorian State Government* <http://www.justice.vic.gov.au/home/justice+system/laws+and+regulation/criminal+law/drone+ban+near+victorian+correctional+and+youth+justice+facilities>.

No aircraft owner … shall operate an aircraft unless, **in respect of every incident related to the operation of the aircraft**, the owner has subscribed for liability insurance covering risks of public liability in an amount that is not less than

(a) $100,000, where the maximum permissible take-off weight of the aircraft is 1 043 kg (2,300 pounds) or less.[21] (emphasis added)

In contrast, European regulations stipulate that aircraft operators must be insured in terms of their aviation-specific liability in respect of third parties.[22]

2.3.5 Registration

A drone by its nature provides its pilot with anonymity. This poses multiple issues where a drone can be used for illegal purposes. States increasingly demand mandatory registration requirements, in part, to ensure accountability. Registration generally involves registering a drone through an official record which enables the owner to be identified.

Jurisdictions that have adopted mandatory registration include the United States, Russia and China. The United States requires all small unmanned aircraft to be registered. China in May 2017 announced that all civil drones weighing more than 250 grams must be registered under *real* names to improve civil aviation safety.[23] Russia amended its Air Code in 2015 to require the registration of all drones.

Other jurisdictions currently have less onerous registration regimes. The approach is either no registration at all or only registration only for certain types of drones. Australia only requires drones weighing over 150 kilograms to be registered. In New Zealand and Italy, drones weighing over 25 kilograms must be registered.

Drones can also be registered as personal property in a number of jurisdictions nationally (for example, on the Australian Personal Property Securities Register) or internationally (on the International Registry of Mobile Assets). The purpose of such registrations is, however, to protect security interests or to provide free and clear title.

2.3.6 Licensing

The role of safety authorities is to ensure that pilots are appropriately qualified and their drones certified as safe to operate. Different types of licences exist. In some jurisdictions there is a distinction between a pilot (the individual who flies

21 *Canadian Aviation Regulations (SOR/96–433)* s 606.02(8).
22 *Regulation (EC) No 785/2004 of the European Parliament and of the Council of 21 April 2004* [2004] L138/1.
23 Xinhua, 'China Requires Real-Name Registration for Civilian Drones' (16 May 2017) The State Council of The People's Republic of China <http://english.gov.cn/news/top_news/2017/05/16/content_281475657535848.htm>.

the drone), and the operator (the company who employs the pilot), with both requiring a separate licence.

Pilot licensing

Unless operations fall within an exception in a particular jurisdiction, such as the small drone exception previously mentioned, pilots are required to undertake appropriate training.

Particular requirements a person must satisfy for a pilot licence varies across jurisdictions. Some jurisdictions may require stringent training before a pilot is licensed while other jurisdictions take a more flexible approach. Australia, New Zealand, the United States, South Africa and the United Kingdom each provide detailed rules on training that pilots must undertake. Other jurisdictions – including Canada, Japan and Romania – take a less stringent approach.

Variations in licensing regimes have legal consequences when a pilot wishes to operate a drone in a foreign jurisdiction. Jurisdictions differ on how they deal with foreign pilots licensed in a foreign State. The United States, for example, does not acknowledge any foreign pilot licences 'because globally recognized RPC standards have not yet been developed'.[24] Contrast this with New Zealand where that State may validate a foreign pilot licence where the issuing country is an ICAO Contracting State, and the pilot holds a medical certificate under that licence, can speak adequate English, and can pass any written examinations or flight tests that a flight official may require.[25]

Drone certification

Drone certification generally involves verification that a drone functions properly and can be operated safely.

The most common approach is to require only larger drones to be certified. In Australia, drones weighing more than 150 kilograms require a 'certificate of airworthiness'[26] to qualify for operation, while France, Italy and the United States only require drones weighing more 25 kilograms to be certified.

2.4 Current international regulations

2.4.1 Introduction

Drone regulations are a national issue concerning individual jurisdictions. However, as manned flight became globalised, so too may unmanned flight. ICAO has been working on harmonising regulatory requirements and the

24 Federal Aviation Administration, 'Unmanned Aircraft Systems (UAS) Frequently Asked Questions' (1 February 2018) United States Department of Transportation <https://www.faa.gov/uas/faqs/>.
25 *Civil Aviation Act Consolidation Part 61 Pilot Licences and Ratings 2017* (Civil Aviation Rules of New Zealand) r 61.9(a).
26 *Civil Aviation Safety Regulations 1998* (Cth) vol 3, reg 101.255.

principles underlying them. At the regional level, the European Union is increasing its regulation of drones. Its focus has been the coordination of operational matters for drones on a wider scale.

2.4.2 The global regulatory regime

As stated elsewhere, for both manned and unmanned aircraft, the foundation for their regulation is the Chicago Convention.[27] The Chicago Convention provides the framework for harmonising aviation regulation for all States. In relation to drones, Article 8 of the Convention provides that:

> No aircraft capable of being flown without a pilot shall be flown without a pilot over the territory of a contracting State without special authorization by that State and in accordance with the terms of such authorization. Each contracting State undertakes to ensure that the flight of such aircraft without a pilot in regions open to civil aircraft shall be so controlled as to obviate danger to civil aircraft.

This Article forms the starting point for regulating drones at the international level. Previously, there was some uncertainty as to whether drones were 'aircraft' within the meaning of the Convention.[28]

ICAO's Global Air Traffic Management Operational Concept (Doc 9854) states that:

> [a]n unmanned aerial vehicle is a pilotless aircraft, in the sense of Article 8 of the Convention on the International Civil Aviation, which is flown without a pilot-in-command on-board and is either remotely and fully controlled from another place (ground, another aircraft, space) or programmed and fully autonomous.[29]

Here, all drones would fall within the definition of 'aircraft' for the purposes of the Chicago Convention.

ICAO's standards and recommended practices

ICAO, amongst other things, is the international body responsible for harmonising aviation law across the globe. ICAO continues to spearhead the global

---

27 *Convention on International Civil Aviation (Chicago Convention)*, opened for signature 7 December 1944, 15 UNTS 295 (entered into force 4 April 1947).

28 Benjamyn I. Scott, 'Terminology, Definitions and Classifications' in Benjamyn I. Scott (ed), *The Law of Unmanned Aircraft Systems: An Introduction to the Current and Future Regulation under National, Regional and International Law* (Wolters Kluwer, 2016) 9–14.

29 International Civil Aviation Organisation, *Doc 9854 AN/458: Global Air Traffic Management Operational Concept* (2005).

effort to create an international regime for drones. ICAO States that the 'principal objective of the aviation regulatory framework is to achieve and maintain the highest possible uniform level of safety'.[30] For drones, this means 'ensuring [that] the safety of any other airspace user as well as the safety of persons and property on the ground'.[31]

ICAO's role is to focus on high level, performance-based standards. This means setting out the minimum requirements for drone performance. ICAO's primary method in achieving harmonisation for all areas of aviation is through its SARPs. These represent minimum requirements and provide some suggestions on how to achieve them. An early focus for ICAO was harmonising terms and definitions. SARPs for drones would represent a significant achievement for ICAO and for the global aviation community.

ICAO has already integrated drone-specific regulations into existing SARPs. Annex 2 – *Rules of the Air* – was amended to include Appendix 4 – *Remotely Piloted Aircraft Systems*. The Annex provides for general operating rules, certificates and licensing, and requests for authorisations. Annex 7 – *Aircraft Nationality and Registration Marks*, now applies to 'RPAS' (included in its definitions).

Circular 328-AN/190 (Circular 328)

Circular 328, ICAO's first major instrument addressing drones at the international level, sets out ICAO's view on integrating drones, considers the fundamental differences between drones and other manned aircraft, and encourages States to provide information on their experience with drones.[32] The document covers all aspects of aviation regulation and provides ICAO's preliminary views on various issues represented by each. It also provides some examples of initiatives undertaken by States and regional authorities in various areas, extending from aeronautical telecommunication procedures to environmental considerations.

Manual on remotely piloted aircraft systems (RPAS)

ICAO's manual on RPAS 'provide[s] guidance on technical and operational issues applicable to the integration of RPA in non-integrated airspace and aerodromes'. The manual focuses on RPAS used for commercial purposes.[33]

---

30 International Civil Aviation Organisation 'Circular 328 AN/190: Unmanned Aircraft Systems (UAS)' (Paper presented at the Seminar on Unmanned Aircraft Systems (UAS), Lima, Peru, 18 April 2012 to 20 April 2012).
31 Ibid.
32 Ibid.
33 International Civil Aviation Authority, *Manual on Remotely Piloted Aircraft Systems (RPAS): ICAO Doc 10019 AN/507* (1st ed, 2015).

The content of the manual provides guidance on developing future RPAS-specific SARPs.

Future developments

In 2007, ICAO constituted a panel for developing drone regulations. The panel expects to complete a new set of SARPs in 2018.[34] The SARPs will relate to airworthiness, operations (including operator certification) and remote pilot licensing. The panel expects to complete another set relating to air traffic and 'detect and avoid' requirements for drones in 2020.[35]

2.4.3 European Union

At the regional level, the EU has made progress in developing drone regulations. While ICAO's focus has been developing high level standards, EASA has focused on operationalising those standards. Specifically, it seeks to develop drone regulations 'in a safe, secure and environmentally friendly manner and at the same time respecting the concerns of the citizen concerning privacy and the protection of data'.[36] One contrast between ICAO and the EU is that ICAO is solely concerned with safety; the EU has taken a broader approach to regulating drones concerning itself also with protecting the environment and privacy.

Regulation 216/2008

Regulation 216/2008 establishes 'common rules in the field of civil aviation ';[37] its primary objective is to set and uphold aviation safety regulations across the EU.[38] It covers essential areas of aviation regulation, including airworthiness, operations, licensing and certification.

Article 4 sets out basic principles and their application. The regulation adopts the term 'aircraft' in its scope of application.[39] Annex II(i) expressly states that 'unmanned aircraft with an operating mass of no more than 150kg' are not covered by the regulation. The regulation only applies to drones that weigh more than 150 kilograms.

Regulation 216/2008 is the first piece of EU law that applies to drones.

---

34 International Civil Aviation Organization, 'Integrating RPAS into Airspace' (2015) 70(2) *ICAO Journal* 4, 5, <https://www.icao.int/publications/journalsreports/2015/7002_en.pdf>.
35 Ibid.
36 Explanatory note for Prototype regulation paragraph 1.1.
37 *Regulation (EC) No 216/2008 of the European Aviation Safety Agency of 20 February 2008 on Common Rules in the Field of Civil Aviation and Establishing a European Aviation Safety Agency, and Repealing Council Directive 91/670/EEC Regulation (EC) No 1592/2002 and Directive 2004/36/E* [2008] OJ L 79/1.
38 Ibid art 2(1).
39 Ibid, art 4.

Prototype regulation

EASA is currently in the process of developing a new prototype regulation that will supersede Regulation 216/2008. Under the current regime, all drones weighing less than 150 kilograms remain within each individual EU member's competence. EASA has admitted '[t]hat this leads to a fragmented regulatory system hampering the development of a single EU market for [drones] and cross-border [drone] operations'.[40] In summary, the prototype regulation's stated purpose is to ensure an operationally centred proportionate risk and performance-based regulatory framework. It also ensures uniform safety for drone use, supports the drone market and contributes to enhancing privacy protection.[41]

Most importantly, it expands EASA's competence to all drones rather than only those weighing more than 150 kilograms.[42] Article 3 of the Prototype Regulation divides drone operations into three risk-based categories: open, specific and certified. Open operations do not require prior authorisation; specific operations do. Certified operations require drone certification, a licensed pilot and an approved operator.

2.5 Making space for drones

The goal for all jurisdictions is to seamlessly integrate drones into their national airspace. In the United States alone, drones are expected to inject USD 82.1 billion between 2015 and 2025 into the US economy if integrated into its national airspace.[43] Consequently, the economic imperative to integrate drones into airspace is clear.

2.5.1 Airspace issues

Airspace is regulated by States through laws and regulations. A State can take a liberal approach and allow increased access to its airspace, or a conservative approach and restrict access. The way in which a State treats its airspace as a resource will determine the airspace issues that emerge. Thus, airspace issues that a drone operation with prior approval will face are very different to the issues that a non-approved drone operation will face.

---

40 *Notice of Proposed Amendment 2017–05 (A): Introduction of a Regulatory Framework for the Operation of Drones* (2017) European Aviation Safety Agency <https://www.easa.europa.eu/system/files/dfu/NPA%202017-05%20%28A%29_0.pdf>.
41 Ibid.
42 Article 2 of the Prototype Regulation defines 'Unmanned Aircraft' as 'any aircraft operated or designed to be operated without a pilot on board'.
43 Fernando Fiallos, 'United States' in Benjamyn I. Scott (ed), *The Law of Unmanned Aircraft Systems: An Introduction to the Current and Future Regulation under National, Regional and International Law* (Wolters Kluwer, 2016) 342.

Drones that require prior permission

The main issue with regulations that require drones to have prior permission is the opportunity cost. From a safety and security perspective, an operation that is subject to prior approval is preferable because the operation has been reviewed by the competent authority. As a result, the operation is known and the appropriate arrangements can be made to ensure that it will be conducted safely and in a secure manner. For example, Russia and South Africa subject all commercial drone operations to prior approval.[44]

The more common approach is to strike a balance where States subject certain drone operations to prior approval while others are not depending on the risk to safety (usually dictated by weight). One reason for the more moderate approach is because the more airspace is restricted, the more opportunity cost a State incurs as a result. As previously mentioned, drone operations are a source of significant economic revenue for States and can be utilised by industry for a wide variety of reasons.

Drones that do not require prior permission

Some States have taken a more liberal approach in allowing drones unrestricted access to uncontrolled airspace. Examples include Australia, the United States, New Zealand, Canada and France. Inevitably, the result of this is more issues pertaining to airspace usage. And these issues arise precisely because the operation itself is unregulated, allowing far more freedom and the potential for abuse. Again, States undertake a balancing act to maximise the enjoyment and economic potential of drones while also ensuring safe and secure use.

States can either restrict access to airspace through operating rules, for example, generally restricting drones to a maximum height of around 400 feet to ensure that the pilot can see potential hazards and conduct avoidance manoeuvres if necessary. Also, States enact regulations which empower the relevant authority to declare certain airspace restricted or prohibited. This can either be for safety or security reasons. By way of example, Italy's drone regulations dictate that different operations are subject to different airspace rules. Generally, drones cannot occupy an 'Air Traffic Zone' (safety) and 'active restricted areas and prohibited areas' (security).[45]

2.5.2 Enforcement issues

Another significant issue States face is in enforcing drone regulations that restrict airspace usage. Given the open nature of the skies, States cannot prevent all unauthorised or illegal drone operations from occurring. And these

---

44 *Federal Law on Amendment of the Air Code of the Russian Federation on Use of Unmanned Aircraft No. 462-FZ* (30 December 2015).
45 *Remotely Piloted Aerial Vehicles Regulation*, art 24(4)(c) (Italian Civil Aviation Authority).

operations can have serious consequences for safety and security. For example, a drone can impact safety if flown near an aerodrome, risking collision with an aircraft, or it can impact on security where a drone surveys a classified military installation. Therefore, States look to other methods to enforce drone regulations – technology to ensure safety and security and facilitate the integration of drones into everyday life.

Technological requirements

Drones must be at least as safe as other manned aerial vehicles.[46] Drones have been officially recognised as 'aircraft' at international law. However, while the law formally treats all aircraft equally, they are substantively different vehicles with different requirements. Individual technologies required to ensure drones are safe and secure differ from other aerial vehicles. Researchers estimate that the software size required to integrate autonomous drones for unrestricted operations 'is in excess of 1 million lines of code, which is an order of magnitude greater than manned aircraft equivalents'.[47] Consequently, drones require new and improved systems to achieve the same level of safety as manned aircraft in national airspace.

Geofencing

A geofence is a virtual boundary for a real-world geographic area. It uses a combination of a GPS and Wi-Fi or Bluetooth to track a drone in real time; the technology has been available for years. Initial versions were used to monitor cattle with the help of GPS collars which provided geographical information and alerts when cattle left pre-defined boundaries. Drones use this technology at a much more concentrated level. Information can be continuously broadcast in real time enabling real-time tracking. An official authority can establish pre-defined boundaries at various locations and prevent a drone from crossing those boundaries. China has implemented a system where drone pilots must input geofencing data to avoid venturing into dangerous areas.[48]

Command and control (C2)

As drones are remotely piloted, reliable command and control systems are essential. NATO defines command and control as 'the exercise of authority and direction by a properly designated [individual] over assigned [resources] in the

---

46 International Civil Aviation Authority, *Manual on Remotely Piloted Aircraft Systems (RPAS): ICAO Doc 10019 AN/507* (1st ed, 2015).

47 Ella Atkins, Anibal Ollero and Anonios Tsourdos, *Unmanned Aircraft Systems* (Wiley, 2016) 491.

48 Jon Fingas, *Drone Pilots in China have to Register with the Government* (17 May 2017) Engadget <https://www.engadget.com/2017/05/17/china-drone-registrations/>.

accomplishment of a [common goal].[49] In terms of drone operations, 'a C2 data-link is a telecommunications link over which data is transmitted and electronically connects the [drone and its remote pilot]'.[50] The better a command and control system is, the more responsive and reliable a drone is.

Detect and avoid systems (DAA)

As the name implies, detect and avoid are designed to ensure that a drone can 'detect' and 'avoid' incoming hazards automatically. ICAO defines DAA as 'the capability to see, sense or detect conflicting traffic or other hazards and take the appropriate action'.[51] Pilots are usually within the aircraft and in the appropriate position to undertake this function, perhaps with assistance from automated systems. But with drones, pilots do not have this luxury. And if the drone is autonomous automatic systems must perform all functions unassisted. Consequently, the need for DAA is integral. No system has been discovered – a 'gold mine' for any developer.[52]

2.5.3 Integration

The integration of these systems has the potential to facilitate drone operations in national airspace, while providing a mechanism for States to enforce airspace regulations.

For example, a State may declare that a certain portion of airspace is prohibited or restricted. Geofencing technologies can provide the necessary means to enforce those regulations. Another example may be regulations where a drone must always give way to manned aircraft. DAA systems can provide the means by which drones will opt to avoid manned aircraft if necessary to ensure safety.

There remains, however, a regulatory gap: how does one ensure that drones are equipped with the necessary technologies to ensure regulations are complied with? The European Prototype Regulation provides an example of how this might be done.

The proto-regulation

The European Prototype Regulation introduces mandatory product requirements to ensure safety and security in its airspace. The Regulation contains

49 Neville A. Stanton, Christopher Baber, Don Harris, *Modelling Command and Control: Event Analysis of Systemic Teamwork* (Ashgate, 2008).
50 Ron Bartsch, James Coyne and Katherine Gray, *Drones in Society: Exploring the Strange New World of Unmanned Aircraft* (Routledge, 2017) 62.
51 International Civil Aviation Authority, *Manual on Remotely Piloted Aircraft Systems (RPAS): ICAO Doc 10019* (1st ed, 2015).
52 Ron Bartsch, James Coyne and Katherine Gray, *Drones in Society: Exploring the Strange New World of Unmanned Aircraft* (Routledge, 2017) 60.

various provisions which mandate drones to be equipped with certain technologies and capabilities.

For example, Article 4 deems it mandatory for drones that fit within a certain operational category to be equipped with geofencing capabilities. Geofencing is divided into two classes: class 2 and class 3. Geofencing class 2 is a permanent boundary which limits access to airspace areas,[53] and class 3 is a 'selectable' boundary which can be used at different times.[54]

Further, the Regulation stipulates that EASA will develop acceptable means of compliance (AMC) and certification specifications (CS) which can be used to comply with its requirements. It also specifies the operational obligations for certain bodies who must assess drones for compliance with the technological requirements.[55] The Regulation is still subject to further development and AMCs and CSs have yet to be published. It does, however, provide an example of how drone laws and regulations can incorporate technological requirements to ensure airspace is used safely and effectively.

2.6 Industry comment

The authors include original industry comment to discuss industry thinking in relation to drones. Comment from international thought leaders addresses the implications of drones for the aviation industry, how to strike an appropriate balance between regulatory protection and technological advancement, and how the future for drones is viewed.

Airlines

The airline industry has obvious concerns with regard to drones and their operation in airspace currently occupied by manned aircraft. Integration of drones into existing airspace will be one of the most important issues for the aviation industry in the next decade. For an airline industry perspective, Auguste Hocking, Assistant General Counsel at IATA, the organisation of the world's airlines, says as follows:[56]

> Drones are of obvious interest for professionals in the airline sector. While the pace of development and state of flux in regulatory arrangements make a comprehensive treatment difficult, it is possible to recount some of the assumptions, concerns and opportunities frequently cited in industry circles. This short note will address drones as "aircraft" within the existing regulatory

53 *'Prototype' Commission Regulation on Unmanned Aircraft Operations* (22 August 2016) European Aviation Safety Agency <https://www.easa.europa.eu/system/files/dfu/UAS%20Prototype%20Regulation%20final.pdf> Appendix I.6 a.
54 Ibid Appendix I.6 b.
55 Ibid Annex II, Article II.29.
56 The views expressed in this commentary are those of the author and do not necessarily reflect the views or policies of IATA.

structure for civil aviation, identify certain concerns for their integration within that structure, comment on harmonisation efforts and make some practical observations for the path ahead.

I.

> Drones are, returning to first principles, simply aircraft with special characteristics. Chief among these is that a pilot is not on board, the drone operating with a remote link to a control station or autonomously via computerisation. Variations on both the large military and smaller consumer drones have different characteristics and promise a wide range of commercial and civil applications, some of which have been realised. While drones are not new technology, a recent upsurge in the availability, capability and affordability of lightweight drones, particularly in the consumer segment, poses difficulties for traditional models of national regulation and enforcement.[57]
>
> As a question of international law, it is generally accepted that drones fall within Article 8 of the Chicago Convention 1944 on 'pilotless aircraft'.[58] That Article states that no pilotless aircraft shall be flown over the territory of a State without 'special authorisation' and must be operated 'in accordance with the terms of that authorisation'.[59] In addition, each State must '[e]nsure that the flight of such aircraft [...] shall be so controlled as to obviate danger to civil aircraft'.[60] Article 8 therefore establishes a precautionary principle in forbidding international operations by default and formalising a duty upon States to eliminate risk to other aircraft, if they allow the use of drones. Consistent with this, and cognisant of airspace standards promulgated at an international level through ICAO, national regulatory responses to drones have centred on concepts of 'segregated' and 'non-segregated' airspace.
>
> Drones are generally only permitted to operate in segregated airspace, invariably below 500 feet, where they are separated from the bulk of air traffic. This separation obviates risk to other airspace users. Certain other provisos are also ubiquitous, including those concerning proximity to built-up or urban areas, line-of-sight operation and protected zones near airports. Approximately 20 jurisdictions have dedicated regulations of this genre, with Australia, Canada, New Zealand, the United Kingdom and the United States being good examples.[61]

57 For an excellent appraisal of the contemporary volume of commercial drone activity, see Gina Y. Chen, 'Reforming the Current Regulatory Framework for Commercial Drones: Retaining American Business' Competitive Advantage in the Global Economy', 37 *Northwestern Journal of International Law & Business* (2017) 513, 515–517.

58 International Civil Aviation Organisation, *Doc 10019: Manual on Remotely Piloted Aircraft Systems* (1st ed, 2015) sections 1.1.1 and 1.2.5; D Marshall, 'Unmanned aerial systems and international civil aviation organization regulations' (2009) *85 NDL Review*, 693, 699.

59 *Convention on International Civil Aviation (Chicago Convention)*, opened for signature 7 December 1944, 15 UNTS 295 (entered into force 4 April 1947) art 8.

60 Ibid.

61 International Air Transport Association, 'Safety of Remotely Piloted Aircraft Systems' (Working Paper to ICAO, HLSC/15-WP/98, 2015) 2.

Criticism of existing regulatory arrangements typically falls into three themes, these being that (i) national legislation is not adapted to deal specifically with drones; (ii) traditional enforcement measures (and resources) are inadequate to address drone misuse and violations of aviation regulations; and (iii) present regulations are too restrictive and stifle the development of drone technology and innovations in commercial application.

Taking just the latter for our purposes, commentators have called for more flexible national regulation, citing the competitive advantages likely to flow to business in jurisdictions seen as first movers.[62] The complexity is therefore in how to unshackle drones so as to allow their useful exploitation and move them away from the constraints associated with 'toys' or 'model aircraft' and localised operations. As aircraft, however, drones are unsuited to non-segregated airspace for the reason that they are unable to comply with traditional rules of the air and bedrock technical standards promulgated under ICAO.

II.

The unshackling is where concerns arise. Drones will have to coexist with other airspace users – including airlines, general aviation, other commercial operators and the military – and assure a level of safety to persons and property on the ground. The regulatory framework and infrastructure that has developed to support civil operations, over the last 70 years, has delivered an impressive safety performance.[63] This framework needs to be carefully adapted to accommodate drones, together with their different categories of application, with an equivalent level of risk mitigation. The integration of drones should not introduce new efficiency and interoperability problems or exacerbate existing ones. Accordingly, work should proceed in incremental terms; to best ensure the safety, efficiency and integrity of existing airspace operations.

The airline industry, for its part, has been keen to voice concerns for integration, identified broadly as those relating to (i) safety; (ii) security; (iii) airspace access; (iv) the communications spectrum; and (v) regulatory considerations.[64] These concerns are cited in turn below:

(i)   Safety deserves first place. As drones are integrated into airspace with other traffic, the standards applicable to drone operators, certification of drone aircraft (and related systems) and airspace management must be introduced. Key incidents of airmanship will have to be translated, including the "see and avoid" concept, the ability to respond to air traffic control instructions and other core responsibilities. The prospect of a collision between a drone

62 R. Olsen 'Paperweights: FAA Regulation and the Banishment of Commercial Drones' (2017) 32(AR) *Berkley Technology Law Journal*, 28–30.

63 In 2017, the major jet accident rate (measure in hull losses per one million flights was 0.11, 'which was the equivalent of one major accident for every 8.7 million flights'. See International Air Transport Association, *IATA Releases 2017 Airline Safety Performance* (22 February 2018) <http://www.iata.org/pressroom/pr/Pages/2018-02-22-01.aspx>.

64 IATA, 'Fact Sheet – Unmanned Aircraft Systems' (December 2017) <https://www.iata.org/pressroom/facts_figures/fact_sheets/Documents/fact-sheet-unmanned-aicraft-systems.pdf>.

and other aircraft must be addressed and mitigated. Drones will have to be tested and certified to high standards of redundancy and reliability, like existing aircraft. Performance-based criteria have been pointed to as possible partial or complete substitutes for traditional standards and should achieve equivalent safety outcomes.

(ii) Security is another issue of prime importance. Beyond the possible exploits of consumer drones, new safeguards are required for the screening and clearance of drone operators, ground station security, physical access control to drones at ground facilities and appropriate encryption or cybersecurity protocols for control links. No doubt high capability drones will prove an attraction for those who would use them as weapons, necessitating adjustments in threat assessment for enforcement authorities. It is conceivable that innovations of design and certification may play a role to build in robust security functionality.

(iii) Increasing airspace congestion in many parts of the world is an acute concern for the airline industry and imposes a real financial cost. Drones promise to add many other individual units to the skies, posing new questions for ANSPs and their ability to 'scale' for new demands. These likely need to be answered with significant investments in infrastructure and, conceivably, new regulation on priorities. Close international cooperation will be essential to prevent congestion and incompatibility between airspace divisions. As such, the industry has called for solutions which are performance-based, enforceable and harmonised across national borders. New standards on geofencing, collision avoidance and noise mitigation are possibilities. Arguably, the integration of drones should be a complement to the general modernisation of aging air traffic control infrastructure in many jurisdictions.[65]

(iv) Drones also place increasing pressure on a limited radio communications spectrum. Like airspace access, an expanding demand for limited allocations on the spectrum implies rationing and a cogent system of priorities. Interference cannot be countenanced. Regulation on priorities in the spectrum will have to be broached and broached in a way that is effective across national boundaries. Clearly existing users of the spectrum, including conventional aviation and government, will have views on the allocation of resources within the spectrum.

(v) Regulatory considerations make up a broad family of issues concerning authorisation and permits for operations, personnel and operator licensing, liability, economic regulation generally, facilitation and related 'doing business' aspects. The technical standards contemplated by ICAO as SARPs, for example, are only part of the picture. A degree of regulatory compatibility needs to be achieved with the conventional aviation sector.

One of the difficulties is that integration is occurring on a double track. There is work at ICAO – which has produced a circular,[66] a manual[67] and

65 See further *Riga Declaration on Remotely Piloted Aircraft – Framing the Future of Aviation*, Riga (6 March 2015) Principle 3 <https://ec.europa.eu/transport/sites/transport/files/modes/air/news/doc/2015-03-06-drones/2015-03-06-riga-declaration-drones.pdf>.
66 *ICAO Circular 328 AN/190 Unmanned Aircraft Systems* (UAS) (2011).
67 International Civil Aviation Organisation, *Doc 10019: Manual on Remotely Piloted Aircraft Systems* (1st ed, 2015).

minor revisions to the SARPs[68] – and work at the national level. ICAO's approach has been incremental, making changes 'as and when required' and seeking to write in drone provisions with as little disturbance to the underlying SARPs as possible. This has been criticised by some as too slow a process.[69] With technology advancing at a rapid clip, vocal drone advocates and governments keen to gain an innovative edge, the risk of disparate national approaches is pronounced. Industry would be the first to argue the benefits of harmonisation, particularly in the nascent period before uniform international standards solidify through ICAO. While some would argue that ICAO needs to take a more proactive role, or perhaps extend scrutiny to all drone activities,[70] it may be sufficient, pragmatically speaking, for regulators to collaborate on common principles with a view to converging at a later date. This has the advantage of offering a choice of national sandboxes for innovators but creates a corresponding burden for the conventional sector in seeking to ensure that concerns are heard by policymakers and legislators. On the other hand, one risk of tardiness is that drone operations, particularly offshore or 'high seas' operations, find a lacuna in which substantive regulation is absent.[71]

III.

A consistent approach to integration is essential in this author's view. Most industry commentators would look to ICAO and to the Chicago Convention system for ultimate, long-term certainty and uniformity in the area. Proposals for a new multilateral treaty on drones, while interesting, do not have the ring of immediate practicality about them. In the nearer term, and before international standards mature, individual governments likely host the most relevant developments. The work for regulators and industry alike is to ensure a degree of practical harmonisation. While jurisdictions are understandably keen to differentiate their individual offerings in order to attract investment and jobs, there is a recognition that regulatory schemes have to be interoperable.[72] A rough consensus appears to be emerging around graduated tiers of regulation, categorising drone operations by the objective risk they present. Most commercial drones, along with their recreational counterparts, will be small and light rather than unmanned approximations of existing aircraft. A regulated envelope is therefore

---

68 Under these changes, 18 of the 19 Annexes to the Chicago Convention were amended.

69 Roger Clarke and Lyria Bennett Moses, 'The Regulation of Civilian Drones' Impacts on Public Safety' (June 2014) 30(3) *Computer Law & Security Review* 263–285 <www.rogerclarke.com/SOS/Drones-PS.html>.

70 See, for this argument, Havel and Mulligan have expressed scepticism on any revolutionary cost savings in the near term, at least in the remotely piloted context. See Brian F. Havel and John Q. Mulligan, 'Unmanned Aircraft Systems: A Challenge to Global Regulators' (2016) 65 *DePaul Law Review* 107, 116–119.

71 D Marshall, 'Unmanned aerial systems and international civil aviation organization regulations' (2009) 85 *NDL Rev.*, 693, 712.

72 *Riga Declaration on Remotely Piloted Aircraft – Framing the Future of Aviation*, Riga (6 March 2015) Principle 2 <https://ec.europa.eu/transport/sites/transport/files/m odes/air/news/doc/2015-03-06-drones/2015-03-06-riga-declaration-drones.pdf>.

conceivable where such drones can operate in a manner where risk and interference to conventional aviation is kept within acceptable limits.

The European Union, through EASA, Australia, Canada and the United Kingdom lean towards this approach, although methodologies differ. Under EASA's Prototype Regulation, as an example, 'open', 'specific' and 'certified' tiers are proposed.[73] The 'open' and 'specific' tiers would allow for low capability activity and devices of up to 25 kilograms in weight, with functionality provisos including a recovery mode (for loss of data link), a 'return home' mode, a geofencing system, altitude limiter and an electronic identifier.[74] Operations are limited to 500 feet, with most devices being electronically limited to 150 feet by design under proposed standards.[75] The certified tier requires, as its name suggests, extensive regulatory approvals for operations outside this envelope.[76]

In Australia, regulation applies by weight with licensing requirements, outside a defined 'excluded' category, are generally applicable for drones over two kilograms in commercial use.[77] Canada allows drone use, subject to conditions, for devices up to 35 kilograms and altitudes to 400 feet.[78] The UK applies restrictions to drones heavier than seven kilograms[79] and thoroughgoing certification requirements for drones that are 20 kilograms or heavier.[80] Most recently, authorities there have signalled a shift in emphasis from weight to functionality in assessing risk for the certification tier.[81]

These schemes are tailored to mitigate risk principally by separating the greatest volumes of drone activity from interaction with airspace traffic, people and property. While the risks posed by smaller drones and recreational users cannot be discounted, measures of education, product design and enforcement,

---

73 *Prototype Commission Regulation on Unmanned Aircraft Operations* (22 August 2016) European Aviation Safety Agency <https://www.easa.europa.eu/system/files/dfu/ UAS%20Prototype%20Regulation%20final.pdf>.
74 *Prototype Commission Regulation on Unmanned Aircraft Operations* (22 August 2016) European Aviation Safety Agency <https://www.easa.europa.eu/system/files/dfu/ UAS%20Prototype%20Regulation%20final.pdf> Appendix I.2–I.6.
75 *Prototype Commission Regulation on Unmanned Aircraft Operations* (22 August 2016) European Aviation Safety Agency <https://www.easa.europa.eu/system/files/dfu/ UAS%20Prototype%20Regulation%20final.pdf> Annex I 'open' and 'specific' categories.
76 See further European Aviation Safety Agency, *Civil drones (Unmanned aircraft)* <https:// www.easa.europa.eu/easa-and-you/civil-drones-rpas>.
77 *Civil Aviation Safety Regulations 1998* (Cth) Part 101; *Advisory Circular 101–10 Remotely Piloted Aircraft Systems – Operation of Excluded RPA (other than model aircraft)* (February 2017) Civil Aviation Safety Authority <https://www.casa.gov.au/file/ 171461/download?token=rD99831v>.
78 See further *Canadian Aviation Regulations* section 602.41, which should be read with exemptions for recreational use. Commercial operations require authorisation.
79 The UK CAA appears to apply an expedited approval processes for commercial operations involving drones of less than 7 kilograms in weight. See United Kingdom Civil Aviation Authority, *Permissions and Exemptions for Drone Flights* (2015) <https://www.caa.co.uk/Consumers/Unmanned-aircraft/Recreational-drones/ Permissions-and-exemptions-for-drone-flights/>.
80 UK Civil Aviation Authority, 'Unmanned Aircraft System Operations in UK Airspace – Guidance' (2015) CAP 722 at 3.
81 Ibid.

of which industry is strongly supportive, should allow for management and mitigation.[82] The higher capacity and weight classes, i.e. those sitting in the upper reaches of the graduated tiers, are likely to be of greater interest from a harmonisation perspective. These are the drones most likely to share airspace and other facilities with manned aircraft in the future. It is beyond the scope of this note to compare approaches in the certification category in detail, suffice to note that industry would praise efforts towards guidance principles, regulatory manuals and initiatives like the Joint Authorities for Rulemaking on Unmanned Systems (JARUS).[83] Within these mechanisms, industry stakeholders would encourage close consideration of the concerns stated earlier. In particular, it should be an uncontested first principle that drones achieve safety outcomes at a level equivalent to manned aviation.

IV.

The utility of drones for a range of applications is clear and the sector offers enormous opportunity for the airline industry, the broader commercial aviation sector and new entrants. As with self-driving motor vehicles, it is easy to imagine a world in which short, Uber-like journeys could occur by autonomous drone or where drones make local delivery rounds.[84] Drones are used at present to deliver specialised freight in remote regions without much in the way of infrastructure.[85] Ancillary applications, like routine airframe inspection, are also of interest and have found application with airlines at the time of writing.[86]

Whether drone technology will be able to 'disrupt' mainline airline operations in the near term, however, is a matter for speculation. Passenger flights on large, wholly automated airliners are certainly not contemplated for the foreseeable future. Even drone delivery operations, in relatively contained local areas, have been slow to find consistent commercial implementation.[87] The prospect of long haul cargo operations by drone has been raised and will be of interest to industry

82 ACI, IATA and IFALPA Joint Statement 'Safety Awareness for Users of Remotely Piloted Aircraft in Close Vicinity of Airports' (February 2016) <www.iata.org/wha twedo/safety/Documents/Safety-Awareness-for-RPA-users-joint-statment.pdf>.

83 For more information of JARUS, see further JARUS, *JARUS – Who We Are & What We Do* (November 2017) <http://jarus-rpas.org/sites/jarus-rpas.org/files/ revision_jarus_who_we_are_what_we_do_v_6_0_version_15112017.pdf>.

84 Gulliver, *Dubai is to Test Passenger-Carrying Drones* (17 February 2017) *The Economist* <https://www.economist.com/blogs/gulliver/2017/02/taxi-take-0> and Uber, *Fast-Forwarding to a Future of On-Demand Urban Air Transportation* (27 October 2016) <https://www.uber.com/elevate.pdf>.

85 Steve Banker, *Drones Deliver Life Saving Medical Supplies in Africa* (13 October 2017) Forbes <https://www.forbes.com/sites/stevebanker/2017/10/13/drones-deliver-li fe-saving-medical-supplies-in-africa>.

86 Dominic Perry, *EasyJet to Roll Out Drone Inspections from 2018* (29 September 2017) Flight Global <https://www.flightglobal.com/news/articles/easyjet-to-roll- out-drone-inspections-from-2018-441652/>.

87 *The Economist, Why the Wait for Delivery Drones May be Longer than Expected* (10 June 2017) <https://www.economist.com/news/technology-quarterly/ 21723002-carrying-cargo-lot-more-complicated-carrying-camera-why-wait>.

in the medium to longer term.[88] Certification of such aircraft will be a challenge, together with regulatory approval for ground station control and autonomous or semiautonomous operation. Claimed cost savings, frequently assumed,
will need to be assessed and confirmed before commercialisation efforts could
attract sufficient capital.[89] Early conventional aircraft, in Saint-Exupéry's day,
carried mail and cargo before making a regular service with passengers and so it
might be similar path for drones.[90]

While the trajectory for drone technology in the airline industry is still
uncertain, lawyers might reason by analogy for the legal principles and regulatory structures required to support such operations. Once global technical
regulations are in place, economic authorisations as required by Article 8 and
other aspects, such as liability and insurance, should present no great conceptual
difficulty to the international community. Beforehand, however, watercooler
wisdom suggests that domestic operations are likely before international operations and remotely piloted arrangements are likely before semiautonomous or
wholly autonomous, rules-based operations.

Final remarks

Drones represent both a challenge and an opportunity for regulators and industry.
Significant advances have been made but significant unanswered questions
remain around technology, regulation and commercialisation. Graduated inclusion
within non-segregated airspace, with appropriate limitations, probably represents
today's answer. Industry would commend close consideration of the concerns on
record and the ICAO work to date. A special emphasis must be placed on risk
mitigation, erring towards incrementalism and full equivalence in safety outcomes. While differences of national approach are inevitable in this early period,
it is hoped that harmonisation efforts may eventually lead to meaningful uniformity
within ICAO.

Commercial operators

As drone technology continues to develop rapidly, corporations continue to
experiment and test such technology. Innovation is a hallmark of drone
development. An experienced drone executive at a prominent *Fortune 500*
technology company (whose identity has been withheld on request) describes
the commercial and regulatory outlook for drone operations as follows:

---

88 Daniel Terdiman, *A Startup's Plan to Cut Air Freight Costs in Half with 777-Size
Drones* (27 March 2017) Fast Company <https://www.fastcompany.com/
3069053/a-startups-plan-to-halve-cargo-shipping-costs-with-777-size-drones>.
89 Havel and Mulligan have expressed scepticism on any revolutionary cost savings in
the near term, at least in the remotely piloted context. See Brian F. Havel and
John Q. Mulligan, 'Unmanned Aircraft Systems: A Challenge to Global Regulators' (2016) 65 *DePaul Law Review* 107, 114–115.
90 Saint-Exupéry's exploits in carrying mail for Aéropostale between Europe and
South America in the 1920s are recounted in his book *Wind, Sand and Stars*
(1939).

As Unmanned Aerial Systems (UAS) proliferate, the effect on the entire community – operators, manufacturers, regulators, the public – can be summarized very simply: it is a clash of cultures. One of the first, and perhaps the most dramatic, examples of this clash is the introduction of the UAS into military operations.

UAS began by chipping away at one of the military's most hallowed traditions: the role and stature of the military aviator. If a military mission could be performed by a UAS almost as well as it could by a manned aircraft, but at a fraction of the cost and with no risk to human lives, did that not detract from the image of the daring fighter pilot or of the unflappable bomber pilot? Military reconnaissance pilots, who proudly – and rightly – boast that they fly into enemy territory 'unarmed, alone, and unafraid', suddenly find some of their missions being performed by a small buzzing contraption carrying a large camera. Take, for example, a Swiss Air Force fighter pilot – truly a member of a small, select group – who was pulled from the cockpit of an F-18 to the ground station of a UAV by a health problem. When asked, he described with a rueful smile his new occupation as that of "chainsaw operator". The US Air Force, two major wars and 15 years after the widespread adoption of UAS, still struggles to give UAS operators a career path and recognition equal to that of their manned aircraft brothers and sisters in arms.

This is only one of many examples of the clash of cultures that UAS have caused. The impact on the engineers who design UAVs, and on the government agencies that regulate their operation and design, is as significant as the impact on those who fly them.

Impact on aircraft designers

> When engineers start the design of a new manned aircraft, one of the first questions they ask is "Under what rules will it be certificated?" These regulations, thousands of lines long, dictate everything from the gusts the airplane's structure must withstand to the number and size of emergency exits. Choosing the body of rules that govern the aircraft's design affects the cost and duration of the development program, so there is an economic incentive to choose the simplest regulatory framework possible. Before the aircraft can be sold, the manufacturer must prove compliance with every applicable rule, sometimes through testing and sometimes through analysis. The rules for how the tests and analyses are to be conducted are equally detailed. The US Federal Aviation Administration publishes regulations for aircraft engines, small airplanes, large airplanes, balloons, small helicopters, and large helicopters. These are themselves subdivided into land airplanes, seaplanes, etc. but the total number of different aircraft categories amounts to a dozen or so. These certification rules, evolved over decades of experience by very qualified engineers, are primarily intended to ensure the safety of the aircraft's occupants, but of course also benefit those who live under the flight paths of these aircraft.
>
> The regulations for the certification of UAVs, on the other hand, are in their infancy. Not only is the field too new, it's also too broad. The UAV industry

today builds 100 gram toy multicopters as well 15 ton Global Hawks. One can spend $30 on a toy UAV or $30 million on a large military UAV. The missions vary from indoor-only play to Suppression of Enemy Air Defense (SEAD) using precision guided munitions. It would be very difficult to write just one regulation to cover the design of all of these aircraft. More likely, regulators would revert to what they know, and write one regulation for small multicopters, one for large multicopters, one for large fixed-wing unmanned airplanes and so forth. While that may indeed happen someday, in their absence we see another clash of cultures.

The engineers bred by the traditional aerospace industry want to design to a regulation. Not only is it legally required, it's also the only way they know to build a safe aircraft. They live or die by their ability to design it, certify it, and sell it. At the other extreme are the consumer quadcopter builders. They do not necessarily come out of the traditional aerospace industry. They are as likely to come from the electronics industry. They just want to sell it! In large quantities! And now, before the competition does!

While it's tempting to group all UAS, and their designers, into one category, that's ill-advised. Some UAS are thought of as semi-disposable toys…it's expected that they'll be unwrapped on Christmas morning and lost or broken by New Year's Eve. Others are treated as serious hardware, and while their design and operation is subject to less scrutiny than manned aircraft, they are still expensive, valuable mission-critical assets and are treated accordingly.

The 'drone engineers' see themselves as a disruptive force. While they may learn from the aerospace industry, they have more in common with Silicon Valley than with the builders of 'heavy iron'. The aerospace industry's engineers see themselves as the protectors of airworthiness, safety, and the tradition of long-lasting, slow, step-wise, cautious evolution linking the 1903 Wright Flyer to today's airliners.

After we remove the risk to occupants, the safety threat posed by UAS is the same – qualitatively if not quantitatively – to the threat posed by manned aircraft. A UAS can collide with other aircraft, it can crash into the terrain (CFIT, or Controlled Flight Into Terrain, is the term of art) and it can simply crash due to an error or a failure. Again, manned aircraft are also susceptible to all these failures. The impact on designers of UAS is that they must make the probabilities of these failures low enough for UAS to be accepted while keeping the cost lower than that of manned aircraft.

Labor drain and opportunity

There are many in the aerospace industry who long to move faster, to innovate, to break free from the tried-and-true. The UAS industry is the perfect haven for them – and this poses a staff retention challenge for the traditional aerospace industry.

They've been trained in the fundamental skills of designing, building, and operating aircraft and now they've come to the UAS industry, where the design cycles are much shorter. It's not uncommon for an engineer to arrive at a large aircraft company long after the program has started, work on a complex machine for five years, and then leave the company before the first flight. In the UAS industry, on the other hand, one might take one UAS from a blank sheet of paper to first flight every year or two.

While aerospace companies are very process-driven, UAS companies often operate as small startups, with processes – if they exist at all – written on the fly. At a typical large aircraft company, the Engineering Department will have a Bracket Design Manual, written from long experience and intended to ensure compliance with the relevant FAA regulations, that the engineers have to follow. Thus to 'design' a bracket becomes little more than following a recipe. At a small UAS start-up, there is no manual...for anything. Engineers are free, even required, to figure out how to design the bracket on their own.

The challenge for regulators

The world's aviation regulators also face a burden due to the UAS-inspired clash of cultures. Aviation regulators are primarily concerned with keeping airline travel safe and efficient. Ensuring the safety of the flying public is their primary duty.

It's therefore natural for regulators to see UAS, or indeed any innovation, as a risk. However, aviation regulators have proven that they are up to the challenge. For example, for the first 25+ years of jet airline travel, crossing an ocean – or otherwise being far from an airport – required three or more engines. Presented with years of data that proved the reliability of twin-engine airliners, starting in the 1980s, regulators approved ETOPS (Extended-range Twin-engine Operational Performance Standards) and the airlines were able to use more efficient twin-engine airliners on transatlantic and transpacific routes. It is crucial to note that ETOPS was approved in stages. Before ETOPS, airliners with fewer than three engines had to have an alternate airport within 60 minutes at all times, a requirement that barred twin-engine airliners from many long-range routes. With ETOPS, twin-engine airliners were allowed to operate 120 minutes form an alternate. After several years of successful operation, that was increased to 180 minutes.

Another example is cockpit crew size. Long-range airliners used to have four-person crews, until better navigation systems allowed for the removal of the navigator, leaving a three-person cockpit. Then reliable automation allowed for the removal of the flight engineer, leaving today's two-person cockpit. The airline industry, the aircraft industry, and the airline pilot unions worked hand-in-hand with regulators to bring both ETOPS and two-person cockpits into existence. In both cases, the restrictions were decreased in stages, backed up by extensive data showing it was safe to do so.

Both these innovations took decades to be accepted, a timeline that many in the UAS industry would find difficult to understand, let alone accept. The fundamental method, however, is sound and unlikely to change: (a) involve the regulators, labor, industry, and any other stakeholders, (b) make it safe, (c) provide data that proves it's safe, (d) give the regulators a chance to evaluate the data and the risk, and (e) plan on step-wise relaxation of the restrictions.

However, the world's civil aviation authorities face a looming crisis. More UAS, more uses for UAS, and more operators are all clamoring for instant response to their operating approvals. Meanwhile, budgets and staff size are relatively static. Both regulators and industry therefore share an incentive to find ways to follow the above process – all agree that safety cannot be compromised – but to do so at a higher rate.

A faster, cheaper alternative that we can offer regulators is to reduce what airspace they choose to regulate. Some UAS advocates point to the USAir "Miracle on the Hudson" accident, in which an airliner ingested a large number of birds, as a *reduction ad absurdum* argument against regulating UAVs. Since you can't regulate birds, the argument goes, why regulate UAVs? The fact is humans tend to manage what we *can* manage, and thus we tend to regulate what we *can* regulate. A better argument would be since we can't regulate everything, let's only regulate what we can regulate *well*. A UAV-to-airliner collision – a scenario we can all agree is the worst case – can be regulated well, and of course should be. Airliners operate in well-defined airspace that UAVs can easily be required to avoid.

For a more challenging example, one might argue that operating a UAV in an urban canyon – below the tops of buildings, but above people, cars, buses, and trucks – makes use of airspace that is not useful to manned aircraft. No manned aircraft would operate in that regime, so the risk of a mid-air collision is low. If the UAVs can avoid colliding with obstacles and with one another, and if the risk of causing injury is thus provably low, one might argue that they are more like tall ground vehicles than low-flying aircraft. Relaxing the definition of airspace to exclude the urban canyon environment might ease the approval process for package delivery UAVs. A similar argument might be made for UAS operation at very high altitude. Currently, no civil aircraft is certificated for flight above FL510, and Class A airspace ends at FL600. One might argue that the risk presented by operating UAVs above FL600 is thus easily managed, the obvious requirement being to deconflict with military aircraft, balloons, and other users of this useful, lightly occupied, but not quite empty airspace.

One might also consider urging regulators to relax their definition of what constitutes an aircraft. Virtually anything that flies, no matter how small or how low, is subject to being regulated today. The current regulations in the United States affect UAVs that do indeed weigh less than birds, which are of course not subject to any regulation.

Yet another new burden on regulators is already looming as UAS-inspired technologies are migrated into manned aviation. For example, there are robotic copilots under development – see the DARPA ALIAS program – that use computer vision to read the instruments and uses a robot arm to actuate the controls in a manned aircraft cockpit, under the command of what is effectively a UAV's flight computer. There are optionally pilot aircraft for sale, that may be flown with a crew, without a crew, or with a pilot onboard merely as a monitor of the UAV's systems while the aircraft is controlled from the ground. These may be thought of as UAVs with an optional onboard pilot, or as a manned aircraft with an avionics suite capable of automating the operation of the entire aircraft. Finally, many aerial taxis are under development around the world intended to carry passengers…but not pilots. These aircraft will fly as autonomously as any UAV, except they won't be unmanned, just unpiloted. Now the cultures are *really* clashing, perhaps even merging.

The future of UAS

There's no question that the demand for UAS will continue to grow, as new applications are found and markets are opened. The versatility, low cost, and fast reaction to emerging needs are just too compelling a force to be held back by the concerns mentioned above. This industry has not yet achieved steady state. New uses for UAS are still being found. Undoubtedly, some use cases currently being contemplated will be discarded as impractical or uneconomical. Others will lay dormant waiting for a technological breakthrough that will make them practical or cost-effective. Even the most mature space for UAS, that of military application, is still not static; new missions are being developed and new UAS for existing missions are being deployed. The civilian space, being newer, offers even greater opportunities, and inevitably, more possibilities for the clash of cultures to manifest, and eventually be resolved.

Drone technologists

Technical Director at Unmanned Aircraft Systems International and former ICAO UAS Panel Representative, James Coyne, provides comment from the perspective of managing future drone technologies:

> The introduction of drones into the aviation industry is considered to be as significant and revolutionary as the advent of the jet engine. Some have even gone so far as to suggest that drones are the greatest aviation innovation since the Wright brothers' Flyer back in 1903.[91]
>
> In the past, unmanned aircraft were primarily used by the military, first as target drones and later as sophisticated reconnaissance and air attack aircraft. For the military, drones are a means of protecting the lives of their pilots and other flight crew by removing them from the onboard cockpits and thus the active war zone and have them now operate the unmanned aircraft from a remote location. Military drones have the ability to stay in the air for longer periods of time than their manned counterparts. An average sortie for a modern fighter aircraft is of the order of approximately two to three hours. Compare this with the unmanned MQ-9 Reaper which has an endurance of between 25 to 30 hours.
>
> However, in more recent years unmanned aircraft have become far more affordable and usable. They have proven themselves in many civilian applications such as conducting surveillance, patrolling borders, agricultural spraying, searching for missing persons, aerial photography and monitoring of emergency situations like bushfires, floods and cyclones. Future use will see the use of drones for the delivery of medical and emergency supplies to remote communities in the event of floods or other disasters (as well, the delivery of pizza and beer).
>
> Drones are neat pieces of technology that every kid – the young and the not so young – would like to own. They are easily accessible to hundreds of thousands if not millions of people. However, with their easy accessibility, governments, regulators and law enforcement agencies the world over have before

---

91 Ron Bartsch, James Coyne and Katherine Gray, *Drones in Society: Exploring the Strange New World of Unmanned Aircraft* (Routledge, 2017).

them an industry segment growing at epidemic rates, presenting a challenge of epic proportion.

So, what are some of the effects that drones are currently having on the aviation industry, how are regulators coping with this new technology, and what does the future look like for drones?

What are the implications of drones for the aviation industry?

When we look at the implications of drones for the aviation industry, we need to examine both the recreational and commercial use of drones. Recreational use appears to be the cause of most of the concerns from invasion of privacy to the potential risks to commercial manned aviation. The operators of recreational drones are generally not trained and have little or no aviation experience. While the operators of drones used for commercial operations may have some training and are generally at least aware of the aviation industry, such knowledge and exposure varies dramatically from operator to operator depending on the size of the drone and the complexity of the operation.

Recreational users of model aircraft fly for fun and their own entertainment. Most of them fly in parks or in wide open spaces and are at least cognisant that if they hit someone or something with their aircraft, they could cause injury or damage. Thus, most of these recreational pilots generally act as responsible citizens.

People flying model aircraft do not have to get approval to do so from their regulator in most countries, nor do they need to join a hobby flying organization (such as the Model Aircraft Association of Australia in Australia). While the Association has over 10,000 members, it is reasonable to guess that there are probably three or four times that number of people operating model aircraft who are not members of a dedicated club. Recreational drones come in all sizes and types. Once upon a time they were either fixed-wing aircraft or helicopters, generally built by an enthusiast. These days there are commercial off the shelf aircraft that come as fixed-wing, helicopters or quad copters for as little as $30. Moreover, people can buy them from Aldi or indeed from pop up stalls in the middle of shopping centres at Christmas.

In terms of commercial operators of small drones with a mass of 2 kg or less, no formal approval or training is required. One can assume that, as they are in 'business' to make an income, they are inclined to act responsibly. However, in many cases, they do not know what they don't know, and could cause an accident through ignorance of the regulations.

Moving up the mass scale, operators of drones with a mass greater than 2 kg are required by CASA to have a remote pilot licence. Further, if they wish to operate commercially, they are required to hold, or work for a person who holds, a Remote Pilot Operators' Certificate (ROC), which is akin to a manned aviation Air Operators' Certificate (AOC) that the likes of Qantas hold. The license and the ROC are expensive and while CASA has issued in excess of 4000 licences and 1200 ROC's, there are still many operators who are doing odd jobs or doing aerial photography of houses for real estate agents without any approvals. They are operating close to people, over houses, beaches and near airports with little regard for people's safety.

So, whether people are operating legally, either for fun or commercially for hire and reward, or illegally, there is always the potential for accidents to happen. We also need to be conscious of the fact that the majority of unmanned aircraft are small and are very hard to spot. So, if operators choose to fly these small drones near airports, particularly in the flight path of manned aircraft during landing and take offs, they pose a great danger to the aviation industry at large.

The most significant implication to be addressed is the seamless integration of unmanned aircraft alongside manned aircraft in civil airspace. To do this we need an air traffic management (ATM) system for unmanned aircraft that complements the current ATM system for manned aviation. This concept will be known as Unmanned Aircraft Systems Traffic Management (UTM) and many organisations, such as Google, Amazon and Facebook are currently working on this technology.

How do we strike an appropriate balance between regulatory protection and technological advancement?

Drones represent a game-changing development for the aviation industry. The current estimate of expenditure on the civilian drones in the world, compared to manned aircraft, is only about two percent. However, that percentage is expected to increase exponentially over the next decade. Notwithstanding the low costs associated with unmanned platforms, there are more unmanned aircraft in the world today than their manned counterpart. This will only increase.

Regulations can have both a positive and negative effect on advancements in technology and innovation. While it is generally considered that the aviation industry is safer because of regulation rather than in spite of it, this message is difficult to get across to most people. It costs money to comply with the regulations. However, there is an old adage in the industry, "If you think safety is expensive, try an accident". Many people do not realise that they would benefit from complying with the regulations and spending a little money on safety and training rather than cost-cutting.

A term used to describe the relationship between technology and regulations is the notion of 'law lag'. Regulators always find themselves a few steps behind technological advancements and constantly struggle to 'keep up'. A good case in point: the first successful controlled manned flight by the Wright brothers occurred in 1903 and it took another 23 years for the USA to pass the *Air Commerce Act* which created a new Aeronautics Branch within the Department of Commerce. This landmark legislation, approved in 1926, made the Secretary of Commerce responsible for advancing air commerce, issuing and enforcing air traffic rules, licensing pilots, certifying aircraft, establishing airways, and operating and maintaining aids to air navigation.

When it comes to drones, the first unmanned aircraft – the Ruston Proctor – flew in 1916. However, the first drone regulation in the world was published in Australia in 2002 – 86 years later. It took the FAA a further 14 years to issue its drone regulations, i.e. 100 years after that first flight of a drone.

The International Civil Aviation Organization (ICAO) was probably the first regulatory body to come to grips with the fact that drone technology was advancing faster than the world could keep up. So, rather than follow its usual process of developing Standards and Recommended Practices (SARPs), a six to seven year process, it chose to develop guidance material to teach States how to develop their own regulations – a three year process. It did this through the Unmanned Aircraft Systems Study Group.

States picked up on this idea and instead of developing regulations that can take years to complete, they published guidance material that was quick to develop and easy to amend so that regulators could get valuable common sense and practical information out to the aviation industry quickly.

This development and publication of well thought out, practical guidance material coupled with targeted education and training can provide a good balance between regulatory protection and technological advancement, however, it is still very much an attempt in progress.

How do you see the future for drones?

This question can be approached in a systematic or methodical manner, or we can look at it as a speculative fiction that deals with imaginative concepts such as futuristic science and technology (science fiction). Science fiction often explores the potential consequences of scientific and other innovations, and has been called a "literature of ideas". Writers stretch imagination beyond provable, into the truly creative space. Innovators of today can draw on these futuristic notions and the uses of drones is only limited by our imagination.

The Teal Group predicts an exponential growth in the value of the drone market. So, we will see them more often, doing more tasks, and we will know more people who own one.

The ease of operation of unmanned aircrafts makes them an obvious choice for the delivery of things. There are many organisations – Google, Amazon and Facebook to name a few – who are working to deliver goods by drone. Google's Project Wing has commenced the commercial delivery of food to a remote farming community in Royalla NSW. Trials have been underway for the past few months. This is just the beginning. Soon, drones will be delivering medical and pharmaceutical products to remote locations around Australia. We may even see, in the not too distant future, delivery of the following:

- a gourmet dinner from your favourite restaurant
- an organ for transplant, bypassing traffic jams
- novel delivery of flowers and chocolate to your picnic spot
- last-minute gift to mum
- a crate of snow brought in from New Zealand
- a new luxury car, direct from Europe, in just days.[92]

We will also see drone 'roads and highways'. Today, manned aircraft follow main routes in the sky just as cars, buses and trains follow their terrestrial routes.

92 Ron Bartsch, James Coyne and Katherine Gray, *Drones in Society: Exploring the Strange New World of Unmanned Aircraft* (Routledge, 2017).

This maintains traffic separation, which minimises accidents and incidents. In order to function with and around us on a large scale, drones will need to have similar traffic management strategies. Before this can happen in a safe fashion, there are still a number of technologies to be developed, such as 'Detect and Avoid' and a viable UTM system. These are just around the corner.

3 Development of aviation laws and regulations

3.1 Introduction

This chapter outlines and examines the development of aviation laws and regulations. It begins with the Paris Convention of 1919, the first multilateral treaty to provide for the regulation of international flight. The Convention establishes the key principle of sovereignty over State airspace and is the foundation of civil aviation law generally, and was succeeded by the Chicago Convention of 1944. It then traces the course of international air carrier liability, safety and security conventions beginning with the Warsaw Convention of 1929 and ending with the Montreal Convention of 1999 (which deal with passenger liability). In terms of passenger liability, the Montreal Convention brought to an end the long battle for adequate levels of passenger compensation in the event of an accident on board an aircraft. It is and will continue to be the enduring treaty in terms of international passenger liability. Finally, the international protection of civil aviation is examined.

Not all of these treaties have direct relevance or applicability to drones. They do, however, provide the basis for domestic and international air law – the law upon which drone laws and regulations build.

3.2 From Paris to Chicago

In order for international flights to operate efficiently, a comprehensive set of international regulations is needed. The first section of this chapter examines the evolution of civil aviation regulation from the origins of flight itself to the development of the two most important international regulatory regimes: the Paris Convention of 1919 and the Chicago Convention of 1944.

3.2.1 Origins of flight

The first documented designs of aircraft including machinery such as turbines and propellers can be traced to the works of Leonardo da Vinci in the late

1400s.[1] These designs, however, were never realised.[2] Centuries later, in 1783, the Montgolfier brothers experimented with lighter-than-air balloon flights in Paris[3] and were responsible for the first successful and documented manned flight. As a direct result of this achievement, the first air laws were promulgated a year later.[4] These laws came in the form of a decree made by Parisian police, which prohibited balloon flights without a permit in order to protect civilians on the ground.[5]

Next came the development of heavier-than-air aircraft, with the works of Otto Lilienthal providing the basis for future developments with regard to manned aircraft. Before he died due to injuries sustained during one of his flights, Lilienthal's designs produced one of the first gliders to successfully transport a person.[6]

Lilienthal's legacy endured through the work of the Wright brothers who studied the early developments of flight, and were encouraged by the highly publicised gliding experiments conducted by Lilienthal.[7] In 1903 they achieved the first authenticated flight in a power-driven machine.

Twentieth-century advances in aviation stem from the Wright brothers' test flight.[8]

3.2.2 The 1919 Paris Convention

The Convention Relating to the Regulation of Aerial Navigation 1919 (the 'Paris Convention') was convened in 1919 by the French Government as part of the Versailles Peace Conference, about six months after the first regular international commercial flights commenced in Europe. The Paris Convention was the first international legal agreement to address the topic of international flight, and comprised a series of regulations relating to the flight of aircraft over and between the territories of different States. While this Convention was intended to be globally applicable, it was only ever ratified by 38 countries.[9]

Notwithstanding the number of ratifications, the Paris Convention is obviously significant given its originality and its important principles, many of

 1 Jacques Richardson, 'Leonardo: Why the Inventor Failed to Innovate' (2005) 7 *The Journal of Futures Studies, Strategic Thinking and Policy* 56, 57.
 2 Ibid 58.
 3 William Harper, 'A Lesson from Minerva' (2012) 51 *Quest* 102, 102.
 4 C. N. Shawcross and K. C. Beaumont, *Shawcross and Beaumont: Air Law* (London: LexisNexis Butterworths, 1997) I 1.
 5 I. H. Ph. Diederiks-Verschoor, *An Introduction to Air Law* (Wolters Kluwer, 9th ed, 2012) 2.
 6 Viktor Harsch, Benny Bardrum and Petra Illig, 'Lilienthal's Fatal Glider Crash in 1896: Evidence Regarding the Cause of Death' (2008) 79 *Aviation, Space and Environmental Medicine* 993, 993.
 7 'The Wright Brothers' and Langley's Aeroplanes' (1928) 122 *Nature* 930, 930.
 8 Ibid.
 9 C. N. Shawcross and K. C. Beaumont, *Shawcross and Beaumont: Air Law* (London: LexisNexis Butterworths, 1997) I 67.

which provided the foundations for the regulation of international flight. For example, the Paris Convention included detailed rules regarding the nationality of aircraft, their fitness for flight, and the competency of their air crews.[10]

Its fundamental principle is that of airspace sovereignty.

3.2.3 The central role of airspace sovereignty

There is little customary law which regulates the use of airspace as there was little need or opportunity for regulations of this nature to be developed prior to the commencement of regular international flights.[11] With regular international flight came the need to determine how the use of airspace should be governed. There were two broad options: to follow existing maritime law principles and allow airspace to be essentially free, or declare that airspace should be exclusively governed by the State beneath.[12] The main arguments for each of these theories were respectively made by Paul Fauchille and John Westlake. Fauchille, a French scholar, based his arguments on his own 'freedom of the air' doctrine. Westlake, however, was of the view that a States' sovereignty should have no vertical limits. After much deliberation, the latter option was decided upon. The Paris Convention established that States were to have complete and exclusive sovereignty over the airspace existing above their territory.

Together with such sovereignty comes the need to define the limits of a State's airspace, both horizontally and vertically, in order to establish the limits of its rights. With regard to the vertical limits of a State's airspace, there is no clear definition. There have been many proposals as to what this limit should be, including the limit of the Earth's atmosphere, the limit of the Earth's gravitational effect, or even simply the area over which a State could effectively exercise control.[13] Regardless, in terms of civil aviation, it has been accepted that this limit is above the height at which an aircraft can fly.[14]

Regarding the horizontal limits of a State's airspace, it has been universally accepted that a State has complete and exclusive sovereignty over the airspace above its national boundaries, which includes the area above its territorial sea.[15] There have previously been many variations on what 'territorial sea' actually includes, with the *United Nations Convention on the Law of the Sea* providing a clearer definition. This Convention provides that a territorial sea is deemed to extend up to 12 nautical miles from the defined baseline of the coastal State.[16]

---

10 Ibid.
11 Ibid IV 1.
12 I. H. Ph. Diederiks-Verschoor, *An Introduction to Air Law* (Wolters Kluwer, 9th ed, 2012) 3.
13 C. N. Shawcross and K. C. Beaumont, *Shawcross and Beaumont: Air Law* (London: LexisNexis Butterworths, 1997) IV 1.
14 Ibid.
15 Ibid IV 2.
16 *United Nations Convention on the Law of the Sea*, opened for signature 10 December 1982, 1833 UNTS 3 (entered into force 16 November 1994) arts 3, 5.

In addition, there is a contiguous zone which extends up to 24 nautical miles from the relevant baseline within which the coastal State may only exercise limited powers relating to customs and immigration.[17] There is also a broader 200 nautical mile zone referred to as the exclusive economic zone.[18] Within this zone the coastal State has even further limited sovereign rights, relating to the government of activities such as the exploration, exploitation and conservation of the natural resources present within that area.[19]

With regard to the application of these zones to airspace, it has been established that the State only has exclusive sovereignty over the airspace above its defined territorial sea, and not over the airspace above its contiguous zone or exclusive economic zone. This is so notwithstanding that its rights relating these zones would technically allow it to impose some restrictions.[20]

3.2.4 The 1944 Chicago Convention

In 1944, immediately prior to the end of World War II, representatives from 52 States convened in Chicago in order to discuss necessary developments to the regulation of international aviation.[21] As a result of this Conference, the *Convention on International Civil Aviation 1944* (the 'Chicago Convention') replaced the Paris Convention. This subsequent treaty was limited to civil aircraft. The Chicago Convention was, and remains, the most significant document relating to the regulation of civil aviation. Like its predecessor treaty, it began with the unequivocal declaration of the principle of State sovereignty. The Chicago Convention also outlined core principles regarding international air transport, based on the principles outlined in the earlier Paris Convention.

The Chicago Convention also established the International Civil Aviation Organisation (ICAO) as an independent aviation body and a specialised agency of the United Nations. ICAO has since been responsible for developing the principles governing international air navigation, and to foster the peaceful growth and sustainability of the civil aviation industry throughout the world.[22]

3.2.5 The basic principles of the Chicago Convention

The most fundamental principles relating to the regulation of international commercial aviation, as set out in the Chicago Convention, are examined below.

---

17 Ibid art 33.
18 Ibid art 57.
19 Ibid art 56.
20 Kay Hailbronner, 'Freedom of the Air and the Convention on the Law of the Sea' (1983) 77 *The American Journal of International Law* 490.
21 I. H. Ph. Diederiks-Verschoor, *An Introduction to Air Law* (Wolters Kluwer, 9th ed, 2012) 10.
22 *Convention on International Civil Aviation (Chicago Convention)*, opened for signature 7 December 1944, 15 UNTS 295 (entered into force 4 April 1947) art 44.

Part I – Air navigation

Part I of the Chicago Convention outlines the basic principles regulating international aviation.

GENERAL PRINCIPLES

As previously discussed, the Chicago Convention begins with the core principle of airspace sovereignty: every contracting State has complete and exclusive sovereignty over the airspace above its territory.[23] 'Territory' is defined as the land areas and adjacent territorial waters under the sovereignty or protection of the relevant State.[24]

Article 3 outlines the scope of the Chicago Convention. All relevant principles are applicable only to civil aircraft, not State aircraft.[25] State aircraft is defined within the treaty as any aircraft used in military, customs or police services.[26] This list, however, is not considered to be exhaustive. Article 3 is one of the most contentious articles in the Chicago Convention, and has been subject to some criticism.

FLIGHT OVER TERRITORY OF CONTRACTING STATES

The Chicago Convention makes a distinction between 'scheduled' and 'non-scheduled' flights. Non-scheduled flights include private flights and charter operations, and comprise a small component of all international air services. Article 5 States that each contracting State agrees that all aircraft belonging to other contracting States, which are not engaged in scheduled international air services, have the right to make flights into, or in transit non-stop across their territory without the necessity of obtaining prior permission. Scheduled flights make up the majority of international air services, and are subject to much more stringent restrictions. Scheduled international air services are not defined within the Chicago Convention, however, a definition has since been provided by ICAO:

> A scheduled international air service is a series of flights that possesses all of the following characteristics:

a   it passes through the air space over the territory of more than one State;
b   it is performed by aircraft for the transport of passengers, mail or cargo for remuneration, in such a manner that each flight is open to use by members of the public;

---

23   *Convention on International Civil Aviation (Chicago Convention)*, opened for signature 7 December 1944, 15 UNTS 295 (entered into force 4 April 1947) art 1.
24   Ibid art 2
25   Ibid art 3.
26   Ibid.

c   it is operated, so as to serve traffic between the same two or more points, either

    i   according to a published timetable, or

    ii   with flights so regular or frequent that they constitute a recognisable systematic series.[27]

Article 6 of the Chicago Convention addresses scheduled international flights, and provides that any scheduled international air service cannot be operated over, or into the territory of, another contracting State unless they have the authorisation of that State.

The Chicago Convention outlines restrictions in relation to cabotage which is the right of a foreign carrier to operate domestic services within another State. The Convention provides that a contracting State has the right to refuse permission of aircraft registered in another contracting State to take on passengers, mail or cargo destined for another point within its territory.[28]

The Chicago Convention also outlines rules regarding the procedures for landing an aircraft in a foreign State. Every aircraft which is scheduled to land in the territory of another State is to land and depart at a designated airport for the purposes of customs and other examinations.[29] Each contracting State must adopt sufficient measures to ensure that every foreign aircraft manoeuvring within its territory, along with every aircraft carrying its nationality mark, complies with the relevant rules and regulations relating to flight and man-oeuvre of aircraft, and that any persons who fail to comply with these rules and regulations are prosecuted.[30] Each contracting State must also take effective measures to prevent the spread of disease by means of air navigation from or into their territory,[31] and has the right to search aircraft belonging to another State upon landing or departure.[32]

NATIONALITY OF AIRCRAFT

Set out in the Chicago Convention are the relevant rules relating to nationality of an aircraft. Aircraft are determined to hold the nationality of the State in which they have been registered.[33] An aircraft cannot be registered in more than one State,[34] but its registration can be changed from one State to another

---

27 International Civil Aviation Organisation, *Doc 7278-C/841: Definition of Scheduled International Air Service* (1952).
28 *Convention on International Civil Aviation (Chicago Convention)*, opened for signature 7 December 1944, 15 UNTS 295 (entered into force 4 April 1947) art 7.
29 Ibid 10.
30 Ibid art 12.
31 Ibid art 14.
32 Ibid art 16.
33 Ibid art 17.
34 Ibid art 18.

in accordance with relevant laws and regulations.[35] Every aircraft engaged in international air navigation must bear appropriate nationality and registration marks.[36] Each contracting State must also supply on demand to any other contracting State, and to ICAO, information regarding the registration and ownership of any aircraft registered in that State.[37]

MEASURES TO FACILITATE AIR NAVIGATION

The Chicago Convention outlines the basis for relevant air navigation formalities, including customs and immigration procedures.[38] Each State party agrees to adopt all practicable measures to facilitate and expedite navigation of aircraft between States, and to prevent any unnecessary delays, particularly with regard to immigration, quarantine, customs and clearance procedures.[39] In addition, the Convention outlines relevant procedures in the event that an aircraft is in distress, or in the event of an accident.[40]

CONDITIONS TO BE FULFILLED IN RESPECT TO AIRCRAFT

The Convention also sets out various conditions which must be fulfilled with regard to the international operation of civil aircraft. These conditions relate to the documents which are to be carried on aircraft in service,[41] including journey log books,[42] the installation and use of aircraft radio equipment,[43] the issue of certificates of airworthiness,[44] and licences of personnel.[45] The Chicago Convention also outlines some restrictions as to the cargo that can be carried on board civil aircraft. No munitions or implements of war may be carried in or above the territory of a State without that State's permission.[46] The Convention further provides that each State party may prohibit or regulate the use of photographic apparatus within aircraft while flying over its territory.[47]

INTERNATIONAL STANDARDS AND RECOMMENDED PRACTICES

The Convention contains articles relating to the adoption of international standards and procedures,[48] the endorsement of various certificates and

35 Ibid art 19.
36 Ibid art 20.
37 Ibid art 21.
38 Ibid arts 23, 24.
39 Ibid art 22.
40 Ibid arts 25, 26, 27.
41 Ibid art 29.
42 Ibid art 34.
43 Ibid art 30.
44 Ibid art 31.
45 Ibid art 32.
46 Ibid art 35.
47 Ibid art 36.
48 Ibid art 37.

licences,[49] the recognition of existing standards of airworthiness,[50] and competency of personnel.[51]

Part II – The International Civil Aviation Organisation

Part II of the Chicago Convention establishes ICAO. The Convention essentially serves as a constitution for ICAO, and includes articles which outline the composition,[52] objectives,[53] and the legal capacity of the organisation.[54]

Annexes to the Chicago Convention

There are 18 Annexes to the Chicago Convention, which work to implement the articles of the Convention. The Annexes regulate:

1   Personnel Licencing
2   Rules of the Air
3   Meteorological Service for International Air Navigation
4   Aeronautical Charts
5   Units of Measurement to be Used in Air and Ground Operations
6   Operation of Aircraft
7   Aircraft Nationality and Registration Marks
8   Airworthiness of Aircraft
9   Facilitation
10 Aeronautical Telecommunications
11 Air Traffic Services
12 Search and Rescue
13 Aircraft Accident Investigation
14 Aerodromes
15 Aeronautical Information Services
16 Environmental Protection
17 Security – Safeguarding International Civil Aviation against Acts of Unlawful Interference
18 Safe Transport of Dangerous Goods by Air

3.2.6 Liberalisation of air services, and the right to fly post-Chicago

The right of an air carrier to fly passengers or cargo over and within a State can have significant commercial benefits. In order for these operations to occur, there are certain 'freedoms of the air' which must be exchanged between relevant States.

---

49 Ibid art 39.
50 Ibid art 41.
51 Ibid art 42.
52 Ibid art 43.
53 Ibid art 44.
54 Ibid art 47.

Freedoms of the air have been exchanged by States through air services agreements. Two of the most significant agreements of this nature were produced in addition to the Chicago Convention during the 1944 Chicago Conference.[55] The first of these documents is the International Air Service Transit Agreement, also known as the 'Two Freedoms Agreement'. This Agreement outlines the first and second freedoms of the air, which are often referred to as 'transit rights'.[56] These rights allow an air carrier to operate services through the airspace of a foreign State, and to land in a foreign State for purposes such as refuelling.[57] The majority of ICAO States have exchanged first and second freedom rights through this agreement, which has been ratified by 131 parties.

The second agreement is the International Air Transport Agreement, also known as the 'Five Freedoms Agreement'. In addition to the first and second freedom rights, this Agreement outlines three additional 'traffic rights', which allow the operation of international commercial air services to, and between, foreign countries.[58] This Agreement, however, has only been ratified by 11 States.

The first five rights are said to be 'official' as they are specifically set out in the Chicago Convention. In addition to these five freedoms, there are other rights which have been exchanged through State-to-State bilateral or multilateral services agreements.

There are nine commonly recognised freedoms of the air, which set out the right or privilege, in respect of international air services, granted by one State to another to:

- fly across its territory without landing (First Freedom Right);
- land in its territory for non-traffic purposes (Second Freedom Right);
- put down, in the territory of the first State, traffic coming from the home State of the carrier (Third Freedom Right);
- take on, in the territory of the first State, traffic destined for the home State of the carrier (Fourth Freedom Right);
- put down and take on, in the territory of the first State, traffic coming from or destined to a third State (Fifth Freedom Right);
- transport, via the home State of the carrier, traffic moving between two other States (Sixth Freedom Right);
- transport traffic between the territory of the granting State and any third State with no requirement to include on such operation any point in the territory of the recipient State (i.e. the service need not connect to, or be an extension of any service to or from the home State of the carrier) (Seventh Freedom Right);

---

55 International Civil Aviation Organization, *Manual on the Regulation of International Air Transport* (2004) <https://www.icao.int/Meetings/atconf6/Documents/Doc%209626_en.pdf> 3.2–3.
56 Erlinda M. Medalla, *Competition Policy in East Asia* (Routledge, 2005) 146.
57 Ibid.
58 Ibid.

- transport cabotage traffic between two points in the territory of the granting State on a service which originates or terminates in the home country of the foreign carrier or (in connection with the so-called Seventh Freedom of the Air), outside the territory of the granting State (Eighth Freedom Right, or 'consecutive cabotage'); and
- transport cabotage traffic of the granting State on a service performed entirely within the territory of the granting State (Ninth Freedom Right or 'stand alone' cabotage).

3.3 From Warsaw to Montreal

As with any form of transport, accidents involving aircraft, passengers, and cargo, are inevitable. The establishment of commercial aviation brought with it the need for rules defining the responsibility of carriers and the rights of passengers, including limits of air carrier liability, for any damage that may be caused to passengers, baggage or cargo. This area of law is governed primarily by treaties, and also by common law.[59] This section examines the development of the various regimes which have been established which govern air carrier liability, beginning with the Warsaw Convention of 1929, and culminating in the Montreal Convention of 1999.

3.3.1 The Warsaw System

When the first passenger aircraft began regular commercial services in the early twentieth century, there were no universally applicable rules of law which concerned the carriage of passengers, their baggage and goods.[60] There were various legal systems within individual States which considered matters of this nature, however, their laws were not consistent.[61] The presence of conflicting domestic laws, along with the absence of international law, led to the need for the development of a universal system of rules, thus, the Warsaw System. This system comprises a complex series of international treaties, together with various amending and supporting documents. Generally, each successive amending or supporting document provides a higher limit to compensation in terms of passenger injury, and for loss, damage or delay in terms of baggage (both checked and unchecked), or cargo.

3.3.2 The Warsaw Convention 1929

The origins of the Warsaw System lie in the early 1920s, with several international aeronautical organisations advocating for the development of an international legal regime for the rapidly developing industry of commercial aviation.

---

59 C. N. Shawcross and K. C. Beaumont, *Shawcross and Beaumont: Air Law* (London: LexisNexis Butterworths, 1997) VII 101.
60 Ibid VII 103.
61 Ibid VII 104.

The International Conference on Private Air Law, the *Conférence Internationale de Droit Privé Aérien* (CIDPA), was organised by the French government, and held in Paris in 1925. During this conference, the notion of a universally applicable system of rules relating to aircraft liability was discussed and recognised as a necessity. Particular concerns from airlines were also addressed. Due to the new and developing nature of the aviation industry, airlines had voiced concerns about being particularly vulnerable to legal action. Airlines needed investors in order to maintain operations and develop further; without limits to their liability in the event of an accident, such investors would likely be deterred. However, it was also recognised that any rules of this nature could not possibly be established successfully if national courts continued to apply inconsistent conflict of laws (choice of law) rules in the event of international disputes.

The conference ultimately resulted in the establishment of a committee, the *Comité International Technique d'Experts Juridiques Aériens* (CITEJA). This committee consisted of a range of legal specialists, designated with the task of drafting a document relating to the issues discussed during the conference.

Four years later, the second meeting of the CIDPA was held in Warsaw, where the document prepared by the CITEJA was examined. This document became the *Convention for the Unification of Certain Rules Relating to International Carriage by Air* (the 'Warsaw Convention'), and was signed by 23 States on 12 October 1929. The Warsaw Convention was the first treaty which provided regulations regarding air carrier liability for international carriage of passengers, baggage and cargo. This Convention has ultimately been ratified by 152 States.

The Warsaw Convention was successful in providing a universally applicable framework which worked to eliminate choice of law issues. The Convention also settled issues regarding jurisdiction and provided a limitation period.[62] Most significantly, the Warsaw Convention provided principles applicable to air carrier liability. Passengers benefited with a presumption of liability against the air carrier, established by a reversal of the burden of proof. As liability of an air carrier is based on the principle of negligence, normally a plaintiff would have the burden of establishing liability.

However, the Warsaw Convention provided that, in the event of an accident involving aircraft, carrier liability could be established by proof of damage which did not have to be established by the plaintiff. In order to avoid liability, the air carrier would then have to demonstrate that it took all necessary measures to avoid the damage. As this principle largely benefited the passenger, a balance was struck by placing limitation on the carrier's liability. This limitation was set at a maximum of 125,000 Poincaré francs in the event of injury caused to a passenger.[63] This amount was approximately equal to £1,000, or US $5,000 at the time the Convention was drafted in 1929.[64]

---

62 C. N. Shawcross and K. C. Beaumont, *Shawcross and Beaumont: Air Law* (London: LexisNexis Butterworths, 1997)) VII 105.
63 Ibid VII 105A.
64 Ibid VII 105B.

Notwithstanding the significance of this Convention, it fell short in a number of areas. For example, many key terms were not defined, including the words 'injury' and 'accident'.

3.3.3 The Hague Protocol 1955

In the 1920s, airline passengers were often wealthy enough to self-insure in case of an accident. However, as air travel became more and more accessible to the general population, the need for consumer or passenger protection in this area increased.[65] Rapid developments within the aviation industry, along with ambiguities and omissions in the 1929 Warsaw Convention, led to the need for further amendments and supporting documents. A revision of the Warsaw Convention initially began in 1938, and continued in the post-World War II period through the efforts of both CITEJA and ICAO.

Initial proposals for amendment were submitted at a conference organised by ICAO at The Hague in 1955. The result of these proposals was the *Protocol to Amend the Convention for the Unification of Certain Rules Relating to International Carriage by Air* (The 'Hague Protocol'). The Hague Protocol was the first amending document to the Warsaw Convention. It included minor changes relating to terminology, along with the addition of entirely new provisions relating to the carriage of baggage and cargo. Most significantly, The Hague Protocol significantly increased the limit of liability for the carriage of passengers, from 125,000 to 250,000 Poincaré francs. This Protocol was signed by 27 States on 28 September 1955, and was ultimately ratified by a total of 137 States.

3.3.4 The Guadalajara Convention of 1961

The Convention Supplementary to the Warsaw Convention for the Unification of Certain Rules Relating to International Carriage by Air Performed by a Person other than the Contracting Carrier (the 'Guadalajara Convention') was introduced in 1961 as a supplement to the Warsaw Convention. The need for this Convention came about due to the development of charter flights and code-sharing operations. As liability attaches to the air carrier, a need arose for a clear definition of 'carrier' in situations where the air carrier performing the flight is not the contracting carrier. Ultimately, the Guadalajara Convention worked to ensure that the actual air carrier was afforded the same rights and liabilities as the contracting carrier under the Warsaw Convention.[66] Essentially, this Convention extended the rules established in the Warsaw Convention to any carrier performing an international flight, even if that air carrier did not have a valid contract of

---

65 I. H. Ph. Diederiks-Verschoor, *An Introduction to Air Law* (Wolters Kluwer, 9th ed, 2012) 199.

66 C. N. Shawcross and K. C. Beaumont, *Shawcross and Beaumont: Air Law* (London: LexisNexis Butterworths, 1997)) VII 165.

carriage with the relevant passenger. This Convention was ultimately ratified by a total of 18 States.[67]

3.3.5 The Montreal Agreement of 1966

The *Montreal Agreement 1966* is not an international treaty but, rather an intercarrier agreement resulting from a series of decisions made by the United States. Although the United States signed The Hague Protocol, its ratification required the 'advice and consent' of the United States Senate.[68] This process comprised a series of long and complex arguments, from a number of major parties involved in the aviation industry.[69] Despite the increase in liability established by The Hague Convention, a majority of parties involved in aviation litigation strongly argued that these limits were too low.[70]

The United States subsequently gave notice to denounce the Warsaw Convention in 1965 and, in response, ICAO held a conference in Montreal in 1966. This conference failed to result in an agreement between States. However, an interim agreement was reached between air carriers. This agreement resulted in the Montreal Agreement – an *Agreement Relating to Liability Limitation of the Warsaw Convention and The Hague Protocol*, which convinced the United States to retract their notice to denounce the Warsaw Convention only two days before it would have come into effect.

The Montreal Agreement is a private agreement signed by each airline that operated services to, from, or through the territory of the United States. This agreement essentially waived the liability limitations provided by the Warsaw Convention, and substituted limitations that the United States could agree to. The Montreal Agreement raised the liability limits applicable in these circumstances to US $58,000 for any sustained passenger damage or US $75,000 including legal fees and costs.[71]

3.3.6 The Guatemala City Protocol of 1971

Significant amendments to the *Warsaw Convention as amended by The Hague Protocol 1955* were proposed during a conference organised by ICAO in Guatemala City in 1971. The result of this conference was the Guatemala City Protocol, a protocol intended to be read together with the *Warsaw Convention as amended by The Hague Protocol 1955* – thus, a single document, the *Warsaw Convention as amended by The Hague Protocol 1955, and at Guatemala City, 1971*.

The main principles outlined in the Guatemala City Protocol were an unbreakable per passenger limit of liability of 100,000 Special Drawing Rights

---

67 Ibid.
68 Ibid VII 125.
69 Ibid.
70 Ibid.
71 I. H. Ph. Diederiks-Verschoor, *An Introduction to Air Law* (Wolters Kluwer, 9th ed, 2012) 209.

(SDRs are examined below), and provision of a supplementary compensation plan in order to allow for the payment of damages in excess of this limit. The Guatemala City Protocol was signed by 21 States on 8 March 1971, but never came into effect.[72] However, its contents were adopted and built upon in later documents.

3.3.7 *The Montreal Additional Protocols of 1975*

The final documents contributing to the Warsaw System came about during a conference convened by ICAO in Montreal in 1975. During this conference, four additional Protocols relating to the Warsaw Convention were produced. Additional Protocols 1, 2 and 3 each amended a different version of the 1929 Warsaw Convention. Additional Protocol 1 amended the original Warsaw Convention, Additional Protocol 2 amended the Warsaw Convention as amended by The Hague Protocol, and Additional Protocol 3 amended the Warsaw Convention as amended by The Hague Protocol and the Guatemala City Protocol. Additional Protocol 3, however, never entered into force. The main purpose of each of these amendments was to replace the unit of measurement used to set liability limits from the Poincaré franc to an SDR.

An SDR is an international reserve asset, the value of which is currently based on the market exchange rates of five major currencies: the US dollar, the Euro, the British pound, the Chinese yuan and the Japanese yen.

Additional Protocol 4 also worked to modify the Warsaw Convention as amended by The Hague Protocol.[73] The purpose of Additional Protocol 4 was to modernise the provisions relating to carriage of cargo in the Warsaw Convention, by outlining documentation and liability relating to cargo and postal items. Among other things, this Protocol simplified cargo documentation, and introduced strict liability for cargo.[74]

These protocols were the final attempts made to amend the original Warsaw Convention. They did not, however, eliminate the need for future changes.

3.3.8 *The Montreal Convention of 1999*

The various protocols which amended and added to the original Warsaw Convention resulted in a patchwork – and often inconsistent – set of rules governing air carrier liability. Rather than amend the Warsaw System, a new convention was drafted to replace and modernise it. *The Unification of Certain Rules for International Carriage by Air* (the Montreal Convention), worked to consolidate and clarify all internationally accepted principles and rules

---

72 C. N. Shawcross and K. C. Beaumont, *Shawcross and Beaumont: Air Law* (London: LexisNexis Butterworths, 1997) VII 141.

73 International Civil Aviation Organization, *Manual on the Regulation of International Air Transport* (2004) <https://www.icao.int/Meetings/atconf6/Documents/Doc%209626_en.pdf> 3.2–4>.

74 Ibid.

established by the Warsaw System. As a result, many of the rules which had been established through the Warsaw System remained in substance.

In addition to consolidating the Warsaw System, the Montreal Convention also provided better protection to passengers striking a better balance between their interests and those of carriers. The Montreal Convention increased compensation to passengers in the event of an accident. In part as a result of this change, it is unlikely that any successor passenger compensation treaty will be formed any time soon.

3.3.9 Further developments

The Montreal Convention ended the patchwork of legal regimes governing the topic of air carrier liability by consolidating relevant principles. 127 out of 191 ICAO member States have ratified this Convention.

Although this is a considerable number, the Montreal Convention is, of course, ineffective in situations where either or both the departure and ultimate arrival States of a given ticketed journey have not ratified it. In these cases, passengers are left without the protection of the Montreal Convention in the event of an accident. And some States yet to ratify the Montreal Convention include ones with rapidly growing aviation markets such as Thailand and Vietnam.[75] The Montreal Convention also does not provide comprehensive definition of some key terms including both 'accident' and 'delay'. While it is not expected that there will be need for creation of another major document relating to air carrier liability in the near future, it can reasonably be expected that amendments will occur.

3.4 Aviation safety and security

In addition to air carrier liability, passenger safety has also been a prominent and ongoing concern within the aviation industry. Early in the development of commercial aviation, it was clear that international operation of commercial aircraft can facilitate serious crimes from drug smuggling, currency offences and theft to aircraft hijacking. Hijacking is the 'seizure by force of control of an aircraft in flight by a person on board'.[76] The first officially recorded hijacking of a commercial aircraft occurred in Peru in 1930, not long after the first regular commercial flights began.[77] Additional difficulties regarding crimes committed on board aircraft arose in terms of jurisdiction and extradition.[78] Common law countries claimed territorial jurisdiction, while civil law countries claimed

---

75 International Air Transport Association, *The Montreal Convention 1999* (MC99) (2017) <www.iata.org/policy/smarter-regulation/Pages/mc99.aspx>.
76 C. N. Shawcross and K. C. Beaumont, *Shawcross and Beaumont: Air Law* (London: LexisNexis Butterworths, 1997) VIII 1.
77 Ibid.
78 Ibid.

jurisdiction over offences committed by their own nationals, whether they were on home soil or abroad.[79]

Over time, there have been various regimes established to protect passengers in the event of air hijackings or major air disasters, along with the various other criminal offences which may be committed on board an aircraft. These regimes have endeavoured to solve jurisdictional issues, and cover both safety of passengers on board an aircraft and civilians on the ground.

There have been several treaties produced to address safety on board aircraft relating to parties who have a contractual relationship with an air carrier. These conventions extend from the 1963 Tokyo Convention to the 1991 Montreal Convention, and have each been ratified by most of ICAO member States.

Tokyo Convention 1963

The Convention on Offences and Certain Other Acts Committed on Board Aircraft (the 'Tokyo Convention') was the first comprehensive legal instrument to address the issue of crimes committed on board an aircraft. This Convention applies to civil aircraft only, and makes an offence of any act which jeopardises the safety of an aircraft (or persons or property on board the aircraft), or any act which may jeopardise good order and discipline on board an aircraft. The Tokyo Convention also provided that the State where an aircraft is registered establishes jurisdiction relating to any offences committed on board that aircraft. Additionally, the Convention provides permission for a State other than the State in which an aircraft is registered to interfere with an aircraft in flight. The State may interfere in cases where an offence committed on the aircraft has affected the territory of that State, was committed against one of its citizens, is against its security, or breaches any of its rules or regulations relating to the flight or manoeuvre of an aircraft, or if necessary in order to fulfil an obligation arising under a multilateral international agreement.

This Convention outlines the powers that the aircraft commander may exercise upon reasonable suspicion that a person has committed or is about to commit any offence or act which could jeopardise the safety of the aircraft or persons or property on board. It also sets out the powers and duties of States in relation as to how offenders should be dealt with.

The Tokyo Convention came into effect on 4 December 1969, and has been ratified by 186 States.

Hague Convention 1970

The Convention for the Suppression of Unlawful Seizure of Aircraft (The 'Hague Convention') was introduced in 1970, in response to a significant increase in aircraft hijacking which occurred during the late 1960s. The aim of this Convention is to provide more specific provisions relating to hijacking than were

79 Ibid VIII 2.

outlined in the Tokyo Convention, in order to eliminate possible refuge for hijackers. The Hague Convention made it an offence to unlawfully seize or exercise control of an aircraft while it is in flight, to attempt to do so, or to be an accomplice in doing so. The Convention also provided certain exclusions for this offence, including military, customs and police aircraft. The Convention does not apply unless either the place of departure or arrival is a State other than that of aircraft registration. The Convention also outlines that each contracting State involved must take all necessary measures to establish jurisdiction, and that criminal jurisdiction may be exercised in accordance with relevant national laws.[80]

This Convention came into effect on 14 October 1971, and has been ratified by 185 States.

Montreal Convention 1971

The Convention for the Suppression of Unlawful Acts against the Safety of Civil Aviation (the '1971 Montreal Convention') was drafted to complement both the Tokyo Convention and The Hague Convention by outlining matters which had previously failed to be addressed. These matters included sabotage and unlawful acts committed against the safety of civil aviation, including acts committed outside an aircraft. These matters extend to any acts any likely to endanger the safety of an aircraft in service. The Convention makes it an offence to unlawfully and intentionally perform an act of violence against a person either when that person is on board an aircraft in flight and the act is likely to endanger the safety of the aircraft, or if that person is at an international airport and the act is likely to cause serious injury or death, to destroy an aircraft in service, or to damage it so as to make flight unsafe or impossible. For the Convention to apply, either the place of departure or the place of actual or intended arrival must be situated, or the offence committed, or the offender found, outside the State of registration of the aircraft.

This Convention came into force on 26 January 1973, and has been ratified by 188 States.

Montreal Convention 1991

The need for a convention relating to more specific aspects of crimes committed on board an aircraft arose following the bombing of Pan Am Flight 103 in 1988. During the Boeing 747's flight from New York City to London, a timer-activated bomb made of an odourless, plastic explosive was detonated while the aircraft was flying over Lockerbie, Scotland.[81] The resulting

---

80 C. N. Shawcross and K. C. Beaumont, *Shawcross and Beaumont: Air Law* (London: LexisNexis Butterworths, 1997) VIII 22.

81 *Pan Am Flight 103* (16 November 2017) Encyclopaedia Britannica <https://www. britannica.com/event/Pan-Am-flight-103>.

explosion caused the deaths of all 259 passengers and crew on board, along with an additional 11 people on the ground who were killed by falling wreckage.[82] This event led to the development of the *Convention on the Marking of Plastic Explosives* (the '1991 Montreal Convention'). The main objective of this Convention was to reduce acts of terror using plastic explosives. State parties are required to prohibit and prevent the manufacture of unmarked plastic explosives within their territory, along with the movement of those explosives in or out of their territory. The Convention outlines provisions relating to the regulation, monitoring, manufacturing, possessing, importing and exporting of plastic explosives.

This Convention came into force on 21 June 1998, and has been ratified by 153 States.

3.4.1 Compensation conventions for damage to third parties

There have also been several conventions dealing with damage caused by foreign aircraft to third parties on the ground – those who do not have a contractual relationship with the air carrier. These conventions date from the Rome Convention 1933 to Conventions drafted in Montreal in 2009.

Rome Convention 1933

The Convention for the Unification of Certain Rules Relating to Damage Caused by Foreign Aircraft to Third Parties on the Surface (the '1933 Rome Convention'), was ratified by only five countries (Belgium, Brazil, Guatemala, Romania and Spain) and is now obsolete. Nevertheless, the Convention set out fundamental principles relating to damage caused to third parties, which were developed by future conventions. These principles include that:

• liability attaches to the operator, rather than the owner of an aircraft;
• strict liability is imposed on the operator of an aircraft;
• exoneration of the liability of an aircraft operator can only occur if it is proved that a third party had intervened;
• the limit of liability is determined in reference to the weight of the aircraft involved; and
• financial guarantees must be obtained by aircraft operators involved in international operations.

Rome Convention 1952

In 1948, ICAO decided that it was necessary to amend the 1933 Rome Convention. A draft of a new convention was considered during an international

---

82 Nancy Jean Strantz, 'Aviation Security and Pan Am Flight 103: What Have We Learned' (1990) 56 *Journal of Air Law and Commerce* 413.

conference held in Rome in 1952 and, as a result, the *Convention on Damage Caused by Foreign Aircraft to Third Parties on the Surface* (the '1952 Rome Convention'), came into effect the same year. The aim of this Convention was much the same as the original Rome Convention. Some of the most significant improvements included the addition of definitions of key terms such as 'operator' and 'in-flight', along with more comprehensive details regarding liability and the determination of liability limits. However, like its predecessor, the 1952 Rome Convention never achieved widespread international recognition, and has only been ratified by 49 States.

Convention on Compensation for Damage Caused by Aircraft to Third Parties 2009 and the Convention on Compensation for Damage to Third Parties Resulting from Acts of Unlawful Interference Involving Aircraft 2009

Air carrier liability regarding third parties on the ground became far more significant following the September 11, 2001 attacks in the United States. Although this event occurred entirely within the United States, eliminating the need for the application of any internationally applicable rules of law, the negative impacts of this event were felt throughout the world. As a result, it was decided that international air safety laws and security regimes needed to be further modernised in order to return a sense of security to the aviation industry. In response, two new instruments on third-party liability were adopted at the International Conference on Air Law held under the auspices of ICAO in Montreal in 2009.[83]

The first of these was the *Convention on Compensation for Damage Caused by Aircraft to Third Parties 2009* (the 'General Risks Convention'). This Convention was intended to modernise the 1952 Rome Convention. It aims to ensure that adequate compensation is awarded to third parties who suffer damages caused by any events involving an aircraft in flight. The Convention established that the aircraft operator is presumed to be liable for any damage suffered by a third party, provided that the relevant damage was caused by an aircraft in flight. The damage must also be directly attributable to the aircraft; it is not considered relevant if the damage was a direct consequence of armed conflict or civil disturbance, or caused merely by the lawful passage of an aircraft through airspace. This Convention also outlines the relevant limits to the aircraft operator's liability, calculated based on the mass of the aircraft involved and provided in SDRs.

The second treaty adopted at the 2009 Conference in Montreal was the *Convention on Compensation for Damage to Third Parties Resulting from Acts of Unlawful Interference Involving Aircraft 2009* (the 'Unlawful Interference Compensation Convention'). There were several objectives of this Convention,

83 Gilles Lauzon, 'The New ICAO Conventions on Third Party Liability' (2009) 14 (3) *Uniform Law Review-Revue de droit uniforme* 676, 676 <http://109.168.120.21/siti/Unidroit/index/pdf/XIV-3-0676.pdf>.

including to balance the protection of innocent parties and the liability of blameless air carriers, and to neutralise the economic consequences of unlawful interference with aircraft.[84] Another was to provide a long-term environment for civil aviation that was stable in terms of war risk insurance, by ensuring that operating costs are predictable and that the aviation industry is free from uninsurable catastrophic losses that occur due to events beyond their control.[85] This Convention also aimed to ensure that airlines can compete on a level playing field, regardless of the degree of wealth of the country in which they are based.[86]

These Conventions, opened for signature in 2009, have not yet come into force due to lack of sufficient support and it appears to the authors unlikely that they ever will.

84 Ibid 686–687.
85 Ibid 688.
86 Ibid.

4 Regulation of aviation at the national and international levels

4.1 Introduction

This chapter provides background to the regulation of aviation law in both an international and national framework – such framework critical to an understanding of current and emerging drone law in federal and unitary jurisdictions. At the international level, aviation law is regulated overwhelmingly by treaties, custom and guiding principles. These sources of law have both advantages and disadvantages and are therefore used to achieve different purposes.

By way of example, we look at the complexities of implementing international law into domestic law in Australia (a federal, common law system). It involves the balancing of powers between the national and sub-national levels of government, and then between the legislative, judicial and executive arms of government. Australia's approach to international law will be compared to other States including the United States, the United Kingdom and France.

What will become apparent from these comparisons is not only the different processes that States employ to implement international law but also the different views of States on the authority and importance of international law generally. This, in turn, has implications for drone law.

4.2 Treaties and international instruments

States are committed to a range of international aviation agreements and arrangements around the world.[1] These international agreements involve a complex web of issues including traffic rights, ownership and control of airlines, tariffs, competition policy and security. They come from different sources including treaties, custom, guiding principles and other international instruments as agreed by States. The main source of international aviation law is treaties, the focus of the first part of this chapter.

---

1 *Australia's Air Services Agreements/Arrangements* (23 August 2017) Australian Government: Department of Infrastructure and Regional Development <https://infrastructure.gov.au/aviation/international/agreements.aspx>.

4.2.1 The Vienna Convention on the Law of Treaties

The Vienna Convention on the Law of Treaties (the 'Vienna Convention') is the primary instrument that regulates treaties. Its entry required 35 ratifications and came into force on 27 January 1980. The Vienna Convention applies to treaties between States (Article 1). It was created because of the need to reformulate the law with coherence and consistency given the growing importance of treaties for relations between States. The Vienna Convention provided clarity on a number of issues that were uncertain or the subject of disagreement. It defines what a treaty is, how it is made, amended, operates and terminated. For that reason, the Vienna Convention is often referred to as the 'treaty of treaties'. It incorporates the notion of good faith as revealed in the preamble:

> [T]he present Convention will promote the purposes of the United Nations set forth in the Charter namely, *the maintenance of international peace and security, the development of friendly relations and the achievement of co-operation among nations* (emphasis added).

It is not, however, concerned with the substance of any specific treaty and the rights and obligations created by it; the content of any treaty is a matter largely negotiated by States.

4.2.2 Treaties

Treaties are the primary source of international aviation law.[2] A treaty is defined in the Vienna Convention, Article 2, as 'an international agreement between States in written form and governed by international law, whether embodied in a single instrument or in two or more related instruments and whatever its particular designation'.[3] Emphasis is given to States because treaties do not cover (or rarely cover) commercial agreements involving individual persons or companies.[4] The fact that this definition requires a treaty to be 'written' does not mean that oral agreements under international law are invalid. Oral agreements can still be valid but will not, however, be governed by the Convention.

In theory, international treaties share equal status with other sources of international law such as custom. In practice, however, international treaties are preferred to other sources of international (aviation) law because of their capacity to express nuances, caveats, idiosyncrasies, exceptions and particularities.[5]

---

2 I. H. Ph. Diederiks-Verschoor, *An Introduction to Air Law* (Wolters Kluwer, 9th ed, 2012).
3 *Vienna Convention on the Law of Treaties*, opened for signature 23 May 1969, 1155 UNTS 331 (entered into force 27 January 1980) art 2(1)(a).
4 C. N. Shawcross and K. C. Beaumont, *Shawcross and Beaumont: Air Law* (London: LexisNexis Butterworths, 1997).
5 Brian F. Havel and Gabriel S. Sanchez, *The Principles and Practice of International Aviation Law* (Cambridge University Press, 2014).

When a State adopts a treaty, such adoption can also be used to signify that State's position on the law. Therefore, it is considered more than just an agreement between two or more States; it is also seen as a legitimate instrument to demonstrate a State's internal political cultures.

Treaties create binding legal obligations. Parties to a treaty are, therefore, not allowed to act (or omit to act) in a way that would be contrary to that treaty. This is emphasised in Article 18 of the Vienna Convention which provides that a State is obliged to refrain from acts which would defeat the object and purpose of a treaty when it has:

a   signed the treaty or has exchanged instruments constituting the treaty subject to ratification, acceptance or approval, until it shall have made its intention clear not to become a party to the treaty; or
b   expressed its consent to be bound by the treaty, pending the entry into force of the treaty and provided that such entry into force is not unduly delayed.

Treaties are generally only binding on States party to a treaty and do not create obligations or rights for a third State without its consent pursuant to Article 34 of the Vienna Convention. A third State is defined in the Vienna Convention as a State that is not a party to the treaty. However, a treaty can provide for obligations for a third State if there is a provision of the treaty which intends to establish that obligation. Where such a provision exists, the third State must expressly accept that obligation in writing under Article 35 of the Vienna Convention.

How are international treaties adopted?

Treaties are adopted by the consent of the States and international organisations that are party to it.[6] Consent of a State is defined in Article 11 of the Vienna Convention as expressed by signature, exchange of instruments constituting a treaty, ratification, acceptance, approval or accession, or by any other agreed means. It was once considered that ratification was the final, official 'stamp' of consent on the part of a State. However, the modern view holds that treaties will only require ratification if specifically required in the treaty.[7] Other forms of consent will still be valid, binding forms of adoption.

If treaty-making takes place at an international conference, the treaty will be adopted in accordance with the procedure agreed upon by the participants at that conference.[8] Where there is no agreement, the treaty is adopted by the

---

6 *Vienna Convention on the Law of Treaties*, opened for signature 23 May 1969, 1155 UNTS 331 (entered into force 27 January 1980) art 9(1).
7 *Treaties* (August 2010) House of Commons Information Office <https://www.parliament.uk/documents/commons-information-office/p14.pdf>.
8 *Vienna Convention on the Law of Treaties*, opened for signature 23 May 1969, 1155 UNTS 331 (entered into force 27 January 1980) art 9(2).

vote of two-thirds of the participants present and voting.[9] The appropriate person to give consent will depend on the circumstances of the treaty and the constitutional framework of the State. Such person may be the head of State, head of government, foreign minister, or such other properly accredited representative.[10]

Reservation

A State party to a treaty may not be legally bound to a specific provision in a treaty to which it objects. The concept of 'reservation' in the context of international treaties exists in customary law, but it was not until the advent of the Vienna Convention that reservation became an established, codified 'right' available to States. It is defined in the Vienna Convention to mean a unilateral statement by a State which purports to exclude or to modify the legal effect of certain provisions of the treaty in their application to that State. This right of reservation is found in Article 19 of the Vienna Convention which provides that:

> a State may, when signing, ratifying, accepting, approving or acceding to a treaty, formulate a reservation unless:
>
> a   The reservation is prohibited by the treaty;
> b   The treaty provides that only specified reservations, which do not include the reservation in question, may be made; or
> c   In cases not falling under sub paragraphs (a) and (b), the reservation is incompatible with the object and purpose of the treaty.[11]

When a State makes a reservation, Article 20 of the Convention provides that the other contracting State or States do not need to subsequently authorise the reservation unless the treaty so provides. A State will automatically be deemed to have accepted the reservation simply by not objecting to it by the end of 12 months after notification.

Reservation is an important part of treaty law. States have the option to reserve to certain provisions of a treaty. This enables States to a treaty to adjust gradually and progressively to rules.[12] It is also argued that the ability to make reservations also enhances the depth and breadth of treaty commitments for all States. This is because it provides a transparent and accurate representation of the State's propensity to comply with the treaty. This can be seen as a form of

---

9 Ibid.
10 C. N. Shawcross and K. C. Beaumont, *Shawcross and Beaumont: Air Law* (London: LexisNexis Butterworths, 1997).
11 *Vienna Convention on the Law of Treaties*, opened for signature 23 May 1969, 1155 UNTS 331 (entered into force 27 January 1980) art 19.
12 Enzo Cannizaro, *The Law of Treaties Beyond the Vienna Convention* (Oxford University Press, 2011).

'risk management'; it lowers the risk of a State 'defaulting'.[13] From a broader policy perspective, reservation is important to prevent smaller States feeling pressured to agree to treaties that they cannot feasibly comply with for social, economic or political reasons. Reservation is a useful, modern 'tool' that assists in the promotion of inter-state cooperation.

Bilateral treaties

Bilateral treaties are agreements made between two States. They are used perhaps most commonly in an aviation context for air service agreements. For example, when a national airline of one State flies to another State, the governments of both States have entered into a bilateral air service agreement generally containing provisions regarding traffic rights, capacity, tariffs, safety, control and other relevant issues that will govern that flight. Australia, for example, has negotiated over 90 air service agreements and associated arrangements and, as globalisation continues to grow, the number of these agreements will also grow.[14]

Multilateral treaties

Multilateral treaties are agreements between three or more States and are the most common source of international aviation law.[15] The first multilateral aviation treaty was the Paris Convention of 1919 which sought for the first time to regulate international aviation law. It was replaced by the Chicago Convention of 1944, an international treaty with over 190 ratifications. Other examples are the Warsaw Convention of 1929 and the Montreal Convention of 1999, both of which established a uniform rule of law concerning international carriage by air and carrier liability.

Amending treaties

As aviation-related technology continues to change rapidly, treaties can become quickly outdated and incapable of addressing twenty-first century issues. Parties to a treaty must, therefore, update their obligations to each. The Chicago Convention, for example, has been amended from time to time; the latest amendment to Annex 17 was made as recently as August 2017. Unless otherwise provided in the relevant treaty, amendment to a treaty is governed by the

---

13 Laurence R. Helfer, 'Not Fully Committed? Reservations, Risk and Treaty Design' (2006) 31 *Yale Journal of International Law* 367.
14 *The Bilateral System – How International Air Services Work* (25 June 2014) Australian Government: Department of Infrastructure and Regional Development <https://infrastructure.gov.au/aviation/international/bilateral_system.aspx>.
15 I. H. Ph. Diederiks-Verschoor, *An Introduction to Air Law* (Wolters Kluwer, 9th ed, 2012).

Vienna Convention under Articles 39 (for treaties generally) and 40 (for multilateral treaties).[16]

For bilateral treaties, amendment is made by agreement between the two parties. Multilateral treaties are more complex in this regard, requiring as they do all parties to be notified of the proposed change(s) and the opportunity for all parties to participate in the negotiation, decision and conclusion of the proposed amendment(s).

Grounds for terminating or withdrawing from a treaty

The Vienna Convention contemplates circumstances where a party which has accepted a treaty is no longer able to perform its obligations.

Article 61 of the Vienna Convention provides that a party may invoke 'supervening impossibility of performing a treaty' as a ground for terminating or withdrawing from a treaty if the impossibility results from the permanent disappearance or destruction of an object indispensable for the execution of the treaty. If the impossibility is *temporary*, it may be invoked only as a ground for suspending the operation of the treaty. However, this will not be available if the impossibility of performance is the result of a breach by that party either of an obligation under the treaty or of any other international obligation.

Further, Article 62 of the Vienna Convention provides that a party may terminate or withdraw from a treaty it has accepted on the grounds that there has been a 'fundamental change of circumstances'. The circumstances must not have been foreseen by the parties at the time of the treaty's conclusion. Therefore, this ground for termination of withdrawal will not be available unless the existence of those circumstances constituted an essential basis of the consent of the parties to be bound and the effect of the change is to radically transform the extent of obligations.

However, under Article 63 of the Vienna Convention, severance of diplomatic or consular relations between parties to a treaty will not affect the legal relations established between them by a treaty. Parties to a treaty cannot, therefore, terminate or withdraw from a treaty *merely* because of a change in political relations. Nevertheless, these grounds under the Vienna Convention demonstrate that, while international treaties generally contain binding obligations, such obligations will not be enforced in circumstances where enforcement would cause undue hardship on a State. In this respect, there is a degree of flexibility afforded to international treaties.

4.2.3 Customary international law

Absent any express or formal agreement, if a State commonly follows a practice for an extended period of time, those States may consider themselves bound by

---

16 *Vienna Convention on the Law of Treaties*, opened for signature 23 May 1969, 1155 UNTS 331 (entered into force 27 January 1980) art 40.

that practice.[17] Customary international law is the set of general principles widely accepted and adhered to by States. If a State party has, from the outset, clearly and consistently expressed objection or disapproval of a particular rule, it will not be bound by customary international law.

There are two elements to customary international law. Firstly, it must be established that States do or do not do something in a matter that is certain and virtually uniform. This is an objective assessment and will require consideration of various other sources of those States' laws including domestic legislation, General Assembly resolutions, Security Council resolutions, treaties and court decisions. Second, it must be shown that the practice is accepted as law in that State and not merely a coincidence or obscure practice (that is, not custom). To show that a practice is accepted as law it must be established that States are legally obliged to follow that practice.

This second element of customary international law is difficult to establish.

Jus Cogens

The most important rule of customary international law is *Jus Cogens* or 'compelling law'. It is derived from customary international law and refers to the highest and most fundamental form of international law. It has also been described as the 'ethical minimum' recognised by the international community.[18] States are customarily bound to it and no exceptions or derogation are permitted.

4.2.4 Guiding principles

Guiding principles are a non-binding (but important) source of international aviation law. Guiding principles outline a number of provisions to be followed. Guiding principles may be proposed or drafted where it is unclear what the law is or as a preliminary step to a convention.

The International Civil Aviation Organisation (ICAO) is an example of a body that establishes guiding principles (as well as standards). ICAO was, as previously mentioned, established by the Chicago Convention and works to uphold the principles underlying that Convention. Its primary objectives are the promotion of safety and the orderly development of civil aviation. It also addresses security matters through continuous auditing and monitoring of member States' aviation security performance. It collates and publishes information on international civil aviation so as to ensure transparency and access to information. It is integral to the achievement of international cooperation and coordination in civil aviation.

---

17 *Treaty-Making Options for Australia* (1996) Parliament of Australia <https://www.ap h.gov.au/About_Parliament/Parliamentary_Departments/Parliamentary_Library/ Publications_Archive/CIB/cib9596/96cib17>.

18 Alfred Von Verdross, 'Forbidden Treaties in International Law: Comments on Professor Garner's Report on "The Law of Treaties"' (1937) 31(4) *American Journal of International Law* 571, 574.

ICAO works with other bodies to create internationally agreed standards and recommended practices (SARPs). 'Standards' are considered to be mandatory obligations; 'recommendations' are not. The purpose of SARPs is to achieve safety, regularity and efficiency in international civil aviation.[19] ICAO makes recommendations to the Air Navigation Committee which then invites all ICAO Member States to comment on its proposals before placing them before the Council for adoption by vote. The Chicago Convention requires a two-thirds majority vote of the SARP before they are published by ICAO as Annexes to the Chicago Convention. Once they have been adopted, it is up to each member State to implement the SARPs through its own domestic arrangements. For example, in 2010, ICAO released the Machine Readable Travel Document (MRTD) Programme which developed a worldwide standard for machine readable passports. Over 180 States now comply with these standards.

Guidance materials are produced separately by ICAO to clarify the understanding of SARPs and to facilitate their implementation. Such materials do not form part of the Annexures to the Chicago Convention but are often issued as attachments to Annexes or as manuals or circulars. Guidance materials are reviewed periodically to ensure consistency and up to date practices.

Guiding principles can easily be amended, for example, in light of new threats and technological developments. Not only are guiding principles efficient, they are also cost-effective. However, guiding principles are only a guide; they are not legally binding and States, therefore, are not obliged to follow them.

4.2.5 Breaches of international aviation law

Under Article 60 of the Vienna Convention, breaches of bilateral and multi-lateral treaties are dealt with separately. In relation to bilateral treaties, Article 60(1) provides that a material breach by one of the parties entitles the other party to invoke the breach as a ground for terminating the treaty or suspending its operation in whole or in part. Breaches of multilateral treaties, however, are more complicated. Article 60(2) provides that a material breach of a multilateral treaty by one of the parties entitles the other parties by unanimous agreement to suspend the operation of the treaty in whole or in part or to terminate it either in terms of the relations between themselves and the defaulting State or as between all of the parties.

If a party is specifically affected by the breach of a multilateral treaty, that State can invoke the breach as a ground for suspending the operation of the treaty in whole or in part in the relations between itself and the defaulting State without unanimous agreement. Further, if the breach radically changes the position of every party with respect to the future performance of its obligations under the treaty, any party can invoke the breach as a ground for suspension without unanimous agreement.

---

19 *Making an ICAO Standard* (1 November 2011) International Civil Aviation Organisation <https://www.icao.int/safety/airnavigation/Pages/standard.aspx>.

4.3 Domestic implementation of international law

4.3.1 Relationship between international and domestic law

In some instances, there may be inconsistencies between a State's domestic law and its obligations under international law.

The International Court of Justice and other various international tribunals take the view that international law cannot merely be avoided because of a contradiction in domestic law. A nation must still uphold its international obligations despite inconsistencies that may arise between the nation's international obligations and the nation's domestic obligations.

In some countries, however, the interrelationship between domestic and international law is not so clear cut. In Australia, for example, former Chief Justice of the High Court, Sir Anthony Mason, quoting legal academic Geoffrey Sawer, once said that in relation to these circumstances:

> There must exist a judicial discretion in the Australian courts to ignore international law rules not so far 'received' on some ground of their inconsistency with general policies of our law, or lack of logical congruence with its principles[20]

Such need for consistency and transparency is emphasised in international treaties. In terms of aviation, Article 37 of the Chicago Convention provides that States must 'secure the highest practicable degree of uniformity in regulations, standards, procedures and organisation in relation to aircraft, personnel, airways and auxiliary services'. Further, if a State cannot for some reason comply with its international obligations, that State is required to disclose its non-compliance to ICAO.[21]

4.3.2 Monism and dualism

The relationship between international and national law is a complex one. Competing theories with regard to this relationship fall into two main groups, monists and dualists. For the monist, international law is but one element of domestic law. A dualist, however, believes that they are two, separate legal systems existing side by side with different spheres of action – 'the international plane and the domestic plane'.[22]

---

20 Anthony Mason, 'Should the High Court Consider Policy Implications When Making Judicial Decisions?' (1997) 57(1) *Australian Journal of Public Administration* 77–80.
21 *Convention on International Civil Aviation (Chicago Convention)*, opened for signature 7 December 1944, 15 UNTS 295 (entered into force 4 April 1947) art 38.
22 www.hcourt.gov.au/assets/publications/speeches/former-justices/kirbyj/kirbyj_weeram.htm#FOOTNOTE_3

Whether a nation adopts a more monist or dualist approach is largely influenced by the culture of the nation. Justice Higgins found that jurisdictions such as those which derive their legal systems from England tend to adhere more towards the dualist approach.[23] Former Australian High Court Justice Michael Kirby takes this further by suggesting that the traditional view of most common law countries has been that 'international law *is not part* of domestic law'.[24] Dualists often raise concerns that international law undermines the sovereignty of a State without the authority of the State's democratic law makers. Further, although international law is theoretically binding, it is not enforceable in practice. Dualists, therefore, often place less importance on international law. Other jurisdictions, however, view international law as embodying norms superior to those of domestic law and argue for its greater recognition.

4.3.3 Australia's position

The position in Australia, for example, again a federal, common law jurisdiction, is predominately dualist. However, over time, there has been increasingly more acceptance of the authority of international law. Traditionally, as in many other common law countries, Australia did adhere strictly to a dualist approach. In 1982, Mason J explained the traditional position in *Koowarta v Bjelke-Petersen* as follows:

> it is a well settled principle of the common law that a treaty not terminating a State of war has no legal effect upon the rights and duties of Australian citizens and is not incorporated into Australian law on its ratification by Australia... To achieve this result, the provisions have to be enacted as part of our domestic law, whether by a Commonwealth or State statute.[25]

More recently, evidence suggests that Australia has relaxed its dualist approach. The movement towards relaxation started in 1988 at the Bangalore meeting in India between lawyers and judges from various Commonwealth countries. It was agreed that national courts should have regard to international obligations which a country undertakes – whether or not they have been incorporated into domestic law – for the purpose of removing ambiguity or uncertainty. Since then, Australia and other States have made significant progress in accepting the authority of international law in each branch of government.

---

23 Michael Kirby, 'The Impact of International Human Rights Norms: A Law Undergoing Evolution' (1995) 25 *Western Australian Law Review* 1, 206–7.
24 Antony Anghie and Garry Sturgess (eds), *Legal Visions of the 21st Century: Essays in Honour of Judge Chirsotpher Weeramantry* (Kluwer Law International, 1998) 339.
25 (1983) 153 CLR 168, 224–225.

Judicial branch

In *Mabo No 2*,[26] a decision of the High Court of Australia, Justice Brennan said that 'customary international law or an unimplemented treaty can be a legitimate influence on the development of the common law'. Further, international law can also indirectly assist a court when interpreting ambiguous legislation by application of constitutional or statutory provisions reflecting universal principles stated in international treaties.[27] In *Polities v the Commonwealth*, the Australian High Court said that there was a presumption of conformity with international law – that is, municipal law will be construed as far as the language permits so as to be in conformity with international law.[28] Justice Dixon, in a frequently cited passage, said that 'international law is not a part, but is one of the sources of English law'.[29]

Legislative branch

Following the 1988 Bangalore meeting, various pieces of Australian legislation make reference to Australia's international obligations. For example, s 11 of the *Civil Aviation Act* (Cth) 1988 States that the Civil Aviation Safety Authority is required to perform its functions in a manner consistent with Australia's international obligations.

Executive branch

Australia's constitutional framework enables the executive branch of government to commit Australia to treaties on an international level through s 61 of the Australian Constitution. Treaties are negotiated by the relevant minister, signed by the head of State or authorised delegate and ratified by the Governor-General. The Executive is not obliged to liaise with any other body before exercising this power.

However, Parliament enacts these treaties through legislation courtesy of the external affairs power in s 51(xxix) of the Australian Constitution. This power refers to matters that are:

i   outside Australian territory;
ii affecting Australia's relations with other countries;
iii regulated by treaties;
iv of customary international law; or
v   otherwise of 'international concern'.

26 (1992) 175 CLR 1.
27 Michael Kirby, 'Constitutional Law and International Law: National Exceptionalism and the Democratic Deficit?' (2010) 98(2) *The Georgetown Law Journal* 433, 439–440.
28 (1945) 70 CLR 60.
29 *Chow Hung Ching v The King* (1949) 77 CLR 449, 477.

The external affairs power is interpreted broadly and does not require the executive to conclude that there be a treaty before it can enact legislation committing Australia to an international obligation. The power extends to any matter relating to 'other nations or things external to Australia'[30] or to a matter that is 'of international concern'.[31] In *Minister for Immigration and Ethnic Affairs v Teoh*,[32] the High Court of Australia said generally international law is crystallised when it is implemented in domestic legislation, but that was not a necessary condition. In *Tasmanian Dam*[33] it was said that implementing legislation must 'conform to the treaty and carry its provisions into effect'.

4.3.4 Implementation of international treaties at the sub-national level

Generally, international treaties are implemented at a national level and not at a state level. This is mainly for efficiency reasons. As former Australian High Court Chief Justice, Sir Anthony Mason has said:

> conduct of international affairs would be a nightmare if legislative implementation of Australia's treaty obligations were to become a matter for each State to decide.[34]

States should (and in some cases, must) be consulted on the negotiation and ratification of treaties.[35]

4.3.5 Differences between federal and unitary systems

In federal systems of government, power is distributed between the central government and other levels of government. Such levels of government refer to provincial and local administrations. In Australia, these are the state and territory authorities. In unitary systems of government, power resides with one, central government. And in unitary systems, the State, nation, or country is essentially administered by one government.

The United States

While the United States also has a federal system of government, there are significant differences between Australia and the United States as to how they deal

---

30   *Commonwealth v Tasmania* (1983) 158 CLR 1.
31   *Koowarta v Bjelke-Petersen* (1982) 153 CLR 168.
32   (1995) 128 ALR 353.
33   (1983) 158 CLR 1.
34   Anthony Mason, 'The Australian Constitution 1901–1988' (1988) 62 ALJ 752, 755.
35   *Treaty Making Process* (2017) Australian Government: Department of Foreign Affairs and Trade <http://dfat.gov.au/international-relations/treaties/treaty-ma king-process/pages/treaty-making-process.aspx>.

Regulation of aviation at all levels 95

with treaties. In the United States, treaties are implemented through ratifi-cation. This means that, if a treaty is made by the decision of the President and with the advice and consent of two-thirds of the Senate, the treaty becomes part of the 'supreme law of the land' and is equal in status to federal legislation.

The United Kingdom

The United Kingdom adopts a dualist approach to international law. For individuals to rely on the protection of international law, Parliament must first implement the international provisions into domestic law through ratifi-cation. Treaty-making remains the exclusive responsibility of the executive, acting on behalf of the Crown. Parliament has limited control over the process unless the treaty itself expressly requires it or else in certain other circumstances.

France

International treaties in France are considered hierarchically superior to French domestic law.[36] Unlike the United States or the United Kingdom, in France international treaties are self-executing and do not require ratifi-cation or any other enabling act by Parliament to have domestic effect. This means that once a treaty has been ratified or otherwise approved, it becomes part of domestic French law. Individuals in France can rely on the protection of international law so long as the treaty is sufficiently precise and does not specifically require the creation of domestic measures of enforcement.[37]

4.4 Domestic law and sovereignty

Sovereignty is defined as the international legal status of a State that is not subject, within its territorial jurisdiction, to the governmental, executive, legis-lative or judicial jurisdiction of a foreign State or to foreign law other than public international law.[38] This means that, within the limitations of interna-tional law, a sovereign nation can administer its own laws free from outside influence. Sovereignty is recognised reciprocally meaning that sovereign nations accept the sovereignty of other nations. Sovereignty is acquired mainly by conquest, cession or settlement.

---

36 *La Constitution du octobre 1985* [French Constitution of 4 October 1958] art 55.
37 Ibid.
38 James Crawford, 'The Criteria for Statehood in International Law' (1977) 48 *Brit-ish Yearbook of International Law* 93, 103.

Australia, for example, has sovereignty to enact domestic aviation laws and regulations insofar as they are not inconsistent with its international obligations.

It has been argued that international treaties result in a loss of sovereignty because it is seen as a handing over of domestic power to an international power. Nevertheless, in terms of drones, a truly global solution to the myriad of issues surrounding drone regulation requires some level of uniformity and consistency, which can only be achieved – at least in part – by a top-down international approach.

5 Guiding Principles

5.1 Rationale

These Guiding Principles provide a general framework, based on principles of aviation and international law and best practice, within which the operation of drones can be regulated. Such regulation would ensure the integration of drones into existing airspace both within States and across borders. The Guiding Principles set out overarching principles to inform rules and regulations including SARPs, treaties and domestic legislation.

The foundations of these Guiding Principles include the following:

- an international treaty to regulate drones at this point is unwise and unlikely given the rapid development of drone technology which continues to outpace drone regulation and the length of time taken to negotiate a treaty;
- over time, based on these foundations, it is not impossible that more formal arrangements, such as a treaty can be agreed between States once the common characteristics of drone technology are more certain;
- there is a need for a consistent approach to drone regulation across borders, as the integration of drones into airspace is a matter of global significance;
- the international community has safety, security, social and financial interests in addressing the integration of drones into airspace in a timely, coordinated and targeted manner;
- there has been no significant coordinated response by States to address drones, whether temporary or permanent in nature; and
- there is a need for a globally applicable framework to provide a coherent and principled approach for the collaborative and universally accepted regulation of drones.

5.2 Principles for the regulation of drones internationally by States

5.2.1 Preamble

Noting that these Guiding Principles build on and contextualise ICAO's efforts, and existing domestic laws in various jurisdictions.

Realising that the international community has safety, security, social and financial interests in addressing the integration of drones into airspace in a timely, coordinated and targeted manner.

Realising further that there has been no significant coordinated response by States to address drones, whether temporary or permanent in nature.

Recognising the work being undertaken by ICAO and other inter-governmental and non-governmental organisations to address drone integration and related matters, including the development of drone-related SARPs.

Realising the need for a globally applicable framework to provide a coherent and principled approach for the collaborative and universally accepted regulation of drones.

Noting that these Guiding Principles, addressing the challenges to drone regulation both within States and across borders, necessarily complement other efforts to address such challenges.

5.2.2 Introduction

Principle 1: Scope and purpose

These Guiding Principles:

a   *provide a general framework, based on principles of aviation and international law and best practice, within which the operation of drones can be regulated to ensure the integration into existing airspace of drones both within States and across borders; and*

b   *set out overarching principles to inform rules and regulations including SARPs, treaties and domestic legislation.*

Principle 2: Definitions

For the purposes of these Guiding Principles:

a   *'Drone' means an aircraft and its associated elements which operate with no pilot on board, the same definition as ICAO's preferred term 'unmanned aircraft systems' (UAS).*

b   *'ICAO' means the International Civil Aviation Organisation.*

c   *'SARPs' mean ICAO's Standards and Recommended Practices.*

Principle 3: Interpretation

a   *These Guiding Principles shall not be interpreted as limiting, altering or otherwise prejudicing rights recognised in international aviation law or rights consistent with aviation laws and standards as recognised under domestic law, including civil aviation, privacy, safety and security.*

b   *States should interpret these Guiding Principles broadly, be guided by their purpose to harmonize and create uniformity amongst States to facilitate safe and effective use of drone technology, and display reasonableness and flexibility in their interpretation.*

5.2.3 Operative provisions

Principle 4: Airspace sovereignty

States recognise that every State has complete and exclusive sovereignty over the airspace above its territory.

Building on the Paris Convention, the Chicago Convention adopts the principle of airspace sovereignty, providing that '[t]he contracting States recognize that every State has complete and exclusive sovereignty over the airspace above its territory' (Article 1).

Drones raise many cross-border operational issues. As with manned aircraft, the principle of sovereignty is paramount with regard to drones.

This overarching principle is consistent with amendments to Annex 2 to the Chicago Convention (Amendment 43 – Appendix 4). The general operating rules which are set out in the new text of Appendix 4 – Remotely Piloted Aircraft Systems – detail the authorisations required for drones to engage in international air navigation. That is, these general operating rules provide the rights to be agreed by States to permit such operations.

Principle 5: Paramount importance of safety

a   *States recognise that safety is the overwhelming priority in the regulation of drones.*
b   *States shall apply existing safety regulations to drones. For matters which must be addressed differently because there is no pilot is on board the aircraft, an alternative means of compliance shall, where possible, be chosen to achieve the same level of safety.*
c   *States shall carry out appropriate risk assessment when considering drone regulations that may compromise safety.*

In 2006, ICAO published the following modern definition of safety:

> the State in which the possibility of harm to person or of property damage is reduced to, and maintained at or below, an acceptable level through a continuing process of hazard identification and safety risk management.[1]

---

1 *Safety Management Manual* International Civil Aviation Organisation (2013) <http s://www.icao.int/safety/SafetyManagement/Documents/Doc.9859.3rd%20Edi tion.alltext.en.pdf>.

ICAO Circular 328-AN/190 references this definition with respect to drones and acknowledges a 'wide array of hazards to the civil aviation system' presented by aircraft operating without a pilot on board.[2] In terms of safety management, it sets out that States should maintain the agreed level of safety through a proper application of SARPs, Procedures for Air Navigation Services (PANS) and guidance material. It notes the responsibility of States to ensure drones are safely introduced into the aviation system.[3]

This principle has been drafted with regard to ICAO's perspective on the safe integration of drones in airspace.

Certain operations – particularly those in the experimental or testing phase – have risks and safety concerns associated with them. While trying to facilitate development of technology for the betterment of society generally, States need to ensure that safety remains the paramount concern. When drafting or interpreting regulations with respect to drones which may compromise safety, States need to undertake comprehensive analysis of the risks.

Principle 6: International drone operation

If States wish to permit cross-border drone operations, States shall cooperate in good faith and use best endeavours to negotiate relevant exchange of rights.

As mentioned, amendments to Annex 2 to the Chicago Convention specifically enunciate this principle. Appendix 4, paragraph 1.2, provides that drones:

> shall not be operated across the territory of another State, without special authorization issued by each State in which the flight is to operate. This authorization may be in the form of agreements between the States involved.[4]

This exchange of rights could facilitate – as with the Freedoms of the Air for manned aircraft – operations from, to, over or in the territory of another State. Such permissions may well break down borders, facilitating 'true' globalisation and enabling industries such as air taxis and drone delivery services (for instance, Amazon) to further expand. Borders become more transparent as a result of this. Indeed, in many ways, drone technology has changed the way we think about borders. Depending on one's perspective, this could be a positive or a negative development.

Appendix 4, paragraph 2, is unsurprisingly silent on the manner in which agreement as to special authorisation is to be reached, reflecting sentiment

---

2 International Civil Aviation Organisation 'Circular 328 AN/190: Unmanned Aircraft Systems (UAS)' (Paper presented at the Seminar on Unmanned Aircraft Systems (UAS), Lima, Peru, 18 April 2012 to 20 April 2012) 5.
3 Ibid 5–6.
4 *Chicago Convention*, app. 4(43) para 1.2.

expressed in the Chicago Convention. Cross-border cooperation in many parts of the world is notoriously difficult to achieve.[5] Indeed,

> [i]n cross border regions … challenges to governance systems are further aggravated by differing cultural, institutional, and legal systems, varying backgrounds, different languages as well as by a lacking knowledge about the different systems involved, which render the conditions for co-operation even more complex.[6]

Nonetheless, there is a real opportunity to contribute to cross-border commerce, aid and other activities through drone operations. To address cross-border challenges, as noted above, States should expressly commit to cooperate in a way that facilitates agreement such as negotiating in good faith and using best endeavours – that is, *if* such States wish to permit cross-border drone operations.

States will likely distinguish between commercial, State-owned and recreational drones in making a determination with regard to cross-border rights.

Principle 7: Air traffic management

States should implement air traffic management plans to ensure the safe and orderly flight of drones, taking into account existing airspace users.

ICAO is in the process of developing 'low-altitude traffic management guidance' for drones at the domestic level. This was a subject of discussion at ICAO's 'Drone Enable' Symposium in September 2017 in Montreal, Canada involving industry, academia and other specialists.[7] A global air traffic management system is vital to establishing the safe and orderly movement of drones – and integrating them seamlessly into existing airspace frameworks.

Various companies, international bodies and associations have put forward proposals for a system of air traffic control for drones and supporting infrastructure, including Uber,[8] myCopter (a project funded by the European Union)[9] and zenAIRCITY (designed to accommodate Airbus' air taxis).[10] These examples are discussed in Chapter 6.

---

5 Kristina Zumbuch and Roland Scherer, 'Cross-Border Governance: Balancing Formalised and Less Formalised Co-Operations' (2015) 4 *Social Sciences* 499.

6 Ibid.

7 International Civil Aviation Organisation, *DRONE ENABLE, ICAO's Unmanned Aircraft Systems (UAS) Industry Symposium* (21 June 2017) International Civil Aviation Organisation <https://www.icao.int/Meetings/UAS2017/Pages/default.aspx>

8 *Fast-Forwarding to a Future of On-Demand Urban Air Transportation* (27 October 2016) Uber <https://www.uber.com/elevate.pdf>.

9 *Lifting Personal Transportation into the Third Dimension* (2017) myCopter <http://www.mycopter.eu>.

10 Beata Cece, *Future of Urban Mobility: My Kind of Flyover* (6 December 2016) Airbus <http://www.airbus.com/newsroom/news/en/2016/12/My-Kind-Of-Flyover.html>.

Principle 8: Right of way

a   *Drones which do not have the size and characteristics of manned aircraft should yield the right of way to all aircraft, airborne vehicles, and launch and re-entry vehicles. Yielding the right of way means giving way to manned aircraft or vehicles and drones may not pass over, under, or ahead of them unless well clear.*

b   *No person may operate such drones so close to another aircraft as to create a collision hazard.*

The wording of this guiding principle is based on the right-of-way rules for small unmanned aircraft systems in the United States (14 CFR Part 107).[11] Amendment has been made to take account of the various interpretations of 'small' drone in multiple, different jurisdictions. To ensure application across jurisdictions, the size and characteristics of the unmanned aircraft should be the paramount consideration in determining right-of-way rules vis-à-vis manned aircraft.

Right-of-way rules are fundamental to bring both manned and unmanned aircraft together safely and in an orderly fashion. ICAO confirms this view in its *Circular 328-AN/190*:

> A fundamental principle of the rules of the air is that a pilot can see other aircraft and thereby avoid collisions, maintain sufficient distance from other aircraft so as not to create a collision hazard, and follow the right-of- way rules to keep out of the way of other aircraft. Integration of RPA may not require a change to the Standards, however, as RPAS technology advances, alternate means of identifying collision hazards will have to be developed with appropriate SARPs adopted. Regardless, **the right–of–way rules will remain essential for the safe operation of aircraft, with or without a pilot on board**. Likewise, for the surface movement of RPA in the aerodrome environment, it is necessary that RPA operations be conducted safely and efficiently without disrupting other aircraft operations. (emphasis added).[12]

Annex 2 Part 4 to the Chicago Convention is silent on right-of-way rules.

Principle 9: Operation over persons on the ground

States should prohibit the operation of drones close to or over a human being unless in the totality of the circumstances it would be considered reasonable from a safety perspective to

---

11   *14 CFR Part 107 – Small Unmanned Aircraft Systems* <http://avsport.org/UAS/ground/PART%20107.pdf> § 107.37.
12   International Civil Aviation Organisation 'Circular 328 AN/190: Unmanned Aircraft Systems (UAS)' (Paper presented at the Seminar on Unmanned Aircraft Systems (UAS), Lima, Peru, 18 April 2012 to 20 April 2012).

allow such operation. This authorisation may be in the form of a waiver from the relevant State regulation(s).

In many countries, domestic legislation provides that unmanned aircraft which meet certain criteria must not fly close to or over persons on the ground. This rule usually applies based on weight (for instance, generally applying to small drones) or use (for instance, generally recreational use). These rules often coincide with drones that can be flown without a remote pilot's licence – obviously, a high-risk category for regulators.

The authors consider that, in determining best practice, such restrictions as to operating drones in close proximity to, or over, persons on the ground should be included.

In certain jurisdictions, regulators are considering waivers to allow small drones to fly directly over people. For example, in the United States, the FAA granted in October 2017 a waiver of its Part 107 regulations to allow CNN to fly a small drone in a range of environments including over crowds of people up to 150 feet above ground.[13] Such exemptions should be contemplated taking into account the totality of the circumstances, including the operator's safety record, the drone's safety features and appropriate test data.[14]

Principle 10: Operation in the vicinity of airports

Drones should not be operated in a manner that interferes with operations and traffic patterns at any airport, heliport or seaplane base or anywhere that an aircraft can take off or land.

Drones operated for *any* reason should not be flown in the vicinity of airports, heliports and seaplane bases – or indeed, anywhere from which an aircraft can take off and land, without prior permission. This rule is widely accepted as ensuring protection to existing airspace users and avoiding collision with manned aircraft in a high-impact environment.

States may also wish to regulate based on a specific vicinity. For instance, in Canada, it is illegal to fly a drone for recreational purposes closer than 5.5 kilometres from aerodromes and 1.8 kilometres from heliports or aerodromes used by helicopters only.[15]

Principle 11: Operation in prohibited or restricted areas

No person may operate a drone in prohibited or restricted areas unless that person has permission from the appropriate using or controlling body.

13 *CNN Receives Breakthrough Part 107 Waiver for Operations over People* (18 October 2017) CNN Communications <http://cnnpressroom.blogs.cnn.com/2017/10/18/cnn-receives-breakthrough-part-107-waiver-for-operations-over-people/>.
14 Ibid.
15 *No Drone Zones* (1 November 2017) Government of Canada <https://www.tc.gc.ca/eng/civilaviation/opssvs/no-drone-zones.html>.

Operators should not be allowed to fly in a prohibited or restricted area without permission given the enormous security risks associated with such an activity, in part, due to the capability of drones to conduct aerial surveillance and deliver packages (including contraband and armaments) as discussed in Chapter 1.

Permission should be sought from the appropriate body, that body being the organisation or authority occupying the prohibited or restricted area, or having responsibility for such area. Similar regulations have been enacted in a number of common law jurisdictions including the United States and Australia.

Principle 12: Security

States shall be responsible for ensuring their own security and should consider geofencing-like systems in locations that might raise an aviation safety or security concern.

Needless to say, States are responsible for managing civil aviation matters, including those related to safety and security. With drones which can easily fly into no-fly zones, prohibited and restricted airspace, and above prisons, military outposts, dangerous and hazardous areas, it is all but impossible for States to ensure that all drones are caught. As such, States should consider the use of technological solutions – such as geofencing – as a mechanism by which to improve national and regional security.

Geofencing is a technology that defines a virtual boundary around an actual geographical area. In doing so, it enables an automatic response when a drone enters or leaves that area.

Some drones include geofencing technology that prevents them from starting up in restricted areas. Ahead of its 'Drone Enable' Industry Symposium in September 2017, ICAO suggested including in its framework:

> geofencing-like systems that will support automatic updates by national authorities on the 28 day aeronautical information regulation and control … cycle to prevent [drone] operation in sensitive security areas and restricted or danger areas such as near aerodromes.[16]

The authors believe that 'geofencing' or similar software or systems will be integral in monitoring – and protecting – our increasingly busy skies. Geofencing is not, however, a complete solution; drones will need a reliable navigation system (for instance, GPS) and autopilot software to create and interact with a fence.

Principle 13: Certificates and licensing

States should avoid rigid entrenched rules for certification and licensing of drones until such time as international standards are developed by ICAO.

---

16 International Civil Aviation Organisation, *Request for Information* (2017) <https://www.icao.int/Meetings/UAS2017/Pages/Request-for-Information.aspx>.

Appendix 4 of ICAO's amended Rules of the Air anticipates that there will be 'the coming into force of international ... [drone SARPs] respecting particular categories, classes or types of aircraft' with respect to certification and licensing standards not yet developed.[17] ICAO has forecast that such SARPs will be adopted by its Council in 2018.[18]

Given this knowledge and ICAO as the appropriate body to address these issues, States should regulate in a manner which allows for adoption of these standards and recommended practices in due course. This is fundamentally important for international consistency – and a priority for drone manufacturers, retailers, owners and operators alike.

Principle 14: Registration

States should implement a system to register all drones. Such a system should take account of the characteristics of the drone and its type(s) of operation in determining the registration requirements. States should work towards an international system of registration.

As with manned aircraft, registration of drones is an important part of ensuring safety and compliance with drone regulations. Registration assists law enforcement through identification of drones, and drone owners and operators. Registration should be mandatory for all drones – again, replicating manned aircraft.

Given the nature of some drones, registration requirements may differ to take account of the characteristics of the drone and its type(s) of operation. The system, however, should be flexible such that it does not stifle growth and development of the drone industry. For example, less onerous registration requirements may attach to small recreational drones – including only the drone's serial number and the owner's name, address, phone number and email address.

In order to identify drones across borders, States should consider implementation of an international drone registration system.

Such a system could be modelled on the International Registry of Mobile Assets established under the *Cape Town Convention* and *Aircraft Protocol 2001* (the 'International Registry').[19] The International Registry is an electronic registry which allows for registration and protection of 'international interests' amongst all ratifying States. As mentioned in Chapter 2, the international Registry is primarily a system designed to protect financial interests in mobile assets (e.g. airframes).[20]

---

17 International Civil Aviation Organisation, *Annex 2 to the Convention on International Civil Aviation: Rules of the Air* (10th ed, 2005) APP 4–1.

18 International Civil Aviation Organisation, 'Integrating RPAS into Airspace' (2015) 70(2) *ICAO Journal* 4 <https://www.icao.int/publications/journalsreports/2015/7002_en.pdf>.

19 *Cape Town Convention and Aircraft Protocol*, opened for signature 16 November 2001, 2307 UNTS 285 (entered into force 1 March 2001).

20 *Welcome to the International Registry* (2017) International Registry of Mobile Assets <https://www.internationalregistry.aero/ir-web/index>.

One of the virtues of the International Registry is that it allows visibility of interests across States in a way that domestic registration systems do not. This would be similarly important for a drone registration system, albeit for a different purpose – to identify drones, their owners and operators for identification and enforcement.

Principle 15: Liability and insurance

a   *The operator shall be liable for damage sustained by third parties upon condition only that the damage was caused by a drone in flight.*

b   *States should require their drone operators to maintain adequate insurance or guarantee covering their liability.*

Adequate protection needs to be afforded to third parties who suffer damage caused by any events involving a drone in flight. Such provision is akin to that contemplated for manned aircraft in the *Convention on Compensation for Damage Caused by Aircraft to Third Parties 2009*. This Convention (discussed in more detail in Chapter 3) establishes strict liability of operators to compensate third-party victims on the ground and requires adequate insurance or guarantee covering their liability under the Convention.[21] It must be noted, however, that this Convention has not entered into force (and may be unlikely to enter into force).

The current regulatory regime relating to the liability of aircraft operators for injuries to victims on the ground is, as previously mentioned, the Rome Convention. This Convention imposes strict liability on operators to compensate victims in accordance with the compensation limits set out therein.[22] Although the Convention does not mention drones, a broad interpretation of 'aircraft' could bring drones within the scope of the Convention.[23] Thus, its third-party liability regime may also apply to drones.

As there is no certainty as to whether 'drones' are caught by the Convention, new or amended rules need to take specific account of drones. Adequate rules need to be in place to address drone liability – as well as insurance matters – in order to protect third parties.

For example, in November 2014 Transport Canada introduced mandatory insurance requiring commercial drone users to have not less than CA\$100,000 worth of liability insurance in case of an accident. As mentioned in Chapter 2, this covers public liability risks.

A new regulation requiring compulsory third-party liability insurance came into effect in Germany in April 2017. Insurers, such as Allianz Global, are introducing new policies for liability insurance for both privately-used flight

21 *Convention on Compensation for Damage Caused by Aircraft to Third Parties 2009* art 9.
22 Anna Masutti, 'Proposals for the Regulation of Unmanned Air Vehicle Use in Common Airspace' (2009) 34 *Air and Space Law* 1, 9.
23 Ibid.

models and commercially-used drones.[24] These policies take account of both States 'required' and 'advisable' insurance as well as increasing risk profiles associated with the operation of drones.[25]

Principle 16: Privacy

States should enact drone-specific regulations for both private and commercial drone operations to address privacy concerns.

As discussed in some detail in Chapter 1, privacy presents a significant societal challenge. Most consider privacy to be a right that is both personal and inviolable.

Many States have approached privacy concerns with a broad interpretation of existing general privacy laws in their application to drones or with amendments to privacy laws to take account of drones. These approaches often fall far short of any framework to regulate privacy issues associated with drone operations.

Drone-specific privacy laws are necessary to adequately address these concerns and issues. This is because of the unique problems which attend drone operations such as the relative ease with which drones can intrude and breach privacy given their size, scale and manoeuvrability and the often anonymous nature of such intrusion.

Germany is one of few regulatory systems which directly incorporate privacy considerations in its drone laws. Germany passed drone-specific laws which entered into force in April 2017 to enforce that drones cannot be flown over residential properties if they weigh more than 250 grams. If the drone is equipped with camera or microphone (that is, a drone which can broadcast or record video or audio), regardless of weight, flying it above another person's property is forbidden – regardless of whether the purpose of the flight is for private or commercial use. German authorities can allow exceptions in justified cases.

In most States, aviation regulatory authorities have no jurisdiction over privacy issues. If such as issue is to be specifically addressed under aviation laws and regulations (as opposed to general privacy laws) it will be up to legislators at the national or subnational levels to determine such laws and the body responsible for enforcing them.

Principle 17: ICAO's role

States should look to ICAO as the international body to provide a regulatory framework for drone operations.

It is well established that ICAO is the appropriate body to provide a framework and guidance for integrating drones into airspace and to assist States with issues that drones present.

---

24 *Drone Insurance* (2015) Allianz <www.agcs.allianz.com/services/aviation/drone-insurance/>.
25 Ibid.

Ahead of its 'Drone Enable' Industry Symposium in late 2017, ICAO stated that it:

> will serve as the global facilitator as States, industry, academia and other interested stakeholders collaborate on conceptualizing a common regulatory framework to support integration of unmanned aircraft into national airspace. This activity is separate from ICAO's on-going work to build a full regulatory framework for the integration of remotely piloted aircraft systems (RPAS) in accordance with instrument flight rules. Although **not traditional work for ICAO**, Member States have requested that ICAO **serve as the global civil aviation facilitator** to assist with the challenge of unmanned aircraft systems (UAS).[26] (emphasis added)

Given ICAO's existing infrastructure, knowledge and position within the global civil aviation community, the authors consider that this is an appropriate role for ICAO to undertake.

Principle 18: Interaction with SARPs

States should consider these Guiding Principles to provide direction for further action on regulating drones.

These Guiding Principles are designed to provide a roadmap and overarching direction for the regulation of drones. They are based on ICAO's analyses, existing and proposed domestic regulations and the global aviation regulatory regime. The virtues of guiding principles generally are explained in Chapter 4.

Ultimately, most effective use of these principles may be to inform rules and regulations including SARPs, treaties and domestic legislation. While we know ICAO is developing SARPs for drones – and that existing SARPs apply to a significant degree[27] – these Guiding Principles are less granular, sit above SARPs and can set the strategic direction and framework for legislative developments. SARPs also take approximately two years to implement.[28]

Principle 19: Development of technology

States should develop regulatory frameworks in such a manner to allow flexibility in accommodating new iterations of drone technology and unmanned flying objects.

Much of drone technology is in testing or experimental phases. New drone developments may present new opportunities and challenges which may well

---

26 International Civil Aviation Organisation, *Request for Information* (2017) <https://www.icao.int/Meetings/UAS2017/Pages/Request-for-Information.aspx>.

27 International Civil Aviation Organisation, 'Circular 328 AN/190: Unmanned Aircraft Systems (UAS)' (Paper presented at the Seminar on Unmanned Aircraft Systems (UAS), Lima, Peru, 18 April 2012 to 20 April 2012)

28 ICAO, 'How ICAO Develops Standards' <https://www.icao.int/about-icao/AirNavigationCommission/Pages/how-icao-develops-standards.aspx>.

require different forms of regulation. States should not implement rigid drone regulations given the attendant danger of such regulations quickly becoming outdated. A key concern for the authors is regulation involving specific weight categories or purposes/use, as increasingly weight will not be a primary item for risk assessment (with micro drones potentially posing more significant safety concerns), and the uses to which drones are put will become more blurred.

5.2.4 General obligations

Principle 20: National implementation measures

a   States should incorporate provisions as set out in these Guiding Principles into domestic law and policies, prioritising airspace sovereignty and the safe integration of drone operations into existing airspace.
b   Local, regional and national levels of government and instrumentalities should implement these Guiding Principles as appropriate.
c   States should ensure the sustainable development of aviation through legislative and administrative mechanisms.
d   All relevant legislation should be consistent with international law.

Principle 21: International cooperation and assistance

a   The integration of drones into airspace is a matter of global importance, and States should cooperate to the fullest extent – as guided by ICAO – to establish an appropriate framework to regulate drones.
b   States may seek cooperation and assistance from other States and relevant international organisations in addressing drone-related matters.

5.2.5 Implementation

Principle 22: Implementation and dissemination

States should implement and disseminate these Guiding Principles without delay and cooperate closely with ICAO, inter-governmental organisations, non-government organisations, the aviation industry, and civil society towards this end.

5.3 A multilateral agreement to regulate drones?

There are inherent problems associated with a multilateral agreement (or treaty) to regulate drones.

States generally lack the political will to negotiate treaties such as these requiring States to meet international standards, especially standards being drafted for the first time. While such an instrument would form the basis of shared responsibility for the integration of drones, States tend to enact domestic measures in line with their existing regulatory frameworks.

Even if the terms of a treaty could be agreed upon, ratification, implementation and enforcement could not easily be guaranteed. Further, treaties are the result of significant compromise and, once entered into force States must demonstrate the necessary will to ratify, implement, adhere to and enforce it.

Further, as previously mentioned, an international treaty to regulate drones at this point is unwise and unlikely given the rapid pace of drone technology development which continues to run ahead of drone regulation. A treaty seems further unlikely given the length of time needed to negotiate, conclude and implement a treaty – rendering it potentially outdated by drone technology prior to it entering into force.

Over time, it is not impossible that more formal arrangements, such as a treaty, can be agreed between States once the common characteristics of drone technology are more certain.

The problem remains, however, that without almost universal adoption of such a treaty, its cross-border application and binding nature – the very virtues of a treaty – are not realised.

Guiding Principles – while non-binding – can provide a roadmap for States, anticipating the future State of drone regulations. This direction is important for planning purposes for governments, regulators, drone manufacturers, retailers, owners and operators alike.

6 The future of drones

6.1 Introduction

This chapter contemplates future advancements in drone-related technology and the impact these technologies may have on the aviation industry. It also considers how the rapid evolution in drone technology may cause international aviation treaties to become outdated.

Drone-related technology is developing exponentially. And future developments in drone technology will have a significant impact on the aviation industry. The authors consider that some of these key developments are as follows:

- the miniaturisation of drones;
- drones as the cheapest and most cost-effective transportation option;
- fully autonomous drone technologies;
- the practice of drone 'swarming';
- more enduring and energy efficient technologies; and
- refining drones as more environmentally friendly platforms.

These are considered in turn.

Views on the evolution of drone technology vary. However, it is undisputed that drones have the potential to impact all levels of society. Drones have already begun to impact the general consumer market. For example, drones are becoming increasingly capable of small-load delivery such as books, medication and even pizza.[1]

Drones, it is argued, will also expand the ability of law enforcement to keep citizens safe by allowing for greater reconnaissance at emergency scenes.[2] Drones may also encourage new perspectives on the natural world; for example, wildlife conservationists have been using drones to track and observe the behaviour of animals in the open ocean.[3] Critics are, however, quick to point

---

1 Roger Clarke, 'Understanding the Drone Epidemic' (2014) 30 *Computer Law & Security Review* 230, 239.
2 Ibid 241.
3 Juliet Eysenck, *How Drones are Changing Our Lives: The Good, the Bad and the Lazy* (25 May 2016) *The Telegraph* <www.telegraph.co.uk/technology/2016/05/23/how-drone-technology-is-changing-our-lives-the-good-the-bad-and/>.

out the societal disruption and risks that will very likely occur as drones become more accessible. The most commonly noted risks relate to infringements on individual privacy. One commentator outlines the risk of 'voyeurnalism' – a form of journalism whereby a drone is used to constantly and invasively monitor a person of interest in a voyeuristic manner.[4] All this to say, it is clear that drone technology is changing – and will continue to change – the face of aviation.

6.2 Key developments

6.2.1 Miniaturisation

Miniaturisation refers to the scaling down of the physical size of a drone. The miniaturisation of fixed-wing and rotary drones allows for faster and more efficient flight, as well as a higher degree of manoeuvrability. Engineers at Harvard University's Robotics Laboratory have developed a miniature drone known as 'RoboBee'. It has a biologically inspired design and resembles an actual insect with flapping wings.[5]

Drones such as the RoboBee are indicative of advancements in drone technology (particularly in terms of aerodynamics) and illustrate the practical issues inherent in scaling down aircraft.[6] For example, certain flight modes such as hovering become more challenging as size is reduced. Small drones also have trouble sustaining flight for an adequate period of time due to the small power packages fitted into miniature frames.

In 2017, Swiss start-up company Wingtra launched a fully autonomous agricultural surveying drone. With a total wingspan of 125 centimetres and total weight of 3.7 kilograms, the drone is incredibly small. It has a payload capacity of 800 grams and is capable of fully autonomous vertical take-off and landing. This small-scale aircraft has the capacity to revolutionise the agricultural industry due to its cost-effectiveness. And it highlights both the significant advancement of drone technology and the many possibilities for drone use.

6.2.2 Autonomy

Technological obstacles: new or improved devices?

Autonomy is the ability to perform intended tasks without human intervention. In terms of drones, full autonomy is constituted by the ability of the craft to access and independently utilise its sensory motors to react to external

---

4 Roger Clarke, 'Understanding the Drone Epidemic' (2014) 30 *Computer Law & Security Review* 230, 240.
5 M. Hassanalian and A. Abdelkefi, 'Classifications, Applications and Design Challenges of Drones: A Review' (2017) 91 *Progress in Aerospace Sciences* 99, 107.
6 Dario Floreano and Robert J. Wood 'Science, Technology and the Future of Small Autonomous Drones' (2015) 521 *Nature* 460, 461.

influences.[7] In some cases, drones use machine learning to inform their autonomy, allowing them to recognise and learn information.

One of the critical developments in autonomous technologies concerns navigation. According to Uber, autonomous operation technologies, together with electronic motor technologies, are considered to be the most important advancements in overcoming challenges related to safety, noise, emissions and vehicle performance.[8] The development of an effective navigation system will be critical in mitigating the risks of possible collisions, as well as improving flight efficiency by taking the most economic routes.

GLOBAL POSITIONING SYSTEMS (GPS)

With widespread drone use, drones will need to be equipped with a control system capable of precisely identifying 'obstacle-free trajectories'.[9] Commentators have raised concerns with simply improving current technologies, such as GPS, in order to determine automated flight paths. Hassanalian and Abdelkefi worry about the possibility of drones losing their GPS connection due to external noise or interference.[10] They suggest utilising ever expanding global tele-communications networks to send flight instructions to drones, as opposed to GPS satellites.

Floreano and Wood share the same concern for the development potential of GPS technology. They explain that GPS technology will fail future drones due to shortfalls in availability and reliability of GPS information, particularly in congested urban areas.[11] Further, they argue GPS navigation systems can identify the location of roads but are unable to identify three-dimensional information such as 'the height of natural structures, buildings, bridges, and the presence of poles…[and] cables'.[12] Floreano and Wood suggest that, in addition to sensors for real-time obstacles, for example, drones will require more complex levels of autonomy for the purposes of navigation.[13]

Some commentators on automated navigation appear to favour development of new navigational technology as opposed to improvement of existing GPS technologies. Countries such as Australia are, however, still seeking to improve current GPS technology.

7 Ibid 462.
8 *Fast-Forwarding to a Future of On-Demand Urban Air Transportation* (27 October 2016) Uber <https://www.uber.com/elevate.pdf> 3.
9 Dario Floreano and Robert J. Wood, 'Science, Technology and the Future of Small Autonomous Drones' (2015) 521 *Nature* 460, 462.
10 M. Hassanalian and A. Abdelkefi, 'Classifications, Applications and Design Challenges of Drones: A Review' (2017) 91 *Progress in Aerospace Sciences* 99, 124–5.
11 Dario Floreano and Robert J. Wood, 'Science, Technology and the Future of Small Autonomous Drones' (2015) 521 *Nature* 460, 462.
12 Ibid.
13 Ibid.

In 2017, the Australian Federal Government announced that it would invest 12 million dollars in a two-year trial to test the Space-Based Augmentation System, a more accurate GPS crucial for 'driverless and connected cars'.[14]

SENSE-AND-AVOID TECHNOLOGY

Accurate and reliable autonomous sense-and-avoid technology for drones is no easy feat. Its widespread experimentation and testing are based on the inherent risk of collisions with other vehicles operating in the same low-altitude airspace. Sense-and-avoidance technology is essential for the successful large-scale commercial operation of drones.

According to aircraft manufacturer Airbus, while there have been some developments in relation to sense-and-avoidance technology for driverless cars, a 'reliable' and 'mature airborne solution' is yet to exist.[15] This is largely due to the small payload of drones and resulting inability to power and use radar or additional active sensors designed to detect other objects and aircraft. Nonetheless, there have been significant steps made in the development of sense-and-avoidance technology. Organisations – NASA and Boeing, for example – are exploring visual collision avoidance systems for drones. These systems contain an image processor that can track obstacles in their field of vision and relay this information to the flight computer. That computer then initiates manoeuvres to avoid possible collision.[16]

Regulatory obstacles

Given the significant changes that automated vehicle technology will bring in the way we operate vehicles, there will be extensive legislative challenges to be addressed. Such challenges will include safety testing, 'driver' liability, what constitutes 'control' of a vehicle, and how these advancements in technology will be integrated into existing transport systems.[17] Essentially, the task is to balance technological innovation with safety concerns.

There has been some regulatory movement so as to accommodate a future of fully autonomous vehicles. A number of Australian state governments, for example, are reviewing the legal landscape with a view to reducing the barriers

14 *$12 Million Boost for Positioning Technology in Australia* (17 January 2017) Matt Canavan <http://minister.industry.gov.au/ministers/canavan/media-releases/12-million-boost-positioning-technology-australia>.

15 Beata Cece, *Future of Urban Mobility: My Kind of Flyover* (6 December 2016) Airbus <www.airbus.com/newsroom/news/en/2016/12/My-Kind-Of-Flyover.html>.

16 Alexander Khvilivitzky, 'Visual Collision Avoidance System for Unmanned Aerial Vehicles' U.S. Patent 5581250A filed February 24, 1995, and issued December 3, 1996 to The United States of America as Represented by the Administrator of the National Aeronautics and Space Administration.

17 *Future Directions Paper: How Victoria Will Continue to Support the Development of Automated Vehicles* (15 December 2016) Victoria State Government <http://apo.org.au/system/files/71905/apo-nid71905-50871.pdf> 3.

to development of automated driving. In 2016, the Victorian government – an Australian state government – announced plans to develop and test 'highly automated vehicle technology' on Victorian roads. The first step to effect the plan was to amend aspects of the current regulatory framework that prohibit the use of automated driving systems.[18]

As we have mentioned, larger drones may fall within the scope of existing regulatory frameworks. This is explained on the basis that larger drones have communication and navigation capabilities that are comparable to piloted air-craft (as well as being manufactured and piloted in line with quality assurance frameworks similar to those applying to those of manned aircraft). However, the same explanation does not apply to smaller 'mini-drones' and the emerging categories of 'micro-drones' and 'nano-drones', as there is no similar applicable regulatory framework to which they can be compared.[19]

Social obstacles: anti-autonomous movements

There has been some backlash with respect to the development of autonomous systems which has led to the creation of 'anti-autonomous movements'. Such backlash stems from a variety of causes, above all, fear for human safety.

Concern is also expressed over the rate at which autonomous vehicle tech-nology has been developing, making it difficult for regulators to stay across such developments. It is clear that, while there does not appear to be staunch opposition to the innovation itself, groups and organisations exist to attempt to stop certain developments in autonomous vehicle technology. For example, the 'Campaign to Stop Killer Robots' is an international organisation 'working to pre-emptively ban fully autonomous weapons'.[20] It works to raise awareness of the ethical, legal, political and technical concerns that arise from the use of autonomous weapons with the capability of determining targets without human intervention.

However, arguments against the development of autonomous technologies appear – for the most part – to be confined to discrete aspects relating to the use of military drones and weapons. Concerns raised in relation to the civil use of autonomous technology appear to be less prevalent.

General concern in a civilian context relates to the avoidance of collisions and harm to human life. However, it can be argued that the use of automated vehicles, at least in a civil context, will be *more* reliable than human decision-making in relation to collision avoidance and vehicle operation. Humans are less consistently safe due to succumbing to the temptation of multi-tasking, for instance, which detracts from a sole focus on the task of driving. Humans, thus,

---

18 PRIYANKAR BHUNIA, A Brief Overview of Vehicles Legislation and Trials in Australia, OpenGov (23 February 2018) <https://www.opengovasia.com/articles/a-brief-overview-of-automated-vehicles-legislation-and-trials-in-australia>

19 Roger Clarke, 'Understanding the Drone Epidemic' (2014) 30 *Computer Law & Security Review* 230, 244.

20 *About Us* (2017) Campaign to Stop Killer Robots <https://www.stopkillerrobots.org/about-us/>.

expose themselves and others to danger on the roads.[21] With autonomous vehicles able to give complete attention to the operation of the vehicle and its navigation – combined with an ability to be updated with improvements – transport safety statistics might improve. Other facets of transport, such as traffic congestion, may also improve.

Integrating autonomous systems into natural systems

A further concern from the development of drone technologies is the inter-action between autonomous and natural systems (such as wildlife and weather); autonomous systems are predictable, natural systems are not. This interaction is the subject of research at Carnegie Mellon University in Pennsylvania.[22]

The social impacts of autonomous vehicle technology are also notable. Society's input with respect to what is 'ethical and acceptable'[23] will radically impact, and may stall, the integration of specific drone technologies into society, particularly in terms of legal use and prevalence. There are growing concerns regarding the use of biologically based drones, such as the RoboBee, and their impact on the natural world. It is possible for biologically based drones to come into contact with natural species in the environment, perhaps through collision.[24] This may result in a societal movement questioning the ethics of a drone-integrated air traffic system.

6.2.3 Swarming

A drone swarm, as the name suggests, is a large group of drones flying together to serve a collective purpose, whether it be to search or survey, for example, or for military operations. From a technological standpoint, drone swarms will form part of developments in autonomy; swarming necessarily involves platforms to operate autonomously.[25]

Boeing has a dedicated Collaborative Autonomous Systems Laboratory for experimenting with the behaviour of multiple unmanned vehicles.[26] The

---

21 Sarah E. Kreps, *Drones: What Everyone Needs to Know* (Oxford University Press, 2016) 156.

22 Brian Heater, 'Teaching Teams of Drones to Work alongside Humans and Nature', *Tech Crunch* (online), 9 June 2017 <https://techcrunch.com/2017/06/08/teaching-teams-of-drones-to-work-alongside-humans-and-nature/>.

23 Vivek Wadhwa and Alex Salkever, *The Driver in the Driverless Car* (Berret-Koehler Publishers, 2017) 122.

24 M. Hassanalian and A. Abdelkefi, 'Classifications, Applications and Design Challenges of Drones: A Review' (2017) 91 *Progress in Aerospace Sciences* 99, 112.

25 Dario Floreano and Robert J. Wood, 'Science, Technology and the Future of Small Autonomous Drones' (2015) 521 *Nature* 460, 463–464.

26 *Swarm Up to the Idea: A Boeing Lab Experiments with Multiple Unmanned Vehicle Behaviours* (11 January 2017) Boeing <www.boeing.com/features/2017/01/casl-lab-01-17.page>.

company has indicated that 'the next big step' for autonomous vehicles is making teams of these vehicles work together, a step that will allow these vehicles to be 'much more capable'.[27] Further, researchers at the Wyss Institute indicate that 'coordinated behaviour in large groups' was one of the core ideas behind the development of the RoboBee.[28] The RoboBee, as previously mentioned, is an autonomous flying 'microrobot' inspired by the anatomy and flight of a bee.[29] Researchers are aiming to assemble a fleet of these drone bees that can operate cooperatively as a unit.[30]

Utility of swarming for particular purposes

The development of swarming is critical in advancing the ability to carry out complex missions and adjust to changes in the swarm. If, as part of a swarm, a drone malfunctions or crashes, the drone will continue to communicate within the swarm such that its formation can be adjusted and the mission can continue. Similarly, where drones may be performing high-power usage tasks, a drone in a swarm is able to take over a task from another drone as its battery becomes depleted. The flight range is, thus, significantly increased in comparison to just one drone performing the task.[31]

The use of a swarm also allows for a larger range of data collection which can be communicated between drones for more effective navigation, as well as a more accurate execution of the specific task.[32] Particularly relevant to military use, swarms allow for greater payload as the payload itself is distributed over a number of drones as opposed to one drone.[33]

With increased mission capabilities that come with operating in drone swarms, however, there are also many technological difficulties to overcome. These difficulties arise in the communication between drones, as well as between drones and ground control, which requires complex communications channels.[34] eVolo, a German start-up company, has developed an electric

---

27 Ibid.
28 *Autonomous Flying Microrobots (RoboBees)* (2017) Wyss Institute <https://wyss.harvard.edu/technology/autonomous-flying-microrobots-robobees/>.
29 Ibid.
30 Ibid.
31 B. Verguouw et al, 'Drone Technology: Types, Payloads, Applications, Frequency Spectrum Issues and Future Developments.' in Bart Custers (ed), *The Future of Drone Use: Opportunities and Threats from Ethical and Legal Perspectives* (T.M.C. Asser Press, 2016) 21, 42.
32 Tommaso Francesco Villa et al, 'An Overview of Small Unmanned Aerial Vehicles for Air Quality Measurements: Present Applications and Future Prospectives' 16 *Sensors* 1072.
33 B. Verguouw et al, 'Drone Technology: Types, Payloads, Applications, Frequency Spectrum Issues and Future Developments.' in Bart Custers (ed), *The Future of Drone Use: Opportunities and Threats from Ethical and Legal Perspectives* (T.M.C. Asser Press, 2016) 21, 42.
34 Ibid.

multicopter called the Volocopter 2X and, as a feature, offers integration of 'air traffic management to coordinate autonomous Volocopter fleets'.[35] It appears that the swarming strategy will allow society to perform 'dull, dirty and dangerous'[36] tasks more easily, quickly and efficiently. Such dangerous tasks may include, for example, entering buildings to search for chemical hazards, in a quick and efficient manner.[37] Researchers from Switzerland's Ecole Polytechnique Federale da Lausanne University have developed swarm software for use in such situations. The software operates by calculating which flight path is better than another in disaster situations.[38]

Issues

While it appears that swarming technology can assist industry, there are challenges to be met, including the need for complex inter-drone communications channels. While the swarming strategy enables tasks to be completed more quickly and efficiently, preparing the drone fleet for operation is time consuming with individual assembly of each drone required.[39] This issue may be overcome once the construction and preparation processes are also automated.

Swarming technology will also be affected by cyber security threats. For example, it cannot be said with certainty that communication between drones will be completely secure against hackers.[40] To address this issue, developers are working on software tools to secure drone swarms.[41] There is no guarantee that these security measures will be sufficiently robust; such measures need updating continually to combat new methods of hacking or reprogramming.

6.2.4 Flight efficiency and endurance

Flight efficiency is paramount to the successful operation of drones. A number of developments in drone technology will serve to improve flight efficiency and endurance of drones. Flight efficiency, however, is affected by a number of factors. These factors are discussed below.

---

35 *Design Specifications Volocopter 2X* (April 2017) Volocopter <https://www.volocopter.com/assets/pdf/2017_04_Design_specifications_2X.pdf>.
36 Dario Floreano and Robert J. Wood, 'Science, Technology and the Future of Small Autonomous Drones' (2015) 521 *Nature* 460, 460.
37 Ibid 461.
38 M. Hassanalian and A. Abdelkefi, 'Classifications, Applications and Design Challenges of Drones: A Review' (2017) 91 *Progress in Aerospace Sciences* 99, 125.
39 A. Kwasniak and A. Kerezman, 'Drones in Transportation Engineering: A Discussion of Current Drone Rules, Equipment and Applications' (2017) 87 *ITE Journal of Transportation Engineers* 40, 43.
40 Bart Custers, *The Future of Drone Use: Opportunities and Threats from Ethical and Legal Perspectives* (T.M.C. Asser Press, 2016) 82.
41 Ibid.

Design-dependent

By virtue of their design, some drones are less flight efficient than others, though their design is also task-specific. Transport company Uber indicated that it avoided a 'multi-copter' approach to its autonomous air taxi due to having 'lower efficiency since they aren't using wing-borne flight'.[42] In general, helicopters have poor energy efficiency compared to conventional aircraft.[43] However, they have more precise landing capabilities necessary, for instance, in city centres where air taxis may operate.

Process of miniaturisation

Scaling down the size of drones has opened up a multiplicity of civilian applications. Smaller size allows for significant improvements in manoeuvrability, resulting in the ability to perform complex aerobatic manoeuvres, as well as to manipulate objects while in flight.[44] However, by reducing size, developers have observed that this also reduces the flight efficiency and endurance of the drone.[45] The scaling down of drones diminishes their ability to sustain flight for an adequate amount of time, which is problematic especially for certain operations.

Further, the scaling down of drones also diminishes maximum velocity capabilities making small-scale drones (at this point) suitable for close range, agile tasks, but making them unsuitable for long distance missions.[46]

There have, however, been a number of developments in improving the energy and flight efficiency of drones. For example, the RoboBee – by virtue of its small airframe – has low aerodynamic efficiency and reduced capacity to store energy, limiting its endurance in flight.[47] Researchers at the previously mentioned Wyss Institute are examining ways to improve the energy efficiency of the RoboBee by experimenting with a perching strategy.[48] In nature, birds perch on surfaces to conserve energy. Researchers hope to enable the RoboBee to imitate the act of perching for the same purpose.[49] Perching would allow

42 *Fast-Forwarding to a Future of On-Demand Urban Air Transportation* (27 October 2016) Uber <https://www.uber.com/elevate.pdf> 15.
43 Stephen Cass, 'Beyond the Quadcopter: New Designs for Drones Showcased at CeBIT' (2016) 53 *IEEE Spectrum* 21.
44 Dario Floreano and Robert J. Wood, 'Science, Technology and the Future of Small Autonomous Drones' (2015) 521 *Nature* 460, 461.
45 Ibid 461.
46 Ibid.
47 D. Mehanovic et al, 'Autonomous Thrust-Assisted Perching of a Fixed-Wing UAV on Vertical Surfaces' in Michael Mangan et al (eds) *Biomimetic and Biohybrid Systems: 6th International Conference, Living Machines, California, 2017* (Springer, 2017) 302.
48 *Autonomous Flying Microrobots (RoboBees)* (2017) Wyss Institute <https://wyss.harvard.edu/technology/autonomous-flying-microrobots-robobees/>.
49 D. Mehanovic et al, 'Autonomous Thrust-Assisted Perching of a Fixed-Wing UAV on Vertical Surfaces' in Michael Mangan et al (eds) *Biomimetic and Biohybrid*

the RoboBee to reduce its power consumption by 'three orders of magnitude'.[50] The RoboBee perches on a surface through electrostatic adhesion.[51] Due to such adhesive technology, it can adhere to a large range of surfaces and further 'perch under overhangs and on ceilings'.[52] Eventually, researchers hope that the RoboBee will be able to perch on any surface.[53]

The ability to perch and conserve energy may hold a key to further improvements in small-scale drone capabilities with the development of charging stations. Companies such as Skysense develop and manufacture autonomous drone charging stations. By combining the ability to perch with charging station technology, small-scale drones may be able to continue performing tasks for extended periods of time.

Adequacy of batteries in future drone technology

The use of batteries in future aerial vehicles will be problematic given that batteries have limited energy density. This may restrict drones to certain routes with capacity to connect and recharge at a power source.[54] This issue invites speculation as to whether the aerial passenger drone system will be a more efficient system overall compared to our current land transportation system, given the frequency at which these vehicles will need to be recharged.

One advantage of a passenger vehicle is that it endures longer than smaller drones merely by virtue of its size. By reducing the size of the airframe, one also reduces the aerodynamic efficiency and energy storage capability of that drone.[55]

6.2.5 Environmentally friendly

As a new technology, many drones have been developed to take account of environmental considerations. The use of solar cells[56] to charge and power drones has been explored by drone researchers and developers. For example,

Systems: 6th International Conference, Living Machines, California, 2017 (Springer, 2017) 302.
50 N. Canter, 'RoboBees: Learning to Perch' (2016) 72 *Tribology & Lubrication Technology* 8, 8.
51 Ibid.
52 *Using Static Electricity, RoboBees Cling to Surface* (19 May 2016) Wyss Institute <https://wyss.harvard.edu/using-static-electricity-robobees-cling-to-surface/>.
53 Ibid.
54 Dario Floreano and Robert J. Wood, 'Science, Technology and the Future of Small Autonomous Drones' (2015) 521 *Nature* 460, 461.
55 D. Mehanovic et al, 'Autonomous Thrust-Assisted Perching of a Fixed-Wing UAV on Vertical Surfaces' in Michael Mangan et al (eds) *Biomimetic and Biohybrid Systems: 6th International Conference, Living Machines, California, 2017* (Springer, 2017) 302.
56 M. Hassanalian and A. Abdelkefi, 'Classifications, Applications and Design Challenges of Drones: A Review' (2017) 91 *Progress in Aerospace Sciences* 99, 120–22.

Facebook has been developing and testing a solar-powered drone, 'Aquila', for the purpose of providing Internet access to remote parts of the world.[57]

Many of the air taxi prototypes proposed by companies are powered by electric motors. A number of companies have promoted eco-friendly or emission-free travel as part of their mission statement. EHang actively advertises its EHang 184 as 'eco-friendly'.[58] eVolo contends that the flight of its Volocopter 2X is 'emission-free'.[59] And Uber advertises its fully electric vertical take-off and landing (VTOL) design as a 'compelling solution' to 'ecologically responsible and sustainable' transport.[60]

Statements by these corporations and drone developers are indicative both of the trend and requirement for environmentally conscious technology to be used in drone production.

6.3 Examples

6.3.1 Robotic flying birds and insects

Introduction

Biologically inspired drones, or 'bio-drones', are at the forefront of developments in drone technology. Indeed, researchers hope to equip drones with the same capabilities as living creatures. These drones cover a wide range of civilian and military applications. Various sensors and cameras for conducting surveillance, reconnaissance and rescue missions can be installed in drones which, combined with their biologically inspired flight methods, invite significant technological advancements. However, developing such drones is more complicated than developing other drones due to the 'complex aerodynamics' associated with natural flight and other factors.[61]

Categories

Robotic flying birds and insects are considered to be smaller unmanned aerial vehicles.[62] These drones can be categorised as 'micro aerial

---

57 *Aquila: Facebook's Solar-powered Internet Drone Takes Flight* (22 July 2016) ABC News <www.abc.net.au/news/2016-07-22/aquila-facebook-solar-powered-internet-drone-takes-flight/7651394>.

58 *EHang 184: Autonomous Aerial Vehicle (AAV)* (6 January 2016) EHang <www.ehang.com/ehang184/>.

59 *Volocopter as an Autonomous Air Taxi in Dubai* (19 June 2017) Volocopter <https://press.volocopter.com/index.php/volocopter-as-an-autonomous-air-taxi-in-dubai>.

60 *Fast-Forwarding to a Future of On-Demand Urban Air Transportation* (27 October 2016) Uber <https://www.uber.com/elevate.pdf> 33.

61 M. Hassanalian and A. Abdelkefi, 'Classifications, Applications and Design Challenges of Drones: A Review' (2017) 91 *Progress in Aerospace Sciences* 99, 105.

62 Ibid 107.

vehicles', 'nano aerial vehicles' and 'pico aerial vehicles'.[63] These biologi-cally-inspired aerial vehicles all have flapping wings, rather than fixed or rotary wings. These flapping wings are flexible and light. Despite the small nature of the vehicle, they allow it to be aerodynamically proficient and stable in flight.[64]

RoboBees

As mentioned, the RoboBee is a micro aerial vehicle developed by researchers at Harvard University's Wyss Institute.[65] Interestingly, a 'drone' by definition also refers to the non-working male bee in a colony of bees.[66]

In terms of the dimensions and design details of the RoboBee, it is half the size of a paperclip and weighs one tenth of a gram. It achieves vertical take-off and landing, and can hover and steer. In operation, the control system causes the flapping wings to rotate.[67]

Future phases of development will see the introduction of RoboBees into commercial industries. RoboBees are currently powered by an external power source via cable. Researchers are aiming to incorporate a power supply on board the RoboBee platform.[68]

Villasenor predicts that RoboBees could fly independently through the use of ultra-light batteries.[69] Through the use of smart sensors and control modules, RoboBees will have the capacity to 'sense and respond dynami-cally to the environment'.[70] The sense and control technologies serve as the eyes and antennae of the RoboBee, although integration of onboard com-putation in the RoboBee will be a challenge given the small size of the drone.[71] To address this, as discussed earlier, researchers are working on the RoboBee colony development[72] and the power-saving technique of perching.

63 Ibid 100.
64 Ibid 105.
65 *Autonomous Flying Microrobots (RoboBees)* (2017) Wyss Institute <https://wyss.harva rd.edu/technology/autonomous-flying-microrobots-robobees/>.
66 M. L. Winston, *The Biology of the Honey Bee* (Harvard University Press, 1991) 41.
67 *Autonomous Flying Microrobots (RoboBees)* (2017) Wyss Institute <https://wyss.harva rd.edu/technology/autonomous-flying-microrobots-robobees/>.
68 Ibid.
69 John Villasenor, 'Drones and the Future of Domestic Aviation' (2014) 102 *Pro-ceedings of the IEEE* 235, 236.
70 *Autonomous Flying Microrobots (RoboBees)* (2017) Wyss Institute <https://wyss.harva rd.edu/technology/autonomous-flying-microrobots-robobees/>.
71 N. Canter, 'RoboBees: Learning to Perch' (2016) 72 *Tribology & Lubrication Tech-nology* 8.
72 *Autonomous Flying Microrobots (RoboBees)* (2017) Wyss Institute <https://wyss.harva rd.edu/technology/autonomous-flying-microrobots-robobees/>.

Bio-drones

Referred to as the 'bio models of micro and nano air vehicles',[73] bio-drones use live or deceased animals for reconnaissance and patrolling missions instead of completely artificial drones.[74] It could be argued that the use of 'live' bio-drones is too severe an interference with natural processes and cannot be justified. And the use of bio-drones further raises significant concerns with regard to the ethical treatment of animals.

Biologically inspired drones may be useful for surveillance and reconnaissance missions given their small size and the possibility of camouflage as insects or birds. Due to flapping wings, these small drones are also optimal for search and rescue missions in that they can hover and transition quickly into forward flight.[75]

6.3.2 Drone copters

Known as 'rotary wing' vehicles, helicopter drones exist in several sizes and for several uses. They are classified by reference to their size and the number of blades. The future of helicopter drones can be divided into two clear lines of development as set out below.

Practical issues and improvements

Whilst helicopter drones can hover and are highly manoeuvrable,[76] their forward flight manoeuvrability is diminished relative to other models or designs, such as the fixed-wing drones.[77] Therefore, developers have looked to hybrid models which exploit the advantages – yet counteract the disadvantages – of the helicopter-inspired design. For example, the Swiss WingtraOne is a hybrid model that combines 'the long-range fuel efficiency of fixed-wing aircraft with the small launch-and-landing footprint of quadcopters'.[78]

Airbus Helicopters, the helicopter manufacturing division of the aeronautical designer and manufacturer, Airbus, recently announced that it is improving its existing helicopter portfolio by making helicopters 'safer, greener and more efficient'.[79]

---

73 M. Hassanalian and A. Abdelkefi, 'Classifications, Applications and Design Challenges of Drones: A Review' (2017) 91 *Progress in Aerospace Sciences* 99, 100.
74 Ibid, 108.
75 Ibid 105.
76 S. Saripalli, J.F. Montogomery and G.S. Sukhatme, 'Vision-Based Autonomous Landing of an Unmanned Aerial Vehicle' (Proceedings 2002 IEEE International Conference on Robotics and Automation, Washington DC, 2002) 2799.
77 Dario Floreano and Robert J. Wood, 'Science, Technology and the Future of Small Autonomous Drones' (2015) 521 *Nature* 460, 460.
78 Stephen Cass, 'Beyond the Quadcopter: New Designs for Drones Showcased at CeBIT' (2016) 53 *IEEE Spectrum* 21.
79 Alexandre Marchand, *One Step Ahead at All Times: Helicopter Innovation at Airbus* (27 July 2017) Airbus <www.airbus.com/newsroom/news/en/2017/07/helicop ter-innovation-at-airbus.html>.

Clearly, these issues have not justified abandoning the design altogether. It has been observed that improvements are made on a case-by-case basis, depending on their specific application.[80]

Autonomy

Researchers are also focusing on making helicopter drones autonomous. It has been said that autonomous features, such as autonomous landing, are critical to the successful functioning of an unmanned helicopter.[81] The developers of Skye, an inflatable drone used for entertainment and aerial photography, aim to create 'a more autonomous version', making it safer for use by the average consumer without a trained operator.[82] The VSR 700, a helicopter-style military drone developed by Airbus Helicopters in conjunction with Hélicoptères Guimbal, utilises autonomous flight technologies, and is currently being tested.[83] The need for autonomous drones extends beyond individual industry application to wide ranging civilian transport. In light of this, developers such as Volocopter are designing autonomous rotary-wing flying taxis.

The future of air taxis: adoption of the dronecopter design

In Dubai, a future in which personal air travel largely features helicopter drones is envisaged. The Road and Traffic Authority in Dubai is testing two helicopter-inspired autonomous air taxi prototypes. Dubai also has a self-driving transport strategy; by 2030, the country aims to make 25 per cent of its passenger transport completely autonomous.[84]

With a view to 'conquer[ing] the market for flying air taxis',[85] German start-up eVolo has developed the Volocopter 2X, a rotary-wing drone that is capable of vertical take-off and landing. Its powerful electric motor and lithium ion batteries allow the craft to cruise for up to 27 minutes at a time and can reach a maximum speed of 100 kilometres per hour. The Volocopter 2X has a two-person passenger capacity and a maximum payload of 160

80 Stephen Cass, 'Beyond the Quadcopter: New designs for drones showcased at CeBIT' (2016) 53 *IEEE Spectrum* 21.
81 S. Saripalli, J.F. Montogomery and G.S. Sukhatme, 'Vision-Based Autonomous Landing of an Unmanned Aerial Vehicle' (Proceedings 2002 IEEE International Conference on Robotics and Automation, Washington DC, 2002) 2799.
82 Stephen Cass, 'Beyond the Quadcopter: New Designs for Drones Showcased at CeBIT' (2016) 53 *IEEE Spectrum* 21.
83 Alexandre Marchand, *One Step Ahead at All Times: Helicopter Innovation at Airbus* (27 July 2017) Airbus <www.airbus.com/newsroom/news/en/2017/07/helicopter-innovation-at-airbus.html>.
84 *Volocopter as an Autonomous Air Taxi in Dubai* (19 June 2017) Volocopter <https://press.volocopter.com/index.php/volocopter-as-an-autonomous-air-taxi-in-dubai>.
85 *Flying Air Taxis from Germany Conquer the World* (1 August 2017) Volocopter <https://press.volocopter.com/index.php/flying-air-taxis-from-germany-conquer-the-world>

kilograms. It flies completely autonomously,[86] with the possibility of integrating extra 'sense and avoid technology' and 'autonomous sub-features'. Since 2017, the Volocopter 2X is engaged in a series of test flights in Dubai which will continue for five years.[87]

The Chinese EHang 184 is a drone designed to provide an electrically powered aerial transportation solution.[88] It carries one passenger; has a rated payload of 120 kilograms; can cruise for up to 25 minutes at a time; can reach a maximum speed of 100 kilometres per hour; and takes one hour to charge on a 'fast charge' and two hours to charge on a 'slow charge'.[89] Ehang 184 is automated through a smart flight system, flying from one pre-set landing target to another in an inverted U-shape, achieved with 'one single click'.[90] The EHang 184 is currently being flight-tested in Dubai.[91]

In February 2017, Airbus Helicopters entered into a memorandum of understanding with the Civil Aviation Authority of Singapore to test its drone, 'Skyways', at the National University of Singapore. Skyways is a vehicle designed to carry cargo, not human passengers.[92] Airbus has chosen a different design approach for their passenger delivery aerial vehicles.

There is, however, a body of commentary questioning the use of helicopter-inspired platforms as air taxis. Uber argues that a VTOL-style aircraft is preferable for practical reasons, as 'helicopters are too noisy, inefficient, polluting and expensive for mass-scale use'.[93] Uber further argues that, for safety reasons, helicopter-inspired designs are not appropriate for passenger travel.[94]

These platforms are highly manoeuvrable; important, for instance, in search and rescue missions because objects can be dropped and retrieved from otherwise inaccessible places.[95] However, increased agility also makes them unstable and dangerous,[96] particularly if operated by a human pilot and for passenger travel.

86 *Volocopter as an Autonomous Air Taxi in Dubai* (19 June 2017) Volocopter <https://press.volocopter.com/index.php/volocopter-as-an-autonomous-air-taxi-in-dubai>.
87 Ibid.
88 *EHang 184: Autonomous Aerial Vehicle (AAV)* (6 January 2016) EHang <www.ehang.com/ehang184/>.
89 Ibid.
90 Ibid.
91 *EHang Partners with Dubai RTA to Boost Smart Transport* (5 February 2017) EHang <www.ehang.com/news/248.html>.
92 Beata Cece, *Future of Urban Mobility: My Kind of Flyover* (6 December 2016) Airbus <www.airbus.com/newsroom/news/en/2016/12/My-Kind-Of-Flyover.html>.
93 *Fast-Forwarding to a Future of On-Demand Urban Air Transportation* (27 October 2016) Uber <https://www.uber.com/elevate.pdf> 3.
94 Ibid.
95 S. Saripalli, J.F. Montogomery and G.S. Sukhatme, 'Vision-Based Autonomous Landing of an Unmanned Aerial Vehicle' (Proceedings 2002 IEEE International Conference on Robotics and Automation, Washington DC, 2002) 2799.
96 Ibid.

6.3.3 Autonomous flying cars

Introduction

While the future looks promising for autonomous flying cars, they are in the early stages of development. Companies that have developed and are testing prototypes appear to have a collective mission or rationale for why they are developing flying cars. Airbus is '…looking skywards to develop three ambitious projects that aim to relieve urban congestion'.[97] Uber aims to 'radically improve urban mobility' and 'alleviate transportation congestion on the ground'.[98]

But first, self-driving cars

Australian statutory authority, VicRoads, and Australian company, TransUrban, have begun testing automated vehicles in Victoria, looking at the vehicles' response to the current infrastructure (signs, for example) and assessing what additional technologies will be required.[99] Both driverless cars and *flying* driverless cars 'address many of the same issues'.[100] If this is indeed the case, the integration of flying autonomous cars into our cities may be more seamless than envisaged, although, needless to say, some time away.

Prototypes in testing phase

Project Vahana by A³ is a 'self-piloted flying vehicle platform' developed by Airbus, which successfully completed its first full-scale test flight in January 2018.[101] A smartphone will be used to book a flight in this vehicle at a given time.[102] It would carry a single passenger or cargo.[103]

CityAirbus is an electrically powered aerial vehicle that is capable of carrying up to four passengers.[104] Developers have focused heavily on reliable sense-and-avoid technology as well as constructing the craft from lightweight composite structures.

97 Beata Cece, *Future of Urban Mobility: My Kind of Flyover* (6 December 2016) Airbus <www.airbus.com/newsroom/news/en/2016/12/My-Kind-Of-Flyover.html>.
98 *Fast-Forwarding to a Future of On-Demand Urban Air Transportation* (27 October 2016) Uber <https://www.uber.com/elevate.pdf> 2.
99 Jane Cowan, *Driverless Cars: Everything You Need to Know about the Transport Revolution* (11 March 2017) ABC News <www.abc.net.au/news/2017-03-11/everything-you-need-to-know-about-driverless-cars/8336322>.
100 Vivek Wadhwa and Alex Salkever, *The Driver in the Driverless Car* (Berret-Koehler Publishers, 2017) 119.
101 Airbus, Vahana Completes First Full-Scale test Flight (February 2018) Airbus <http://www.airbus.com/newsroom/news/en/2018/02/vahana-completes-first-full-scale-test-flight.html>.
102 Beata Cece, Future of Urban Mobility: My Kind of Flyover (6 December 2016) Airbus <www.airbus.com/newsroom/news/en/2016/12/My-Kind-Of-Flyover.html>.
103 Ibid.
104 *Rethinking Urban Air Mobility* (17 June 2017) Airbus <www.airbus.com/newsroom/topics-in-focus/urban-air-mobility.html>.

Uber has been conceptualising the type of infrastructure needed for on-demand VTOLs in a ridesharing network. It has conceived a 'vertiport' – an urban docking station that can accommodate up to 12 VTOLs.[105]

Kitty Hawk is developing an electric, single pilot, personal aircraft. It is an ultra-light rotary-wing design and can reach speeds of 40 kilometres per hour. However, at its current stage of development, the Kitty Hawk can only fly over water. Nonetheless, it represents a significant development in personal flying vehicles.[106]

Lilium is the world's first VTOL jet. Lilium represents a sustainable evolution of the traditional fixed and rotary-wing designs. The craft has 36 small jet turbines which allow for a maximum range of 300 kilometres and maximum speed of 300 kilometres per hour. The craft seats up to two passengers and is supposedly quieter than a motorbike in urban areas.[107]

6.3.4 Air traffic management systems and supporting infrastructure

While this chapter largely focuses on developments in relation to drone platforms themselves, some attention to proposals for air traffic control systems is necessary. As the skies become increasingly congested with disparate aerial devices, it is critical that appropriate infrastructure is in place to ensure effective and safe operations. This may include, for example, safety measures such as 'emergency kill-switches' for drones, dedicated air corridors for drone travel, or systems that can secure schools in the event of drone attack.[108]

Various companies, international bodies and associations have advanced their own versions of a system of air traffic control for drones and supporting infrastructure. Uber proposes an 'urban VTOL network' to host its VTOL vehicle that includes charging infrastructure, hubs with multiple take-off and landing pads and single take-off and landing pads.[109]

myCopter is a project funded by the European Union that aims to create a personal air transport system through the development of technologies concerning obstacle avoidance, path planning and formation flying.[110]

105 *Fast-Forwarding to a Future of On-Demand Urban Air Transportation* (27 October 2016) Uber <https://www.uber.com/elevate.pdf> 54.

106 John Markoff, *No Longer a Dream: Silicon Valley Takes on the Flying Car* (24 April 2017) The New York Times <https://www.nytimes.com/2017/04/24/technology/flying-car-technology.html?hp&action=click&pgtype=Homepage&clickSource=story-heading&module=second-column-region%AEion=top-news&WT.nav=top-news>.

107 *Lilium Celebrates Successful Flight Tests of World's First Electric VTOL Jet* (20 April 2017) Lilium <https://lilium.com/press-releases/lilium-celebrates-successful-flights-tests.pdf>.

108 Vivek Wadhwa and Alex Salkever, *The Driver in the Driverless Car* (Berret-Koehler Publishers, 2017) 120.

109 *Fast-Forwarding to a Future of On-Demand Urban Air Transportation* (27 October 2016) Uber <https://www.uber.com/elevate.pdf> 3.

110 *Lifting Personal Transportation into the Third Dimension* (2017) myCopter <www.mycopter.eu>.

HyperLoop One, the underground tunnel transport system, has been developed to ensure efficient and safe implementation of such new transport technology.[111]

zenAIRCITY is a 'business and mobility concept', which maps out a hypothetical city that will accommodate Airbus Group's CityAirbus air taxis. It also identifies the necessary supporting infrastructure such as 'zenCYBER', designed to protect flights against hacking.[112]

6.3.5 Vehicles for package delivery

Airbus Helicopter's Skyways project is an ambitious project aimed at relieving urban congestion. In February 2017, Airbus Helicopters and the Civil Aviation Authority of Singapore signed a memorandum of understanding allowing Airbus Helicopters to test a drone parcel delivery service on campus at the National University of Singapore.

Since 2013, Amazon has been working on its 'Prime Air' drone delivery service. The company has developed an 'airborne fulfilment center' which is essentially a drone airport where the vehicles can dock, charge and pick up their packages for delivery.[113]

In developing its drone delivery project, Project Wing, Google has created software that will automatically and simultaneously manage different drones from different manufacturers as they conduct deliveries and travel. The software manages the flight paths of different drones and can plan new routes for each aircraft independently if and when conflicts arise.[114]

In terms of the military, the United States Marine Corps has been testing disposable autonomous gliders that could deliver supplies to troops in enemy territory, or to military forces on beaches that are far from resupply ships. In 2017, it was reported that advanced guidance and control systems have been developed to turn cargo boxes into flying trucks, capable of carrying 1,600 pounds of supplies to drop zones up to 74 nautical miles away.[115] This allows a carrier aircraft to deploy a glider drone far from a battlefield and, thus, avoid the risk of enemy fire.

111 A. Hern, *Richard Branson's Virgin Group Invests in Hyperloop One* (13 October 2017) The Guardian <https://www.theguardian.com/technology/2017/oct/12/richard-branson-virgin-group-invests-hyperloop-one>.

112 Beata Cece, *Future of Urban Mobility: My Kind of Flyover* (6 December 2016) Airbus <www.airbus.com/newsroom/news/en/2016/12/My-Kind-Of-Flyover.html>.

113 Ed Oswald, *Here's Everything You Need to Know about Amazon's Drone Delivery Project, Prime Air* (3 May 2017) Digital Trends <https://www.digitaltrends.com/cool-tech/amazon-prime-air-delivery-drones-history-progress>.

114 Julie Bort, *Google's Drone Delivery Project Just Shared Some Big News about its Future* (8 June 2017) Business Insider Australia <https://www.businessinsider.com.au/project-wing-update-future-google-drone-delivery-project-2017-6?r=US&IR=T>.

115 Jeremy Hsu, *Disposable Drones Could Deliver Supplies under Enemy Fire* (5 August 2017) WIRED <https://www.wired.com/2017/05/disposable-drones-deliver-supplies-enemy-fire/>.

6.4 Pilotless commercial aircraft

Introduction

Until recently, pilotless aircraft have been viewed as a novel concept.[116] It appears to us that society has been somewhat reluctant to embrace the possibility of having no human pilot on board, operating the aircraft remotely *or* with no human pilot *at all* where the aircraft is operating fully autonomously.

UBS, however, doubts whether an aircraft will ever be fully autonomous.[117] One reason for this is the psychological impact associated with the removal of a human pilot from the cockpit. Despite autonomous software being far more computationally competent than a human pilot, there is a sense of security which attaches to a human pilot. It must be said, however, that society clearly does adapt to new technologies over time.

Prototypes in testing phase

Boeing's ambition is to develop autonomous aircraft capable of navigating without any human assistance. The company plans to test self-flying technology in a cockpit simulator.[118]

Staged development and implementation

Analysts observe that technology may develop in stages, from 'full pilot control' to 'full autonomy'.[119] It appears likely that the implementation of this technology in the aviation industry will also follow a graduated approach. This seems appropriate in the light of what we consider to be society's hesitation towards the complete removal of the human pilot from aerial vehicles.

The role of the human pilot

One of the more contentious issues in the development of drones has been the actual control of the drone.[120] It has been a longstanding requirement to have a human pilot on board a commercial aircraft to pilot or, at the very least, monitor aircraft systems. Notwithstanding accidents occurring wholly or

---

116 Roger Clarke, 'Understanding the Drone Epidemic' (2014) 30 *Computer Law & Security Review* 230, 231.
117 Jarrod Castle et al, *Q-Series: Flying Solo – How Far Are We down the Path towards Pilotless Planes?* (7 August 2017) UBS <http://nzz-files-prod.s3-website-eu-west-1.amazonaws.com/2017/8/7/93872795-5ab9-4f94-bb3a-f6ed38c6b886.pdf>.
118 Ibid.
119 Roger Clarke, 'Understanding the Drone Epidemic' (2014) 30 *Computer Law & Security Review* 230, 233.
120 Ibid 232.

partially as a result of a pilot's erroneous decision-making[121] or mental vulnerabilities,[122] this requirement remains.

Impact on the aviation industry

Two main impacts that pilotless commercial aircraft may have in terms of the aviation industry are economic and safety-related. Analysis of the aviation industry suggests that meaningful savings can be generated by the removal of pilots. UBS has predicted that aerospace suppliers, manufacturers and commercial airlines can save more than US $35 billion a year overall. If flight optimisation services were implemented, there could be up to US $133 billion saved in fuel.

There is, however, a need for significantly enhanced automated systems to combat cybersecurity threats to aircraft. Despite such threats, there are also potentially significant safety benefits associated with pilotless planes (including the ability of software to sense-and-avoid danger).

6.5 Issues for regulation going forward

Development of technology will continue to outpace the regulatory process,[123] including in relation to privacy, safety, security and airspace. The challenges related to these matters should not be underestimated.

Privacy will continue to be a fundamental concern associated with the use of drones. Consideration must be given to, for instance, whether aerial vehicles will be allowed to fly over residential and other private property, or whether they should be restricted to drone-specific public roads.[124] Will regulations be sufficient to mandate behaviour or will it be necessary to have privacy safeguards (such as geofencing) in place?[125]

The intersection between military and civilian drone regulations may well (in addition to existing concerns) impact on safety. In August 2017, the Pentagon announced that it will permit military personnel in certain domestic US bases to shoot down 'commercial and privately owned small unmanned aerial vehicles'[126]

121 William Langewiesche, *The Human Factor* (October 2014) Vanity Fair <https://www.vanityfair.com/news/business/2014/10/air-france-flight-447-crash>.
122 *Germanwings Plane Crash: Co-Pilot Andreas Lubitz Crashed Plane Deliberately, French Prosecutor Says* (27 March 2015) ABC News <www.abc.net.au/news/2015-03-26/germanwings-co-pilot-andreas-lubitz-crashed-plane-deliberately/6351854>.
123 Bharat Rao, Ashwin Goutham Gopi and Romana Maione, 'The Societal Impact of Commercial Drones' (2016) 45 *Technology in Society* 83, 87.
124 Vivek Wadhwa and Alex Salkever, *The Driver in the Driverless Car* (Berret-Koehler Publishers, 2017) 120.
125 Bart Custers, 'Drones Here, There and Everywhere: Introduction and Overview' in Bart Custers (ed), *The Future of Drone Use: Opportunities and Threats from Ethical and Legal Perspectives* (Springer, 2016).
126 Terri M. Cronk, '*DoD Cracks Down on Use of Drones over Installations*' (7 August 2017) United States of America: Department of Defense <https://www.defense.

that 'endanger aviation safety or pose other threats'.[127] This could, however, have the undesired effect of endangering civilians...

The ability to hack or reprogram flights poses a threat to national security. A drone's GPS may be attacked through 'spoofing' or 'jamming'.[128] Spoofing involves the transmission of fake GPS signals which are so strong that the drone is unable to follow its programmed directions.[129] From a safety perspective, this interference is life-threatening, particularly if the drone is reprogrammed to crash. Arduino circuit boards and open-source software, both of which are very common in drones, make it easy for motivated coders and hackers to enable drones to perform functions that are contrary to the public good.[130] Jamming involves overwhelming the GPS antenna with signal, to the extent that 'collisions become unavoidable'.[131] Needless to say, this presents a danger to human life.

There may be the option to 'opt out' of drones by banning their sale or restricting their operation,[132] but this is likely to be insufficient to countenance misuse of the technology.

Key regulatory questions regarding airspace include whether there needs to be a distinction between non-autonomous, partially autonomous and fully autonomous aircraft. Further, whether airspace can be adequately shared or needs to be segregated is another question. As previously noted, there may be a need for physical infrastructure to ensure adherence to boundaries.

What is clear is that the development of drone technology does – and will continue to – present challenges for lawmakers across the globe.

gov/News/Article/Article/1270758/dod-cracks-down-on-use-of-drones-over-in stallations/>.

127 *Military can Destroy Drones over Domestic U.S. Bases: Pentagon* (8 August 2017) Reuters <https://www.reuters.com/article/us-usa-military-drone-idUSKBN1AN2BP>.

128 Bharat Rao, Ashwin Goutham Gopi and Romana Maione, 'The Societal Impact of Commercial Drones' (2016) 45 *Technology in Society* 83, 86.

129 Ibid.

130 Vivek Wadhwa and Alex Salkever, *The Driver in the Driverless Car* (Berret-Koehler Publishers, 2017) 113–114.

131 Bharat Rao, Ashwin Goutham Gopi and Romana Maione, 'The Societal Impact of Commercial Drones' (2016) 45 *Technology in Society* 83, 86.

132 Vivek Wadhwa and Alex Salkever, *The Driver in the Driverless Car* (Berret-Koehler Publishers, 2017) 119.

Appendix

Principles for the Regulation of Drones Internationally by States

Preamble

Noting that these Guiding Principles build on and contextualise ICAO's efforts, and existing domestic laws in various jurisdictions.

Realising that the international community has safety, security, social, and financial interests in addressing the integration of drones into airspace in a timely, coordinated and targeted manner.

Realising further that there has been no significant coordinated response by States to address drones, whether temporary or permanent in nature.

Recognising the work being undertaken by ICAO and other inter-governmental and non-governmental organisations to address drone integration and related matters, including the development of drone-related SARPs.

Realising the need for a globally applicable framework to provide a coherent and principled approach for the collaborative and universally accepted regulation of drones.

Noting that these Guiding Principles, addressing the challenges to drone regulation both within States and across borders, necessarily complement other efforts to address such challenges.

Introduction

Principle 1: Scope and Purpose

These Guiding Principles:

a   provide a general framework, based on principles of aviation and international law and best practice, within which the operation of drones can be regulated to ensure the integration into existing airspace of drones both within States and across borders; and

b   set out overarching principles to inform rules and regulations including SARPs, treaties and domestic legislation.

Principle 2: Definitions

For the purposes of these Guiding Principles:

a   'Drone' means an aircraft and its associated elements which operate with no pilot on board – the word is given the same definition as ICAO's preferred term 'unmanned aircraft systems' (UAS).
b   'ICAO' means the International Civil Aviation Organisation.
c   'SARPs' mean ICAO's Standards and Recommended Practices.

Principle 3: Interpretation

a   These Guiding Principles shall not be interpreted as limiting, altering or otherwise prejudicing rights recognised in international aviation law or rights consistent with aviation laws and standards as recognised under domestic law, including civil aviation, privacy, safety and security.
b   States should interpret these Guiding Principles broadly, be guided by their purpose to harmonize and create uniformity amongst States to facilitate safe and effective use of drone technology, and display reasonableness and flexibility in their interpretation.

I. Operative Provisions

Principle 4: Airspace Sovereignty

States recognise that every State has complete and exclusive sovereignty over the airspace above its territory.

Principle 5: Paramount Importance of Safety

a   States recognise that safety is the overwhelming priority in the regulation of drones.
b   States shall apply existing safety regulations to drones. For matters which must be addressed differently because there is no pilot on board the aircraft, an alternative means of compliance shall, where possible, be chosen to achieve the same level of safety.
c   States shall carry out appropriate risk assessment when considering drone regulations that may compromise safety.

Principle 6: International Drone Operation

If States wish to permit cross-border drone operations, States shall cooperate in good faith and use best endeavours to negotiate relevant exchange of rights.

Principle 7: Air Traffic Management

States should implement air traffic management plans to ensure the safe and orderly flight of drones, taking into account existing airspace users.

Principle 8: Right of Way

a   Drones which do not have the size and characteristics of manned aircraft should yield the right of way to all aircraft, airborne vehicles, and launch and re-entry vehicles. Yielding the right of way means giving way to manned aircraft or vehicles and drones may not pass over, under, or ahead of them unless well clear.

b   No person may operate such drones so close to another aircraft as to create a collision hazard.

Principle 9: Operation over persons on the ground

States should prohibit the operation of drones close to or over a human being unless in the totality of the circumstances it would be considered reasonable from a safety perspective to allow such operation. This authorisation may be in the form of a waiver from the relevant State regulation(s).

Principle 10: Operation in the vicinity of airports

Drones should not be operated in a manner that interferes with operations and traffic patterns at any airport, heliport, or seaplane base or anywhere that an aircraft can take off or land.

Principle 11: Operation in prohibited or restricted areas

No person may operate a drone in prohibited or restricted areas unless that person has permission from the appropriate using or controlling body.

Principle 12: Security

States shall be responsible for ensuring their own security and should consider geofencing-like systems in locations that might raise an aviation safety or security concern.

Principle 13: Certificates and Licencing

States should avoid rigid entrenched rules for certification and licensing of drones until such time as international standards are developed by ICAO.

Principle 14: Registration

States should implement a system to register all drones. Such a system should take account of the characteristics of the drone and its type(s) of operation in determining the registration requirements. States should work towards an international system of registration.

Principle 15: Liability and Insurance

a The operator shall be liable for damage sustained by third parties upon condition only that the damage was caused by a drone in flight.
b States should require their drone operators to maintain adequate insurance or guarantee covering their liability.

Principle 16: Privacy

States should enact drone-specific regulations for both private and commercial drone operations to address privacy concerns.

Principle 17: ICAO's Role

States should look to ICAO as the international body to provide a regulatory framework for drone operations.

Principle 18: Interaction with SARPs

States should consider these guiding principles to provide direction for further action on regulating drones.

Principle 19: Development of technology

States should develop regulatory frameworks in such a manner to allow flexibility in accommodating new iterations of drone technology and unmanned flying objects.

II. General Obligations

Principle 20: National Implementation Measures

a States should incorporate provisions as set out in these Guiding Principles into domestic law and policies, prioritising airspace sovereignty and the safe integration of drone operations into existing airspace.
b Local, regional and national levels of government and instrumentalities should implement these Guiding Principles as appropriate.
c States should ensure the sustainable development of aviation through legislative and administrative mechanisms.
d All relevant legislation should be consistent with international law.

Principle 21: International and Assistance

a   The integration of drones into airspace is a matter of global importance, and States should cooperate to the fullest extent – as guided by ICAO – to establish an appropriate framework to regulate drones.

b   States may seek cooperation and assistance from other States and relevant international organisations in addressing drone-related matters.

III. Implementation

Principle 22: Implementation and Dissemination

States should implement and disseminate these Guiding Principles without delay and cooperate closely with ICAO, inter-governmental organisations, non-government organisations, the aviation industry, and civil society towards this end.

Bibliography

A Articles/Books/Reports

ACI, IATA and IFALPA, Joint Statement 'Safety Awareness for Users of Remotely Piloted Aircraft in Close Vicinity of Airports' (February 2016) <www.iata.org/whatwedo/safety/Documents/Safety-Awareness-for-RPA-users-joint-statment.pdf>

Anderson, John D., *The Airplane: A History of its Technology* (American Institute of Aeronautics and Astronautics, 2002)

Archibald, Douglas, *The Story of the Earth's Atmosphere* (George Newnes, 1897)

Atkins, Ella, Anibal Ollero and Anonios Tsourdos, *Unmanned Aircraft Systems* (Wiley, 2016)

Australian Government: Department of Infrastructure and Regional Development, *The Bilateral System – How International Air Services Work* (2014) <https://infrastructure.gov.au/aviation/international/bilateral_system.aspx>

Australian Government: Department of Infrastructure and Regional Development, Australia's Air Services Agreements/Arrangements (2017) <https://infrastructure.gov.au/aviation/international/agreements.aspx>

Banker, Steve, Drones Deliver Life Saving Medical Supplies in Africa (13 October 2017) Forbes <https://www.forbes.com/sites/stevebanker/2017/10/13/drones-deliver-life-saving-medical-supplies-in-africa>

Bartsch, Ron, James Coyne and Katherine Gray, *Drones in Society: Exploring the Strange New World of Unmanned Aircraft* (Routledge, 2017)

Bernauw, Kristian, 'Drones: The Emerging Era of Unmanned Civil Aviation' (2016) 66 *Collected Papers of Zagreb Law Faculty* 223

Brown, Ethan N., 'Please, Don't Let Me Drone On: The Need for Federally-Led and State-Collaborated Action to Promote Succinct and Efficient Drone Regulations' 16 *Kansas Journal of Law and Public Policy* 48

Bryant, John H., 'The First Century of Microwaves – 1886 to 1986' (1988) 36 *IEEE Transactions on Microwave Theory and Techniques* 830

Caldwell, Jillian, 'Protecting Privacy Post Lenah: Should the Courts Establish a New Tort or Develop Breach of Confidence?' (2003) 26 *UNSW Law Journal* 90

Cannizaro, Enzo, *The Law of Treaties beyond the Vienna Convention* (Oxford University Press, 2011)

Canter, Neil, 'RoboBees: Learning to Perch' (2016) 72 *Tribology & Lubrication Technology* 8

Cass, Stephen, 'Beyond the Quadcopter: New Designs for Drones Showcased at CeBIT' (2016) 53 *IEEE Spectrum* 21

Chaffey, Douglas C., 'The Right to Privacy in Canada' (1993) 108 *Political Science Quarterly* 117

Chen, G. Y. 'Reforming the Current Regulatory Framework for Commercial Drones: Retaining American Business' Competitive Advantage in the Global Economy', 37 *Northwestern Journal of International Law & Business* (2017) 513, 515–517

Civil Aviation Safety Authority, Advisory Circular 101–10 Remotely Piloted Aircraft Systems – Operation of Excluded RPA (other than model aircraft) (February 2017) <https://www.casa.gov.au/file/171461/download?token=rD99831v>

Clarke, Roger, 'Understanding the Drone Epidemic' (2014) 30 *Computer Law & Security Review* 230

Commercially Unmanned Flight – Remotely Piloted Aircraft under 2kg (2 November 2017) Civil Aviation Safety Authority <https://www.casa.gov.au/standard-page/commercial-unmanned-flight-remotely-piloted-aircraft-under-2kg>

Coyne, Christopher J., and Abigail R. Hall-Blanco, 'The Drone Paradox: Fighting Terrorism with Mechanized Terror' (2016) 16 *GMU Working Paper in Economics* 1

Crawford, James, 'The Criteria for Statehood in International Law' (1977) 48 *British Yearbook of International Law* 93

Crook, Terry M., 'DoD Cracks Down on Use of Drones over Installations' (7 August 2017) United States of America: Department of Defence <https://www.defense.gov/News/Article/Article/1270758/dod-cracks-down-on-use-of-drones-over-installations/>

Current Lists of Parties to Multilateral Air Treaties (2017) International Civil Aviation Organisation <https://www.icao.int/secretariat/legal/Lists/Current%20lists%20of%20parties/AllItems.aspx>

Current Unmanned Aircraft State Law Landscape (25 July 2017) National Conference of State Legislatures <www.ncsl.org/research/transportation/current-unmanned-aircraft-state-law-landscape.aspx#1>

Custers, Bart (ed), *The Future of Drone Use: Opportunities and Threats from Ethical and Legal Perspectives* (Springer, 2016)

DeGarmo, Matthew T., 'Issues Concerning Integration of Unmanned Aerial Vehicles in Civil Airspace' (2004) *MITRE* 4

Diederiks-Verschoor, I. H. Philepina, *An Introduction to Air Law* (Wolters Kluwer, 9th ed, 2012)

The Economist, Why the Wait for Delivery Drones may be Longer than Expected (10 June 2017) <https://www.economist.com/news/technology-quarterly/21723002-carrying-cargo-lot-more-complicated-carrying-camera-why-wait>

European Aviation Safety Agency, *'Prototype' Commission Regulation on Unmanned Aircraft Operations* (22 August 2016) <https://www.easa.europa.eu/system/files/dfu/UAS%20Prototype%20Regulation%20final.pdf>

Eyes in the Sky: Inquiry into Drones and the Regulation of Air Safety and Privacy (July 2014) House of Representatives Standing Committee on Social Policy and Legal Affairs, Parliament of Australia <https://www.aph.gov.au/Parliamentary_Business/Committees/House/Social_Policy_and_Legal_Affairs/Drones/Report>

Fernando, Fiallos, 'United States' in Benjamyn I. Scott (ed), *The Law of Unmanned Aircraft Systems: An Introduction to the Current and Future Regulation under National, Regional and International Law* (Wolters Kluwer, 2016)

Finn, Rachel L., and David Wright, 'Unmanned Aircraft Systems: Surveillance, Ethics and Privacy in Civil Applications' 28 *Computer Law and Security Review* 184

Floreano, Dario, and Robert J. Wood, 'Science, Technology and the Future of Small Autonomous Drones' (2015) 521 *Nature* 460

Flying Drones or Model Aircraft Recreationally (23 October 2017) Civil Aviation Safety Authority <https://www.casa.gov.au/modelaircraft>

Flying Drones/Remotely Piloted Aircraft in Australia (14 November 2017) Civil Aviation Safety Authority <https://www.casa.gov.au/aircraft/landing-page/flying-drones-australia>

Flying Your Drone Safely and Legally (1 November 2017) Government of Canada <https://www.tc.gc.ca/eng/civilaviation/opssvs/flying-drone-safely-legally.html>

Gaining Your Remote Pilot Licence (RePL) and RPA Operator's Certificate (ReOC) (31 October 2017) Civil Aviation Safety Authority <https://www.casa.gov.au/aircraft/standard-page/commercial-unmanned-flight-gaining-your-remotely-piloted-aircraft-pilot>

Getting Started (31 July 2017) Federal Aviation Administration <https://www.faa.gov/uas/getting_started/>

International Civil Aviation Organisation, 'Circular 328 AN/190: Unmanned Aircraft Systems (UAS)' (Paper presented at the Seminar on Unmanned Aircraft Systems (UAS), Lima, Peru, 18 April 2012 to 20 April 2012)

Gibbs-Smith, Charles H., 'Sir George Cayley: "Father of Aerial Navigation" (1773–1857)' (2012) 17 *Notes and Records of the Royal Society of London* 36

Gulliver, Dubai is to Test Passenger-Carrying Drones (17 February 2017) *The Economist* <https://www.economist.com/blogs/gulliver/2017/02/taxi-take-0>

Guttman, Robert, 'Drones: The Hollywood Connection: Actor Reginald Denny was Instrumental in Launching the Target Drone, and His Factory Launched a New Star' (2017) 27 *Aviation History* 48

Hailbronner, Kay, 'Freedom of the Air and the Convention on the Law of the Sea' (1983) 77 *The American Journal of International Law* 490

Harper, William, 'A Lesson from Minerva' (2012) 51 *Quest* 102

Harsch, Viktor, Benny Bardrum and Petra Illig, 'Lilienthal's Fatal Glider Crash in 1896: Evidence Regarding the Cause of Death' (2008) 79 *Aviation, Space and Environmental Medicine* 993

Hassanalian, Mostafa, and Abdessattar Abdelkefi, 'Classifications, Applications and Design Challenges of Drones: A Review' (2017) 91 *Progress in Aerospace Sciences* 99

Havel, Brian F., and John Q. Mulligan, 'Unmanned Aircraft Systems: A Challenge to Global Regulators' (2016) 65 *DePaul Law Review* 107

Havel, Brian F., and Gabriel S. Sanchez, *The Principles and Practice of International Aviation Law* (Cambridge University Press, 2014)

Helfer, Laurence R., 'Not Fully Committed? Reservations, Risk and Treaty Design' (2006) 31 *Yale Journal of International Law* 367

Higgins, Rosalyn, *Problems and Process – International Law and How We Use It* (Clarenden, 1994)

Hodgkinson, David, and Rebecca Johnston, *International Air Carrier Liability: Safety and Security* (Routledge, 2017)

IATA, 'Fact Sheet – Unmanned Aircraft Systems' (June 2017) <https://www.iata.org/pressroom/facts_figures/fact_sheets/Documents/fact-sheet-unmanned-aicraft-systems.pdf>

International Air Transport Association, 'Safety of Remotely Piloted Aircraft Systems' (Working Paper to ICAO, HLSC/15-WP/98, 2015)

International Air Transport Association, IATA Releases 2016 Airline Safety Performance (10 March 2017) <www.iata.org/pressroom/pr/Pages/2017-03-10-01.aspx>

International Air Transport Association, The Montreal Convention 1999 (MC99) (2017) <www.iata.org/policy/smarter-regulation/Pages/mc99.aspx>

International Civil Aviation Organisation, Circular 328 AN/190 Unmanned Aircraft Systems (UAS)

International Civil Aviation Organisation, Doc 7278-C/841: Definition of Scheduled International Air Service (1952)

International Civil Aviation Organization, Doc 9626: Manual on the Regulation of International Air Transport (2004) <https://www.icao.int/Meetings/atconf6/Documents/Doc%209626_en.pdf>

International Civil Aviation Organisation, Doc 9854 AN/458: Global Air Traffic Management Operational Concept (2005)

International Civil Aviation Organisation, Doc 10019: Manual on Remotely Piloted Aircraft Systems (1st ed, 2015)

International Civil Aviation Organisation, 'Integrating RPAS into Airspace' (2015) 70(2) *ICAO Journal* 4 <https://www.icao.int/publications/journalsreports/2015/7002_en.pdf>

International Civil Aviation Organisation, *Manual on Remotely Piloted Aircraft Systems (RPAS): ICAO Doc 10019* (1st ed, 2015)

International Civil Aviation Organisation, DRONE ENABLE, ICAO's Unmanned Aircraft Systems (UAS) Industry Symposium (21 June 2017) *International Civil Aviation Organisation* <https://www.icao.int/Meetings/UAS2017/Pages/default.aspx>

International Civil Aviation Organisation, Request for Information (2017) <https://www.icao.int/Meetings/UAS2017/Pages/Request-for-Information.aspx>

JARUS, JARUS – Who We Are & What We Do (November 2017) <http://jarus-rpas.org/sites/jarus-rpas.org/files/revision_jarus_who_we_are_what_we_do_v_6_0_version_15112017.pdf>

Jha, A. R., *Theory, Design, and Applications of Unmanned Aerial Vehicles* (CRC Press, 2017)

Kakaes, Konstantinet al, *Drones and Aerial Observation: New Technologies for Property Rights, Human Rights, and Global Development* (New America, 2015)

Kirby, Michael, 'The Impact of International Human Rights Norms: A Law Undergoing Evolution' (1995) 25 *Western Australian Law Review* 1

Kirby, Michael, 'Constitutional Law and International Law: National Exceptionalism and the Democratic Deficit?' (2010) 98(2) *The Georgetown Law Journal* 433

Kirby, Richard S., *Engineering in History* (Courier Corporation, 1990)

Kreps, Sarah E., *Drones: What Everyone Needs to Know* (Oxford University Press, 2016)

Kwasniak, Andrew and Anita Kerezman, 'Drones in Transportation Engineering: A Discussion of Current Drone Rules, Equipment and Applications' (2017) 87 *ITE Journal of Transportation Engineers* 40

Large Unmanned Aircraft (2015) UK Civil Aviation Authority <www.caa.co.uk/Commercial-industry/Aircraft/Unmanned-aircraft/Large-unmanned-aircraft/>

Lauzon, Gilles, 'The New ICAO Conventions on Third Party Liability' (2009) 14(3) *Uniform Law Review-Revue de droit uniforme* 676, 676 <http://109.168.120.21/siti/Unidroit/index/pdf/XIV-3-0676.pdf>

Lele, Ajay, and Archana Mischra, 'Aerial Terrorism and the Threat from Unmanned Aerial Vehicles' (2009) 3 *Journal of Defence Studies* 54

Lin, James C., and Paolo Bernadi, 'Editorial: Exposure Hazards and Health Protection in Personal Communication Services' (1997) 3 *Wireless Networks* 435

Lovett, Thomas D., 'Ruling the Skies or Drowning in Rules? A Look at the FAA's Sluggish Progress in Developing Rules and Forces that Might Be Shaping the Future of Drone Use in the United States' (2016) 21 *Barry Law Review* 251

Making an ICAO Standard (1 November 2011) International Civil Aviation Organisation <https://www.icao.int/safety/airnavigation/Pages/standard.aspx>

Marshall, D. 'Unmanned Aerial Systems and International Civil Aviation Organization Regulations' (2009) 85 *NDL Review*, 693

Marston, Philip L., 'James Clerk Maxwell: Life and Science' (2016) 178 *Journal of Quantitative Spectroscopy and Radiative Transfer* 50

Mason, Anthony, 'The Australian Constitution 1901–1988' (1988) 62 *Australian Law Journal* 752

Mason, Anthony, 'Should the High Court Consider Policy Implications when Making Judicial Decisions?' (1997) 57(1) *Australian Journal of Public Administration* 77–80

Masutti, Anna, 'Proposals for the Regulation of Unmanned Air Vehicle Use in Common Airspace' (2009) 34 *Air and Space Law* 1

Medalla, Erlinda M., *Competition Policy in East Asia* (Routledge, 2005)

Mehanovic, Dino, 'Autonomous Thrust-Assisted Perching of a Fixed-Wing UAV on Vertical Surfaces' in Michael Mangan et al (eds) *Biomimetic and Biohybrid Systems: 6th International Conference, Living Machines, California, 2017* (Springer, 2017)

Michaelides-Mateou, Sofia, and Chrystel Erotokritou, 'Flying into the Future with UAVs: The Jetstream 31 Flight' (2014) 39 *Air and Space Law* 111

Milojevich, Allyn K., 'Proliferation of Unmanned Aerial Systems (Drones) and Policy Challenges on the Horizon: A Policy Memorandum to John P. Holdren' (2013) 8 *Journal of Science* 1

Mirza, Muhammad Nadeem et al, 'Unmanned Aerial Vehicles: A Revolution in the Making' (2016) 31 *Research Journal of South Asian Studies* 625

Mistry, Michael et al, *Advances in Autonomous Robotics Systems* (Springer, 2014)

Model Aircraft (2015) UK Civil Aviation Authority <www.caa.co.uk/Consumers/Unmanned-aircraft/Model-aircraft/>

Moor, James H., 'Towards a Theory of Privacy in the Information Age' (1997) 27 *Computers and Society* 27

National Conference of State Legislature, Current Unmanned Aircraft State Law Landscape <www.ncsl.org/research/transportation/current-unmanned-aircraft-state-law-landscape.aspx>

Newcombe, Laurence R., *Unmanned Aviation: A Brief History of Unmanned Aerial Vehicles* (American Institute of Aeronautics and Astronautics, 2004)

No Drone Zones (1 November 2017) Government of Canada <https://www.tc.gc.ca/eng/civilaviation/opssvs/no-drone-zones.html>

Notice of Proposed Amendment 2017–05 (A): Introduction of a Regulatory Framework for the Operation of Drones (2017) European Aviation Safety Agency <https://www.easa.europa.eu/system/files/dfu/NPA%202017-05%20%28A%29_0.pdf>

Olsen, R., 'Paperweights: FAA Regulation and the Banishment of Commercial Drones' (2017) 32(AR) *Berkley Technology Law Journal*

Perritt, Henry H., and Eliot O. Sprague, *Domesticating Drones: The Technology, Law and Economics of Unmanned Aircraft* (Routledge, 2017)

Peterson, Mark E., 'Regulatory Construct for Integration into the National Airspace System' (2006) 71 *Journal of Air Law and Commerce* 521

Powell, Rebecca, NASA and NOAA Fly Unmanned Aircraft into Hurricane Noel (3 April 2008) National Aeronautics and Space Administration <https://www.nasa.gov/centers/wallops/news/story105.html>

Proposed Rules for Drones in Canada (30 August 2017) Government of Canada <https://www.tc.gc.ca/eng/civilaviation/opssvs/proposed-rules-drones-canada.html>

Prototype Commission Regulation on Unmanned Aircraft Operations (22 August 2016) European Aviation Safety Agency <https://www.easa.europa.eu/system/files/dfu/UAS%20Prototype%20Regulation%20final.pdf>

Rachels, James, 'Why Privacy is Important' (1975) 4 *Philosophy and Public Affairs* 323

Rao, Bharat, Ashwin Goutham Gopi and Romana Maione, 'The Societal Impact of Commercial Drones' (2016) 45 *Technology in Society* 83

Rappaport, Theodore S., Wonil Roh and Kyungwhoon Cheun, 'Mobile's Millimeter-Wave Makeover' (2014) 51 *IEEE Spectrum* 34

Recreational Drone Flights (2015) UK Civil Aviation Authority <www.caa.co.uk/Consumers/Unmanned-aircraft/Recreational-drones/Recreational-drone-flights/>

Regulation (EC) No 216/2008 of the European Aviation Safety Agency of 20 February 2008 on Common Rules in the Field of Civil Aviation and Establishing a European Aviation Safety Agency, and Repealing Council Directive 91/670/EEC Regulation (EC) No 1592/2002 and Directive 2004/36/E [2008] OJ L 79/1

Regulation of Drones: Australia (26 July 2016) Library of Congress <https://www.loc.gov/law/help/regulation-of-drones/australia.php>

Regulations Relating to the Commercial Use of Small Drones (2015) UK Civil Aviation Authority <www.caa.co.uk/Commercial-industry/Aircraft/Unmanned-aircraft/Small-drones/Regulations-relating-to-the-commercial-use-of-small-drones/>

Reiman, Jeffrey H., 'Privacy, Intimacy, and Personhood' (1976) 6 *Philosophy and Public Affairs* 26

Richardson, Jacques, 'Leonardo: Why the Inventor Failed to Innovate' (2005) 7 *The Journal of Futures Studies, Strategic Thinking and Policy* 56

Riga Declaration on Remotely Piloted Aircraft – Framing the Future of Aviation, Riga (6 March 2015) <https://ec.europa.eu/transport/sites/transport/files/modes/air/news/doc/2015-03-06-drones/2015-03-06-riga-declaration-drones.pdf>

RPAS, UAV, UAS, Drones and Model Aircraft (March 2016) Civil Aviation Authority of New Zealand <https://www.caa.govt.nz/rpas/>

Safety Management Manual (2013) International Civil Aviation Organisation<https://www.icao.int/safety/SafetyManagement/Documents/Doc.9859.3rd%20Edition.all text.en.pdf>

Saripalli, Srikanth, James F. Montogomery and Gaurav S. Sukhatme, 'Vision-Based Autonomous Landing of an Unmanned Aerial Vehicle' (Proceedings: IEEE International Conference on Robotics and Automation, Washington DC, 2002)

Scott, Benjamyn I. (ed), *The Law of Unmanned Aircraft Systems: An Introduction to the Current and Future Regulation under National, Regional and International Law* (Wolters Kluwer, 2016)

Security (2017) International Civil Aviation Organisation <https://www.icao.int/Security/Pages/default.aspx>

Shawcross, C. N. and K. C. Beaumont, *Shawcross and Beaumont: Air Law* (LexisNexis Butterworths, 1997)

Shelley, Andrew, 'Application of New Zealand Privacy Law to Drones' (2016) 12 *Policy Quarterly* 73

Stanton, Neville A., Christopher Baber and Don Harris, *Modelling Command and Control: Event Analysis of Systemic Teamwork* (Ashgate, 2008)

State Government of Victoria, Future Directions Paper: How Victoria Will Continue to Support the Development of Automated Vehicles (15 December 2016) <http://apo.org.au/system/files/71905/apo-nid71905-50871.pdf>

Stewart, Pam, 'Drone Danger: Remedies for Damage by Civilian Remotely Piloted Aircraft to Persons or Property on the Ground in Australia' (2016) 23 *Torts Law Journal* 290

Strantz, Nancy J., 'Aviation Security and Pan Am Flight 103: What Have We Learned' (1990) 56 *Journal of Air Law and Commerce* 413

Terdiman, Daniel, A Startup's Plan to Cut Air Freight Costs in Half with 777-Size Drones (27 March 2017) Fast Company <https://www.fastcompany.com/3069053/a-startups-plan-to-halve-cargo-shipping-costs-with-777-size-drones>

Treaties (August 2010) House of Commons Information Office <https://www.parliament.uk/documents/commons-information-office/p14.pdf>

Treaty-Making Options for Australia (1996) Parliament of Australia <https://www.aph.gov.au/About_Parliament/Parliamentary_Departments/Parliamentary_Library/Publications_Archive/CIB/cib9596/96cib17>

Treaty Making Process (2017) Australian Government: Department of Foreign Affairs and Trade <http://dfat.gov.au/international-relations/treaties/treaty-making-process/pages/treaty-making-process.aspx>

Uber, Fast-Forwarding to a Future of On-Demand Urban Air Transportation (27 October 2016) <https://www.uber.com/elevate.pdf>

United Kingdom Civil Aviation Authority, Permissions and Exemptions for Drone Flights (2015) <https://www.caa.co.uk/Consumers/Unmanned-aircraft/Recreational-drones/Permissions-and-exemptions-for-drone-flights/>

United Kingdom Civil Aviation Authority, 'Unmanned Aircraft System Operations in UK Airspace - Guidance' (2015) *CAP* 722

Unmanned Aircraft (14 November 2017) European Commission <http://ec.europa.eu/growth/sectors/aeronautics/rpas_en>

Valvanis, Kimon P. (ed), *Advances in Unmanned Aerial Vehicles* (Springer, 2007)

Villa, Tommaso F. et al, 'An Overview of Small Unmanned Aerial Vehicles for Air Quality Measurements: Present Applications and Future Prospectives' (2016) 16 *Sensors* 1072

Villasenor, John, 'Drones and the Future of Domestic Aviation' (2014) 102 *Proceedings of the IEEE* 235

Wadhwa, Vivek, and Alex Salkever, *The Driver in the Driverless Car* (Berret-Koehler Publishers, 2017)

Warwick, Graham, More Airlines Turn to UAVs for Aircraft Inspection (25 September 2015) *Aviation Week Network* <http://aviationweek.com/mro-enterprise-software/more-airlines-turn-uavs-aircraft-inspection>

Webb, Janeen, and Jack Dann, 'Lawrence Hargrave: Unheralded Aeroplane Engineer' 17 *Omni* 24

Winston, Mark L., *The Biology of the Honey Bee* (Harvard University Press, 1991)

Xinhua, 'China Requires Real-Name Registration for Civilian Drones' (16 May 2017) The State Council of The People's Republic of China <http://english.gov.cn/news/top_news/2017/05/16/content_281475657535848.htm>

Zaloga, Steven J., *Unmanned Aerial Vehicles: Robotic Air Warfare 1917–2007* (Bloomsbury Publishing, 2011)

Zumbuch, Kristina, and Roland Scherer, 'Cross-Border Governance: Balancing Formalised and Less Formalised Co-Operations' (2015) 4 *Social Sciences* 499

B Cases

Bernstein of Leigh v Skyviews and General Ltd [1978] 1 *QB* 479

Chow Hung Ching v The King (1949) 77 *CLR* 449

Commonwealth v Tasmania (1983) 158 *CLR* 1

Koowarta v Bjelke-Petersen (1982) 153 *CLR* 168

Mabo v Queensland (No 2) (1992) 175 *CLR* 1

Minister of State for Immigration and Ethnic Affairs v Ah Hin Teoh (1995) 128 *ALR* 353
Polites v Commonwealth (1945) 70 *CLR* 60
United States v Causby, 328 *US* 256(1946)

C Legislation

An Act to Exempt Certain Unmanned Aircraft Systems from the Requirement to be Registered as Aircraft, ch 50–11, §§ 50–11–9, SD Sess Laws 746 (2017)
An Act Relating to Unmanned Aircraft Systems, ch 72, Or Laws 837.340 and 837.365(2017)
Canadian Aviation Regulations (SOR/96–433)
Civil Aviation Act Consolidation Part 61 Pilot Licences and Ratings 2017 (Civil Aviation Rules of New Zealand)
Civil Aviation Regulation, Supplementary Instruction No. 21–002/2012 (2012) (National Civil Aviation Agency of Brazil)
Civil Aviation Safety Regulations 1998 (Cth)
Criminal Code Act 1899 (Qld)
Directive 2009/48/EC of the European Parliament and of the Council of 18 June 2009 on the Safety of Toys [2009] OJ L 170/1
Federal Aviation Regulations, Small Unmanned Aircraft Regulations (2016) CFR
Federal Law on Amendment of the Air Code of the Russian Federation on Use of Unmanned Aircraft, No. 462-FZ (30 December 2015)
La Constitution du octobre 1985 [French Constitution of 4 October 1958]
Regulation (EC) No 785/204 of the European Parliament and of the Council of 21 April 2004 [2004] L 138/1
Remotely Piloted Aerial Vehicles Regulation 2013 (Italian Civil Aviation Authority)

D Treaties

Cape Town Convention and Aircraft Protocol, opened for signature 16 November 2001, 2307 UNTS 285 (entered into force 1 March 2001)
Convention on Compensation for Damage Caused by Aircraft to Third Parties, DCCD Doc No 42 (2 May 2009) International Civil Aviation Organisation
Convention on International Civil Aviation (Chicago Convention), opened for signature 7 December 1944, 15 UNTS 295 (entered into force 4 April 1947)
International Civil Aviation Organisation, *Annex 2 to the Convention on International Civil Aviation: Rules of the Air* (10th ed, 2005)
United Nations Convention on the Law of the Sea, opened for signature 10 December 1982, 1833UNTS 3 (entered into force16 November 1994)
Vienna Convention on the Law of Treaties, opened for signature 23 May 1969, 1155 UNTS 331 (entered into force 27 January 1980)

E Other

Aamoth, Doug, Cryptids: The Saqqara Bird (9 June 2010) *Time* <http://techland.time.com/2010/06/09/cryptids-the-saqqara-bird/>
About Us (2017) Campaign to Stop Killer Robots <https://www.stopkillerrobots.org/about-us/>
Amazon Unveils Futuristic Plan: Delivery by Drone (1 December 2013) CBS News <https://www.cbsnews.com/news/amazon-unveils-futuristic-plan-delivery-by-drone/>

Aquila: Facebook's Solar-powered Internet Drone Takes Flight (22 July 2016) ABC News <www.abc.net.au/news/2016-07-22/aquila-facebook-solar-powered-internet-drone-takes-flight/7651394>

Autonomous Flying Microrobots (RoboBees) (2017) Wyss Institute <https://wyss.harva rd.edu/technology/autonomous-flying-microrobots-robobees/>

Aviation: Commission is Taking the European Drone Sector to New Heights (16 June 2017) European Commission <http://europa.eu/rapid/press-release_IP-17-1605_en.htm>

Bort, Julie, Google's Drone Delivery Project Just Shared Some Big News about its Future (8 June 2017) *Business Insider Australia* <https://www.businessinsider.com. au/project-wing-update-future-google-drone-delivery-project-2017-6?r=US&IR=T>

Canavan, Matt$12 Million Boost for Positioning Technology in Australia (17 January 2017) <http://minister.industry.gov.au/ministers/canavan/media-releases/12-million-boost-positioning-technology-australia>

Carey, Bill, 'ICAO Panel Will Recommend First UAV Standards in 2018' (6 January 2015) AIN Online <www.ainonline.com/aviation-news/aerospace/2015-01-06/icao-panel-will-recommend-first-uav-standards-2018>

Castle, Jarrod, Q-Series: Flying Solo – How Far Are We down the Path towards Pilotless Planes? (7 August 2017) UBS <http://nzz-files-prod.s3-website-eu-west-1. amazonaws.com/2017/8/7/93872795-5ab9-4f94-bb3a-f6ed38c6b886.pdf>

Cece, Beata, Future of Urban Mobility: My Kind of Flyover (6 December 2016) Airbus <www.airbus.com/newsroom/news/en/2016/12/My-Kind-Of-Flyover.html>

Civilian Drones (2017) *The Economist* <www.economist.com/technology-quarterly/ 2017-06-08/civilian-drones>

CNN Receives Breakthrough Part 107 Waiver for Operations over People (18 October 2017) CNN Communications <http://cnnpressroom.blogs.cnn.com/2017/10/18/ cnn-receives-breakthrough-part-107-waiver-for-operations-over-people/>

Cowan, Jane, Driverless Cars: Everything You Need to Know about the Transport Revolution (11 March 2017) *ABC News* <www.abc.net.au/news/2017-03-11/ everything-you-need-to-know-about-driverless-cars/8336322>

Dormehl, Luke, 'The Home-Inspecting Aire Drone Looks like a Flying Amazon Echo ' (19 September 2017) Digital Trends <https://www.digitaltrends.com/cool-tech/a ire-flying-security-guard/>

Dowling, James, Drones to be Banned from Flying Near or Above Prisons (8 May 2017) *Herald Sun* <www.heraldsun.com.au/news/law-order/drones-to-be-banned-from-flying-near-or-above-prisons/news-story/eea583a d5de2d64e1267be4e0e92d74f>

Drone Insurance (2015) *Allianz* <www.agcs.allianz.com/services/aviation/drone-insurance/>

Drones: Reporting for Work (9 October 2016) Goldman Sachs

EHang Partners with Dubai RTA to Boost Smart Transport (5 February 2017) EHang <www.ehang.com/news/248.html>

EHang 184: Autonomous Aerial Vehicle (AAV) (6 January 2016) EHang

EPFL Develops New Origami-Inspired Delivery Drone (14 September 2017) Aerospace Technology <www.aerospace-technology.com/news/newsepfl-develops-new-origami-inspired-delivery-drone-5926689>

European Aviation Safety Agency, Civil Drones (Unmanned aircraft) <https://www.easa. europa.eu/easa-and-you/civil-drones-rpas>

Eysenck, Juliet, How Drones are Changing Our Lives: The Good, the Bad and the Lazy (25 May 2016) *The Telegraph* <www.telegraph.co.uk/technology/2016/05/23/how-drone-technology-is-changing-our-lives-the-good-the-bad-and/>

Facebook Drone That Could Bring Global Internet Access Completes Test Flight (3 July 2017) *The Guardian* <https://www.theguardian.com/technology/2017/jul/02/facebook-drone-aquila-internet-test-flight-arizona>

Farquhar, Peter, China is Using a Flamethrower Drone to Clean Rubbish off Power-lines (20 February 2017) *Business Insider* <www.businessinsider.com/china-is-using-a-flamethrowing-drone-to-clean-rubbish-off-power-lines-2017-2?IR=T>

Fast-Forwarding to a Future of On-Demand Urban Air Transportation (27 October 2016) Uber <https://www.uber.com/elevate.pdf>

Federal Aviation Administration, 'Unmanned Aircraft Systems (UAS) Frequently Asked Questions' (11 July 2017) United States Department of Transportation <https://www.faa.gov/uas/faqs/>

Fingas, Jon, Drone Pilots in China have to Register with the Government (17 May 2017) Engadget <https://www.engadget.com/2017/05/17/china-drone-registrations/>

Flying Air Taxis from Germany Conquer the World (1 August 2017) Volocopter <https://press.volocopter.com/index.php/flying-air-taxis-from-germany-conquer-the-world>

Germanwings Plane Crash: Co-Pilot Andreas Lubitz Crashed Plane Deliberately, French Prosecutor Says (27 March 2015) *ABC News* <www.abc.net.au/news/2015-03-26/germanwings-co-pilot-andreas-lubitz-crashed-plane-deliberately/6351854>

Gibbs, Samuel, World's First Passenger Drone Cleared for Testing in Nevada (8 June 2016) *The Guardian* <https://www.theguardian.com/technology/2016/jun/08/worlds-first-passenger-drone-testing-ehang-nevada>

Gomez, Martin, Aquila's Successful Second Flight: Another Step forward in Bringing the World Closer Together (30 June 2017) <https://code.facebook.com/posts/200887800439084/aquila-s-successful-second-flight-another-step-forward-in-bringing-the-world-closer-together/>

Heater, Brian, 'Teaching Teams of Drones to Work alongside Humans and Nature' (8 June 2016) Tech Crunch <https://techcrunch.com/2017/06/08/teaching-teams-of-drones-to-work-alongside-humans-and-nature/>

Hern, Alex, Richard Branson's Virgin Group Invests in Hyperloop One (13 October 2017) *The Guardian* <https://www.theguardian.com/technology/2017/oct/12/richard-branson-virgin-group-invests-hyperloop-one>

Holman, Brett, The First Air Bomb: Venice, 15 July 1849 (22 August 2009) *Airminded: Airpower and British Society* 1901–1941 <https://airminded.org/2009/08/22/the-first-air-bomb-venice-15-july-1849/>

How an Alleged Voyeur Modified his Drone to be a High-Tech Peeping Tom (17 February 2017) Inside Edition <www.insideedition.com/headlines/21724-how-an-alleged-voyeur-modified-his-drone-to-be-a-high-tech-peeping-tom>

Hsu, Jeremy, Disposable Drones Could Deliver Supplies under Enemy Fire (5 August 2017) WIRED <https://www.wired.com/2017/05/disposable-drones-deliver-supplies-enemy-fire/>

India Delivers First Pizza by Drone, Kind Of… (29 May 2014) NBC News <https://www.nbcnews.com/news/world/india-delivers-first-pizza-drone-kind-n117611>

International Civil Aviation Organisation, Frequently Used Terms <https://www4.icao.int/uastoolkit/Home/FAQ>

International Civil Aviation Organisation, *Background* <https://www4.icao.int/uastoolkit/Home/Narrative>

James, Gregory K., Unmanned Aerial Vehicles and Special Operations: Future Directions (Postgraduate Thesis, Monterey, California Naval Postgraduate School, 2000)

Joshi, Divya, 'Commercial Unmanned Aerial Vehicle (UAV) Market Analysis – Industry Trends, Companies and What You Should Know' (8 August 2017) *Business Insider* <www.businessinsider.com/commercial-uav-market-analysis-2017-8/?r=AU&IR=T>

Khvilivitzky, Alexander, 'Visual Collision Avoidance System for Unmanned Aerial Vehicles' U.S. Patent 5581250A filed 8 June 2006

Langewiesche, William, The Human Factor (October 2014) *Vanity Fair* <https://www.vanityfair.com/news/business/2014/10/air-france-flight-447-crash>

Lauzon, Gilles, 'The New ICAO Conventions on Third Party Liability' (2009) Uniform Law Instruments <http://109.168.120.21/siti/Unidroit/index/pdf/XIV-3-0676.pdf>

Lifting Personal Transportation into the Third Dimension (2017) myCopter <www.mycopter.eu>

Lilium Celebrates Successful Flight Tests of World's First Electric VTOL Jet (20 April 2017) Lilium <https://lilium.com/press-releases/lilium-celebrates-successful-flights-tests.pdf>

Maguire, Yael and Martin Gomez, Reviewing Aquila's First Full-Scale Test Flight (16 December 2016) Facebook <https://code.facebook.com/posts/1186557928107489/reviewing-aquila-s-first-full-scale-test-flight/>

Marchand, Alexandre, One Step Ahead at All Times: Helicopter Innovation at Airbus (27 July 2017) Airbus <www.airbus.com/newsroom/news/en/2017/07/helicopter-innovation-at-airbus.html>

Markoff, John, No Longer a Dream: Silicon Valley Takes on the Flying Car (24 April 2017) *The New York Times* <https://www.nytimes.com/2017/04/24/technology/flying-car technology.html?hp&action=click&pgtype=Homepage&clickSource=story-heading&module=second-column-region%AEion=top-news&WT.nav=top-news>

McSweeney, Kelly, Drones Help with Hurricane Recovery Efforts (26 September 2017) ZD Net <www.zdnet.com/article/drones-help-with-hurricane-recovery- efforts/>

Military can Destroy Drones over Domestic U.S. Bases: Pentagon (8 August 2017) Reuters <https://www.reuters.com/article/us-usa-military-drone-idUSKBN1AN2BP>

Mogg, Trevor, BBC News Launches Hexacopter 'Flying Camera' to Give Viewers the Bigger Picture (29 October 2013) Digital Trends <https://www.digitaltrends.com/cool-tech/bbc-news-hexacopter/>

Mohan, Manimaran, Cybersecurity in Drones (Senior Capstone Thesis, Utica College, 2016)

Oswald, Ed, Here's Everything You Need to Know about Amazon's Drone Delivery Project, Prime Air (3 May 2017) Digital Trends <https://www.digitaltrends.com/cool-tech/amazon-prime-air-delivery-drones-history-progress>

Pan Am Flight 103 (16 November 2017) Encyclopaedia Britannica <https://www.britannica.com/event/Pan-Am-flight-103>

Pre-Aviation UAV's: Perley's Aerial Bomber (USA) NOVA <www.pbs.org/wgbh/nova/spiesfly/uavs_01.html>

Rethinking Urban Air Mobility (17 June 2017) Airbus <www.airbus.com/newsroom/topics-in-focus/urban-air-mobility.html>

Rushe, Dominic, Google Reveals Home Delivery Drone Program Project Wing (30 August 2014) *The Guardian* <https://www.theguardian.com/technology/2014/aug/29/google-joins-amazon-in-testing-home-delivery-drones>

Schladebeck, Jessica, Utah Couple Charged with Voyeurism for Allegedly Recording Unsuspecting People with Drone (16 February 2017) *Daily News* <www.nydaily

news.com/news/crime/couple-charged-voyeurism-recording-people-drone-article-1.
2974236>

Singer, Peter W., The Predator Comes Home: A Primer on Domestic Drones, their Huge Business Opportunities, and their Deep Political, Moral and Legal Challenges (8 March 2013) <https://www.brookings.edu/research/the-predator-comes-home-a-primer-on-domestic-drones-their-huge-business-opportunities-and-their-deep-politica l-moral-and-legal-challenges/>

Swarm Up to the Idea: A Boeing Lab Experiments with Multiple Unmanned Vehicle Behaviours (11 January 2017) Boeing <www.boeing.com/features/2017/01/casl-la b-01-17.page>

Theilmann, Connor A., Integrating Autonomous Drones into the National Aerospace System (Senior Capstone Thesis, University of Pennsylvania, 2015)

The Economic Impact of Unmanned Aircraft Systems Integration in the United States (March 2013) Association for Unmanned Vehicle Systems International <https:// higherlogicdownload.s3.amazonaws.com/AUVSI/958c920a-7f9b-4ad2-9807-f9a 4e95d1ef1/UploadedImages/New_Economic%20Report%202013%20Full.pdf>

'The Wright Brothers' and Langley's Aeroplanes' (1928) 122 *Nature* 930

Using Static Electricity, RoboBees Cling to Surface (19 May 2016) Wyss Institute <https:// wyss.harvard.edu/using-static-electricity-robobees-cling-to-surface/>

Volocopter as an Autonomous Air Taxi in Dubai (19 June 2017) Volocopter <https:// press.volocopter.com/index.php/volocopter-as-an-autonomous-air-taxi-in-dubai>

Wallop, Harry, Drones – How they Became the Gadget of 2014 (9 December 2014) *The Telegraph* <www.telegraph.co.uk/technology/news/11280750/Drones-how-they-became-the-gadget-of-2014.html>

Welcome to the International Registry (2017) International Registry of Mobile Assets <https://www.internationalregistry.aero/ir-web/index>

YouTube, Drone Almost Hits Marcel Hirscher (22 December 2015) <https://www. youtube.com/watch?v=p9T6-KPFRq8>

Zuckerberg, Mark, The Technology behind Aquila (22 July 2016) Facebook <https:// www.facebook.com/notes/mark-zuckerberg/the-technology-behind-aquila/ 10153916136506634/>

Index

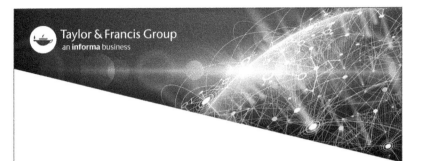

Taylor & Francis Group
an **informa** business

Taylor & Francis eBooks

www.taylorfrancis.com

A single destination for eBooks from Taylor & Francis
with increased functionality and an improved user
experience to meet the needs of our customers.

90,000+ eBooks of award-winning academic content in
Humanities, Social Science, Science, Technology, Engineering,
and Medical written by a global network of editors and authors.

TAYLOR & FRANCIS EBOOKS OFFERS:

A streamlined
experience for
our library
customers

A single point
of discovery
for all of our
eBook content

Improved
search and
discovery of
content at both
book and
chapter level

REQUEST A FREE TRIAL
support@taylorfrancis.com

Routledge
Taylor & Francis Group

CRC Press
Taylor & Francis Group

For Product Safety Concerns and Information please contact our EU
representative GPSR@taylorandfrancis.com
Taylor & Francis Verlag GmbH, Kaufingerstraße 24, 80331 München, Germany

www.ingramcontent.com/pod-product-compliance
Ingram Content Group UK Ltd.
Pitfield, Milton Keynes, MK11 3LW, UK
UKHW020949180425
457613UK00019B/596